Opinion Mining for Software Development

Doctoral Dissertation submitted to the
Faculty of Informatics of the Università della Svizzera italiana
in partial fulfillment of the requirements for the degree of
Doctor of Philosophy

Bin Lin

Research Advisor
Prof. Gabriele Bavota

Research Co-Advisor
Prof. Michele Lanza

Dissertation Committee

Prof. Carlo Alberto Furia   Università della Svizzera italiana, Switzerland
Prof. Paolo Tonella   Università della Svizzera italiana, Switzerland
Prof. Martin Pinzger   Alpen-Adria-Universität Klagenfurt, Austria
Prof. Denys Poshyvanyk   The College of William & Mary, USA

Dissertation accepted on 10 June 2020

ISBN 978-1-716-47087-5

9 781716 470875

Abstract

Opinion mining, which uses computational methods to extract opinions and sentiments from natural language texts, can be applied to various software engineering (SE) tasks. For example, developers can mine user feedback from mobile app reviews to understand how to improve their products, and software team leaders can assess developers' mood and emotions by mining communication logs or commit messages. Also, the growing popularity of technical Question & Answer (Q&A) websites (*e.g.,* Stack Overflow) and code-sharing platforms (*e.g.,* GitHub) made available a plethora of information that can be mined to collect opinions of experienced developers (*e.g.,* what they think about a specific software library). The latter can be used to assist software design decisions.

However, such a task is far from trivial due to three main reasons: First, the amount of information available online is huge; second, opinions are often embedded in unstructured data; and third, recent studies have indicated that opinion mining tools provide unreliable results when used out-of-the-box in the SE domain, since they are not designed to process SE datasets.

Despite all these challenges, we believe *mining opinions from online resources enables developers to access peers' expertise with ease. The knowledge embedded in these opinions, once converted into actionable items, can facilitate software development activities.*

We first investigated the feasibility of using state-of-the-art sentiment analysis tools to identify sentiment polarity in the software context. We also examined whether customizing a neural network model with SE data can improve its performance of sentiment polarity prediction. Based on the findings of these studies, we proposed a novel approach for recommending APIs with rationales by mining opinions from Q&A websites to support software design decisions. On the one hand, we shed light on the limitations researchers face when applying existing opinion mining techniques in SE context. On the other hand, we illustrate the promise of mining opinions from online resources to support software development activities.

Acknowledgments

It has been almost four years since I first arrived in Lugano, but it seems like only yesterday. Although the journey of my Ph.D. is not considered very long, it definitely impacts me significantly. I am truly grateful for everything I have come across and all the kindness I have received during these years.

First of all, I would like to thank my advisors, Prof. Gabriele Bavota and Prof. Michele Lanza. I am extremely lucky to have this opportunity to work with such tremendously supportive advisors. Gabriele, thank you for always providing me with fast and constructive feedback all these years. I have learned so much about research from you, and I am so proud of being your first Ph.D. student. Michele, thanks for always sharing your insightful opinions and senior experience. And very importantly, thank you for showing us the sense of beauty and decency, which benefits us profoundly.

Since I set my foot in the REVEAL group, I have never been alone. People come and go, but it is every one of you who makes these years full of fun. I will never forget those interesting moments in the Via Balestra office. Specifically, I would like to express my gratitude to the following people who have gone through part or all of my Ph.D. journey with me: Andrea Mocci, Luca Ponzanelli, Roberto Minelli, Tommaso Dal Sasso, Emad Aghajani, Jevgenija Pantiuchina, Fengcai Wen, and Alejandro Mazuera Rozo. I am also very glad to see the REVEAL group growing, and I wish all the best to Rosalia Tufano and Luca Pascarella, who just embarked their journey in REVEAL. I would also extend my gratitude to all the members of Software Institute, some of whom have become good friends. It is especially precious to see our institute getting stronger and more united.

I would also like to express my sincere gratitude to the members of my dissertation committee: Prof. Carlo Alberto Furia, Prof. Tonella Paolo, Prof. Martin Pinzger, and Prof. Denys Poshyvanyk. Thank you for accepting my invitation, taking time to review this thesis, and attending my defense.

Many thanks to my collaborators. Indeed, collaboration is one of the most interesting parts in an academic life. It is my great honor and pleasure to have the chance to work with so many excellent fellow students and professors: Simone Scalabrino, Prof. Rocco Oliveto, Fiorella Zampetti, Prof. Massimiliano Di Penta, Prof. Andrian Marcus, Prof. Nikolaos Tsantalis, Maria Caulo, Prof. Giuseppe Scanniello, Nathan Cassee, Prof. Alexander Serebrenik, Prof. Nicole Novielli, Luca Traini, Rungroj Maipradit, Prof. Hideaki Hata, Yutaro Kashiwa, and Prof. Yasutaka Kamei. Particularly, I would like to give a big shout-out to Alexander, who took me into the research field of software engineering. Without his support and encouragement, I would never be able to reach where I am now.

I want to express my profound gratitude to my parents. I have been far away from home for 10 years, but there is not a single moment when I cannot feel their unconditional love and care. Without their support, I would never be able to come this far. Last but not least, I would like to thank my girlfriend Nan, for bringing me so much happiness, and helping me learn how to become a better me. What's past is prologue. I believe we will overcome all the difficulties and reach our dreamland together.

Contents

Figures

Tables

Introduction

In 2003, Dave *et al.* [DLP03] proposed a novel approach which uses a classifier to identify the sentiment of product review sentences, *i.e.,* whether these sentences are positive or negative. They addressed the process as "opinion mining", and in their perspective, *"an opinion mining tool would process a set of search results for a given item, generating a list of product attributes (quality, features, etc.) and aggregating opinions about each of them (poor, mixed, good)."* This is the first time that the term "opinion mining" appeared in the computer science literature. However, researchers' efforts to mine opinions can be dated back even earlier. For example, in a work published in 2002, Pang *et al.* [PLV02] employed three machine learning techniques (*i.e.,* Naive Bayes, Maximum Entropy Classification, and Support-Vector Machines) to classify the sentiment embedded in movie reviews. In the same year, Turney [Tur02] proposed an unsupervised learning algorithm to classify reviews of automobiles, banks, movies, and travel destinations as *recommended* or *not recommended*, leveraging the semantic orientation assigned to the phrases which contain adjectives or adverbs.

Tasks that capture sentiment polarity (positive or negative) are also called "sentiment analysis" in some other studies [NY03, Liu15]. In fact, the terms "opinion mining" and "sentiment analysis" are often used interchangeably [PL07, Liu15].

Meanwhile, the concept of "opinion mining" is also constantly evolving and no longer limited to classifying texts into different polarities. For example, Conrad and Schilder [CS07] analyzed subjectivity (*i.e.,* whether the text is subjective or objective) of online posts when mining opinions from blogs in the legal domain. Hu *et al.* [HCC17] adopted a text summarization approach, which identifies the most informative sentences, to mine opinions from online hotel reviews. These new perspectives pose the requirement for a broader definition of opinion mining. In this dissertation, we refer to "opinion mining" as the process of analyzing *"people's opinions, appraisals, attitudes, and emotions toward entities, individuals, issues, events, topics, and their attributes"*, as proposed by Liu [Liu11].

In recent years, opinion mining has also attracted considerable attention from software engineering (SE) researchers. Studies have seen the usage of opinion mining in collecting informative app reviews, aiming at understanding how developers can improve their products and revise their release plans [IH13, CLH$^+$14, PSG$^+$15,

VBR+16, MKNS16, SBR+19]. Besides, researchers have also applied opinion mining techniques to monitor developers' emotions expressed during development activities [GB13, MTAO14, OMD+16, SLS16, CLN17, Wer18, LA19]. Opinion mining has also been used to assess the quality of software products [DY13, Ato20].

While there is an increasing number of SE studies leveraging opinion mining, many researchers tend to use opinion mining tools designed for other domains, which often leads to unreliable results [TJA14, JSDS17]. Novielli *et al.* [NCL15] also highlighted and discussed the challenges of employing existing sentiment analysis techniques to detect affective expressions from texts containing technical lexica, as typical in programmers' communication. These facts call for opinion mining techniques curated with software-related data to address the problem of low accuracy when applied in SE contexts.

To overcome these limitations, researchers have spent considerable efforts in customizing existing opinion mining techniques or proposing new approaches. Some of these tools (*e.g.,* SENTISTRENGTH-SE [IZ17]) improve the performance of original approaches by enriching built-in vocabularies with domain-specific ones and adding additional heuristic rules, while others (*e.g.,* EMOTXT [CLN17], SENTI4SD [CLMN18]) trained entirely new machine learning classifiers based on software-related data without modifying the existing opinion mining approaches.

Nevertheless, the proposed approaches are not always thoroughly evaluated with different datasets and in different application domains. For instance, an approach working on discussions from Q&A sites might not perform well when applied on bug reports. Therefore, it is necessary to carefully inspect the performance of these techniques before using them.

Additionally, in current studies, opinion mining techniques have only been applied to a few scenarios, while we believe they can benefit many other software development activities. For example, as software systems are becoming increasingly complex, developers often need to obtain relevant information from various online resources (such as Q&A websites, mailing lists, and issue tracking systems). These resources often include opinions valuable in different software development tasks, such as software design (*e.g.,* understanding which libraries to use for certain functionalities) and software maintenance (*e.g.,* learning how to fix a certain bug in software systems).

However, implementing approaches for these tasks remains far from trivial. First of all, the amount of information available in online resources can be overwhelming. For instance, Stack Overflow[1], one of the most popular Q&A websites used by developers, featured around 19 million questions and 28 million answers by the end of March 2020. Moreover, Stack Overflow is just one important source developers might consult during software development. GitHub[2], the most popular code sharing platform, hosts more than 160 million repositories as of March 2020. These repositories also contain huge amounts of opinions embedded in issue reports, commit messages, and comments. Given the fact that these valuable opinions are widely dis-

---

[1]https://www.stackoverflow.com
[2]https://github.com/

tributed, developers often have to invest significant amounts of time on extracting and aggregating useful pieces of information from different resources, which results in constant context switching and reduced productivity. In other words, being unable to efficiently retrieve and reuse this information undermines its value. Furthermore, text information online is often noisy [DH09], and the texts often contain spelling mistakes, grammatical errors, and irrelevant information. Additionally, the format of the media containing information is not uniform, since the text can be embedded in Q&A sites, source files, issue tracking systems, mailing lists, etc. Given all these difficulties, the value of useful opinions embedded in online resources is under-exploited but worth further attention.

1.1 Thesis Statement

We formulate our thesis as follows:

> *Mining opinions from online resources enables developers to access peers' expertise with ease. The knowledge embedded in these opinions, once converted into actionable items, can facilitate software development activities.*

To validate our thesis, we investigated the possibility of applying and customizing existing opinion mining techniques in SE context [LZB⁺18]. We also implemented POME, an approach that, given the functionality developers want to implement expressed in the natural language, is able to recommend to developers the best APIs to use together with a rationale explaining the reason for such a recommendation [LZB⁺19].

Our results can be leveraged to understand the concrete difficulties of applying opinion mining techniques in a software-related context. We also provide a novel approach for mining developers' opinions from online discussions, thus laying the foundations for a novel generation of opinion mining techniques in the SE field.

1.2 Research Contributions

The contributions of our research can be grouped in two high-level categories: i) the performance examination of opinion mining techniques in the SE context [LZB⁺18], and ii) a novel approach for mining opinions from software-related online discussions [LZB⁺19].

1.2.1 Performance Examination of Opinion Mining Techniques

- We re-train a neural network-based sentiment analysis model with Stack Overflow sentences (Section 3.1). The dataset and scripts used for the re-training process are publicly available, such that other researchers can build their own models on top of it.

- We provide two datasets with labeled sentiment polarities, giving researchers more possibilities to evaluate their own sentiment analysis approaches (Section 3.3.1).

- We investigate the accuracy of commonly used tools to identify the sentiment of software-related texts (Section 3.3.3). We also study the impact of different datasets on tool performance (Section 3.3.3).

- We point out the concrete difficulties faced by existing techniques in identifying the sentiment in software-related contexts (Section 3.5).

1.2.2 Approach for Mining Opinions from Online Discussions

- We propose a novel approach to sentiment polarity identification and quality aspect classification, which exhibits a higher precision than a state-of-the-art technique (Section 4.2).

- We implement a tool which takes as input the text describing a functionality developers want to implement, and returns recommendations on which APIs developers can use and what the advantages and disadvantages are regarding different quality aspects (*e.g.*, performance, compatibility) (Section 4.2.5).

- We provide a dataset containing Stack Overflow discussions with labeled sentiment polarities and corresponding quality aspects, allowing researchers to train and evaluate their own approaches (Section 4.3).

- We also evaluate several machine learning-based approaches with different settings, providing an overview of the performance of traditional machine learning approaches for sentiment polarity identification and quality aspect categorization (Section 4.4).

1.3 Outline

This dissertation is structured in the following chapters:

Chapter 2 presents an overview of the state of the art, including the general concepts of opinion mining, the customization of opinion mining techniques in the SE context, and the application of opinion mining in various software development activities.

Chapter 3 describes our attempt to customize a widely used sentiment analysis tool STANFORD CORENLP with software related data. Meanwhile, this chapter also presents the evaluation of the performance of different opinion mining techniques when applied in SE context. This chapter is based on the following publications [LZB+18, LZO+18]:

> **Sentiment Analysis for Software Engineering: How Far Can We Go?**
>
> Bin Lin, Fiorella Zampetti, Gabriele Bavota, Massimiliano Di Penta, Michele Lanza, Rocco Oliveto. In *Proceedings of the 40th International Conference on Software Engineering (ICSE 2018) – Technical Track*, pp. 94–104, 2018

> **Two Datasets for Sentiment Analysis in Software Engineering**
>
> Bin Lin, Fiorella Zampetti, Rocco Oliveto, Massimiliano Di Penta, Michele Lanza, Gabriele Bavota. In *Proceedings of the 35th International Conference on Software Maintenance and Evolution (ICSME 2018) – Artifact Track*, pp. 712, 2018

Chapter 4 presents our plan to build a software API recommender system, which can take as input texts describing what functionality developers want to implement, and recommends the APIs they can use with rationals. To reach this goal, we propose Pattern-based Opinion MinEr (POME), a novel approach that leverages natural language parsing and pattern-matching to mine online discussions and recommend suitable APIs to developers with rationales. This chapter is based on the following publication [LZB$^+$19]:

> **Pattern-Based Mining of Opinions in Q&A Websites**
>
> Bin Lin, Fiorella Zampetti, Gabriele Bavota, Massimiliano Di Penta, Michele Lanza. In *Proceedings of the 41st International Conference on Software Engineering (ICSE 2019) – Technical Track*, pp. 548--559, 2019

Chapter 5 concludes this dissertation by summarizing our work and indicating future research directions based on the results we achieved.

During our research, before we ended up with the research topic presented in this dissertation, we had also explored several different research directions. The relevant studies are presented in our appendices, which are structured as follows:

Appendix A presents a study of the redundancy of several types of code constructs in a large-scale dataset of active Java projects mined from GitHub, unveiling that redundancy is not uniform and mainly resides in specific code constructs. We further investigate the implications of the locality of redundancy by analyzing the performance of language models when applied to code completion. This chapter is based on the following publication [LPM$^+$17]:

> **On the Uniqueness of Code Redundancies**
>
> Bin Lin, Luca Ponzanelli, Andrea Mocci, Gabriele Bavota, Michele Lanza. In *Proceedings of the 25th International Conference on Program Comprehension (ICPC 2017) – Technical Research Track*, pp. 121–131, 2017

Appendix B presents an empirical study which investigates the impact of different types of refactoring operations on the naturalness of the refactored code, *i.e.,* how refactoring operations impact the repetitiveness and predictability of source code. This chapter is based on the following publication [LNBL19]:

> **On the Impact of Refactoring Operations on Code Naturalness**
>
> Bin Lin, Csaba Nagy, Gabriele Bavota, Michele Lanza. In *26th IEEE International Conference on Software Analysis, Evolution and Reengineering (SANER 2019) - Early Research Achievements Track*, pp. 594–598, 2019

Appendix C presents LEAR, which employs a customized version of the n-gram language model to recommend renaming operations for variables declared in methods and method parameters. We also conduct a large-scale empirical study to evaluate the meaningfulness of the renaming recommendations generated by LEAR and other state-of-the-art techniques. This chapter is based on the following publication [LSM$^+$17]:

> **Investigating the Use of Code Analysis and NLP to Promote a Consistent Usage of Identifiers**
>
> Bin Lin, Simone Scalabrino, Andrea Mocci, Rocco Oliveto, Gabriele Bavota, Michele Lanza. In *Proceedings of the 17th International Working Conference on Source Code Analysis and Manipulation (SCAM 2017) – Research Track*, pp. 81-90, 2017

Appendix D presents an empirical study which assesses the quality of identifiers in test code. The study mainly consists of a survey involving participants evaluating the quality of identifiers in both manually written and automatically generated test cases from ten open source software projects. This chapter is based on the following publication [LNB$^+$19]:

> **On The Quality of Identifiers in Test Code**
>
> Bin Lin, Csaba Nagy, Gabriele Bavota, Andrian Marcus, Michele Lanza. In *Proceedings of the 19th International Working Conference on Source Code Analysis and Manipulation (SCAM 2019) – Research Track*, pp. 204–215, 2019

Appendix E presents a mining-based study investigating how and whether the code review process helps developers to improve their contributions to open source projects over time. More specifically, we analyze 32,062 peer-reviewed pull requests (PRs) made across 4,981 GitHub repositories by 728 developers, and verify if the contribution quality of a developer increases over time (*i.e.,* when more and more reviewed PRs are made by that developer). This chapter is based on the following publication [CLB$^+$20]:

> **Knowledge Transfer in Modern Code Review**
>
> Maria Caulo, Bin Lin, Gabriele Bavota, Giuseppe Scanniello, Michele Lanza. In *Proceedings of the 28th International Conference on Program Comprehension (ICPC 2020) – Research Track*, accepted

As we have created several datasets in our studies, to facilitate replication, we describe these datasets in Appendix F. In the end, we list all the acronyms used in this dissertation in "Acronyms".

State of the Art

In this chapter, we present the categories of opinion mining tasks, as well as the customizations and applications of opinion mining techniques in the SE domain. We conclude this chapter by outlining the limitations of current studies and indicating potential directions for improvement.

2.1   Opinion Mining in a Nutshell

While opinion mining covers a wide range of tasks, those tasks can usually be categorized into:

- **Sentiment polarity and positivity degree identification**, which is applied to classify the opinions expressed in the text into one of the distinguishable sentiment polarities (*e.g.,* positive, neutral, or negative). For example, Ranco *et al.* [RAC+15] identified the sentiment in the tweets related to finance, and inspected its impact on stock price returns.

- **Subjectivity detection and opinion identification**, which is applied to decide whether a given text contains subjective opinions or objective information. For example, Satapathy *et al.* [SCC+17] detected the opinionated tweets on the nuclear energy, which serve as a basis to understand whether social media bias exists toward this controversial energy.

- **Joint topic-sentiment analysis**, which consider topics and opinions simultaneously and search for their interactions. For example, Wang [Wan10] proposed a topic sentiment mixture model, which analyzed the sentiment polarity (positive, neutral, or negative) for each of the detected topics (*e.g.,* price, battery life) of mobile phone reviews.

- **Viewpoints and perspectives identification**, which is applied to detect the general attitudes expressed in the texts (*e.g.,* political orientations) instead of detailed opinions toward a specific issue or narrow subject. For example, Pla and Hurtado [PH14] collected politics-related tweets and used sentiment analysis techniques to classify users into three political tendency categories: left, right, and center, with the remaining of the users categorized as undefined.

- **Other non-factual information identification**, which include emotion detection, humor recognition, text genre classification, etc. For example, Barros *et al.* [BMO13] reveal the possibility to leverage emotion detection (joy, sadness, anger, fear) to automatically classify poems into different categories (*e.g.*, love, satire, religious).

2.2   Opinion Mining Techniques for SE

In this section, we first illustrate the potential perils of using existing opinion mining techniques out-of-the-box for SE tasks. We then present the efforts of researchers on customizing opinion mining techniques in SE.

2.2.1   The Perils of Using Opinion Mining Techniques Out-Of-The-Box

Thanks to the pioneers of opinion mining research, there are many existing approaches researchers can use out-of-the-box. These include, for example, SENTISTRENGTH [TBP+10] and Natural Language Toolkit (NLTK) [HG14]. Researchers often use these tools directly without extra tuning, although they are trained on data from completely different domains. For example, a common task of opinion mining in SE is sentiment polarity identification (*i.e.*, classifying text into three polarity categories: positive, neutral, or negative). The most adopted tool by SE researchers is SENTISTRENGTH [TBP+10], which is based on a sentiment word strength list and some heuristics including spell checking and negation handling. Its word list is based on comments taken from myspace.com/, making it unsuitable for SE applications.

Another popular tool, NLTK [HG14], is a lexicon and rule-based sentiment analysis tool leveraging Valence Aware Dictionary and sEntiment Reasoner (VADER), which, in turn, is tuned to social media text (especially micro-blogging).

A different approach is used by STANFORD CORENLP [SPW+13], which leverages Recursive Neural Networks (RNNs) and is able to compute the sentiment of a sentence based on how words compose the meaning of the sentence, and not by summing up the sentiment of individual words. However, STANFORD CORENLP has also been trained on a corpus of documents outside the SE domain, namely movie reviews.

As these existing sentiment polarity analysis tools were not conceived to be applied on SE artifacts, researchers posed questions about their applicability in the software domain. Indeed, several studies have been conducted to verify their reliability when applied in SE contexts.

For example, Tourani *et al.* [TJA14] used SENTISTRENGTH to extract sentiment information from user and developer mailing lists of two major successful and mature projects from the Apache software foundation: Tomcat and Ant. They found that

SENTISTRENGTH achieved a very low precision when compared to human annotated ground truth, *i.e.,* 29.56% for positive sentences and 13.1% for negative sentences. The low precision is caused by the ambiguous technical terms and the difficulty of distinguishing extreme positive/negative texts from neutral ones. Meanwhile, the challenges of employing sentiment analysis techniques to assess the affective load of text containing technical lexica, as typical in the communication among programmers, have also been highlighted by Novielli *et al.* [NCL15].

Jongeling *et al.* [JSDS17] conducted a comparison of four widely used sentiment polarity analysis tools: SENTISTRENGTH, NLTK, STANFORD CORENLP, and ALCHEMY API. They evaluated their performance on a human labeled golden set of JIRA issue comments from a developer emotions study by Murgia *et al.* [MTAO14]. As a result, they found none of them can provide accurate predictions of expressed sentiment in the SE domain. They also observed that disagreement exists not only between sentiment analysis tools and the developers, but also between different sentiment analysis tools themselves. Their experiment also confirmed that disagreement between these tools can lead to contradictory results when using them to conduct SE studies.

A similar study on evaluating sentiment analysis tools was conducted by Imtiaz *et al.* [IMGM18]. Instead of JIRA issue comments, they analyzed the performance of six tools (SENTISTRENGTH, NLTK, STANFORD CORENLP, ALCHEMY API, SENTI4SD, and SENTICR) on 589 manually labeled GitHub comments. Their results also suggested that these tools have a low agreement with human ratings, and even human raters have a low agreement among themselves. In addition to sentiment polarity, this study also evaluates the performance of a politeness detection tool developed by Danescu-Niculescu-Mizil *et al.* [DSJ+13]. The result plotted a similar trend of unreliability.

The performance of some techniques, which require extra training, was also assessed by researchers. Shen *et al.* [SBS19] compared the performance of three machine learning approaches (*i.e.,* Logistic Regression, Support-Vector Machine, Naive Bayes Classifier) for sentiment polarity prediction when trained on technical and non-technical datasets. By testing against a dataset consisting of 4,800 Stack Overflow comments, they found that domain related datasets have a positive impact on the improvement of prediction accuracy.

The results achieved in these studies call for a sentiment analysis technique curated with SE related data to address the problem of low accuracy when dealing with technical terms and specific application contexts.

2.2.2 Customizing Opinion Mining Techniques for SE Tasks

To overcome the limitations of the existing sentiment analysis techniques, researchers have devoted considerable efforts into customizing them for SE tasks. Generally speaking, there are two types of approaches: 1) lexicon and rule-based, and 2) machine learning-based.

Lexicon and rule-based approaches

Lexicon and rule-based approaches identify the sentiment or opinions in the text by leveraging dictionaries and/or heuristic rules. These approaches can usually be used directly without extra tuning for a new task. An intuitive idea for improving their performance in software related tasks is exploiting domain-specific dictionaries and additional heuristic rules.

An example is SENTISTRENGTH-SE [IZ17], built upon the popular sentiment analysis tool SENTISTRENGTH [TR10]. The authors revisited the built-in dictionary of SENTISTRENGTH, and neutralized words usually expressing no sentiment in SE contexts. They also incorporated extra heuristics, such as taking into account the word context to minimize ambiguity. Their evaluation showed that the new tool significantly outperformed SENTISTRENGTH when applied on SE artifacts.

Detecting Emotions in Valence Arousal space in software engineering text (DEVA) [IZ18a], a dictionary-based lexical approach for detecting excitement, stress, depression, and relaxation expressed in SE texts, also integrated two domain-specific dictionaries (Software Engineering Arousal Dictionary and the valence dictionary used by SENTISTRENGTH-SE). Their evaluation showed that DEVA outperforms the approach adopting only general-purpose dictionaries.

Machine learning-based approaches

Most machine learning-based approaches used in SE studies are supervised learning techniques. To use this type of approaches, researchers often need to re-train the classifier. In practice, they either incorporate software related data into the original training set, or only use a new domain-specific dataset.

An example of improving the original classifier by incorporating SE data is SENTIMOJI [CCL+19]. SENTIMOJI is a sentiment polarity prediction approach, which considers the meaning of emojis. This approach is built on DEEPMOJI [FMS+17], a deep learning model trained on tweets with emojis for analyzing sentiment in the text. The authors curated the original DEEPMOJI model with emoji-labeled texts from GitHub posts, and obtained promising performance.

In many other cases, researchers re-trained commonly used machine learning classifiers with only software related data. Support-Vector Machine (SVM) [BGV92] is one of the most popular classifiers in this scenario. Examples include SENTI4SD [CLMN18], EMOTXT [CLN17], and MARVALOUS [IAZ19]. SENTI4SD [CLMN18] is an approach for analyzing sentiments in developers' communication channels. The authors trained a SVM classifier with a dataset of Stack Overflow questions, answers, and comments manually annotated for emotions and sentiment polarities. Trained with the same dataset, the authors of SENTI4SD also built EMOTXT [CLN17], another SVM-based technique for recognizing specific emotions (*e.g.,* joy, love, and anger) in SE texts. Islam *et al.* [IAZ19] trained a SVM classifier with emotion-annotated datasets of 5,122 JIRA and Stack Overflow comments to build MARVALOUS, a tool detecting four emotional states (excitement, stress, depression, and relaxation).

Of course, SVM is not the only classifier used by researchers for opinion mining. For example, SENTICR [ABIR17], a sentiment polarity prediction tool for code review interactions, employed Gradient Boosting Tree [PP11] instead of SVM. SENTICR was trained with 2,000 sentiment polarity-annotated review comments from 20 popular open source software projects.

The results obtained by above approaches indicate that incorporating SE data is a promising direction to move forward to improve the performance of existing opinion mining tools on software-related data.

2.3 Applications of Opinion Mining in SE

In this section, we present how opinion mining techniques are used to support various software development activities. More specifically, we categorize the applications of opinion mining into the following types: 1) supporting software requirements engineering, 2) supporting software design and implementation, 3) supporting software maintenance and evolution, and 4) understanding human aspects of software development.

2.3.1 Opinion Mining to Support Software Requirements Engineering

There are various sources which contain valuable opinions for facilitating requirements engineering. For instance, developers can analyze online discussions to understand users' need. Moreover, they can learn how to shape their software from the documents of other projects.

For example, researchers have applied opinion mining to extract non-functional requirements. Liu *et al.* [LLY+18] proposed CoLlaborative App Permission recommendation (CLAP), which mines the descriptions of similar apps to recommend potentially required permissions (*e.g.*, access to locations). CLAP identifies similar apps by considering their titles, descriptions, permissions, and categories. From app descriptions of the similar apps, CLAP then identifies permission-explaining sentences by verb phrase identification and keyword matching. The evaluation of CLAP on 1.4 million apps exhibited its promise to help developers decide which permissions are required in their apps. Casamayor *et al.* [CGC10] proposed a semi-supervised learning approach to identify non-functional requirements. Unlike traditional supervised learning approaches which require a large amount of annotated training data, their approach only used a small set of annotated requirements (functional or non-functional) in conjunction with unannotated requirements. The underlying idea is that co-occurring words often belong to the same class. Their approach achieved accuracy rates of over 70%. Wang *et al.* [WHGW17] have investigated the possibility of identifying security requirements. They used five metrics (the number of issue comments, the average textual length of issue comments, the quantity of attachments in an issue, the number of types of attachments in an issue, the number of developers involved in an issue) to build a security requirements classifier. Their results indicated that four out of these five metrics are discriminative of security requirements.

A number of other studies exploited opinion mining to identify both functional and non-functional requirements. Liu *et al.* [LLLL19] proposed an approach to mine domain knowledge from the descriptions of similar apps, and recommend developers with potential functional and non-functional requirements. By evaluating 574 apps, their approach achieved a precision of 88.09% and a recall of 74.45%, on average. Kurtanović and Maalej [KM17] adopted the supervised machine learning technique SVM, leveraging lexical features, to classify requirements as functional or non-functional. Their approach obtained a high precision of 92%. They also tried to classify the non-functional requirements into more fine-grained categories (*e.g.*, usability, security) and obtained high precision and recall values (up to 93% and 90%, respectively).

Opinion mining can be also applied to detect the defects in requirements. Ferrari *et al.* [FGR+18] applied rule-based natural language processing (NLP) techniques to detect defects (*e.g.*, vague terms, missing unit of measurement) in the requirement documents of a railway signaling manufacturer. Their experience confirmed that NLP can be used to detect defects even in a very large set of industrial requirements documents.

2.3.2 Opinion Mining to Support Software Design and Implementation

Since developers often share their programming expertise online, mining opinions from their online discussions can effectively support other developers' engineering work, especially when facing a similar task. For example, researchers have investigated the feasibility of mining the knowledge regarding different implementation approaches to support developers design decisions.

Uddin and Khomh [UK17b] proposed OPINER, an approach to mine API-related opinions and give users a quick overview of the pros and cons of APIs when choosing which API to use to implement a specific feature. OPINER is able to detect the polarity of sentences related to libraries by using a customized version of the Sentiment Orientation algorithm [HL04]. The algorithm was originally developed to mine customers' opinions about computer products. Uddin and Khomh customized the tool with words specific to library reviews. OPINER can also classify the mined opinions into "aspects" by exploiting machine learning classifiers using as predictor variables the frequency of single words and of n-grams appearing in the sentences.

Huang *et al.* [HCX+18] proposed DIFFTECH, which compares different software technologies (*e.g.*, TCP v.s. UDP) by applying natural language processing techniques on relevant Stack Overflow discussions. The authors maintain a database of comparable software technologies by mining tags of Stack Overflow posts. With the help of such a database, DIFFTECH extracts sentences related to technology comparisons. These sentences are further processed by TF-IDF to extract keywords (*e.g.*, security, speed) representing the compared aspect.

Some other studies have focused on mining opinions to gain knowledge regarding the usage of APIs. For example, Serva *et al.* [SSPV15] mined negative code examples from Stack Overflow. More specifically, they applied sentiment analysis to the questions on Stack Overflow which contain code segments. By obtaining code examples discussed with negative sentiments, developers can avoid making similar mistakes and possibly improve their code. Zhang and Hou [ZH13] mined online discussions of Oracle's Java Swing Forum to extract problematic API features. Their proposed approach, named HAYSTACK, identified the negative sentences using a sentiment analysis approach, and parsed these negative discussions with pre-defined grammatical patterns to disclose problematic features. Wang *et al.* [WPWZ19] mined Stack Overflow to extract short practical and useful tips regarding API usage from developer answers. Their proposed approach DEEPTIP employed Convolutional Neural Network (CNN) architectures to train a model with a corpus of annotated texts (labeled as "tip" or "non-tip"). Their approach achieved a high precision of over 80%. Ahasanuzzaman *et al.* [AARS20] proposed CAPS, an approach to classify Stack Overflow posts concerning API into issue related and non-issue related. CAPS used a statistical modeling method (Conditional Random Field) to detect issue-related sentences. These sentences, together with the features collected from posts (*e.g.,* the experience of users), are fed into another logistic regression-based classifier to finally decide whether a post is issue-related or not.

Several studies have focused on extracting relevant code snippets by analyzing the text around them. Ponzanelli *et al.* [PBL13] developed an IDE plugin to automatically formulate queries from the current code context and present a ranked list of relevant Stack Overflow discussions. Developers can simply drag & drop code samples from such discussions to speedup their implementation tasks. Nguyen *et al.* [NNN16] as well as Campbell and Treude [CT17] have developed tools to convert natural English texts describing a task (*e.g., "how to read a file in Java"*) into source code snippets implementing the described feature. This is done by matching the textual description to Stack Overflow discussions to then exploit the code snippets in them as "code translations" for the provided description.

Stack Overflow has also been mined to recommend comments for source code. Rahman *et al.* [RRK15] proposed a heuristic-based approach to extract insightful discussions regarding issues, concerns, or tips. The heuristics used include comment popularity, code segment relevance, comment rank, comment word count, and comment sentiment polarity. A ranking mechanism considering all these five heuristics was adopted to produce the final list of comments for source code.

2.3.3 Opinion Mining to Support Software Maintenance and Evolution

Several works have focused on the mining of opinions in reviews posted by users of mobile applications (apps). Analyzing the polarity of apps' reviews is particularly useful to support the evolution of mobile apps [CLH+14, GMBV12, CW13, GM14, PSG+15, SBR+19]. For example, developers can gain insights on what features are desired by users and which bugs are manifesting as application failures.

Indeed, it has been proven that applying opinion mining techniques to app reviews helps developers to find useful information for app maintenance and evolution. Goul *et al.* [GMBV12] applied a sentiment analysis tool to over 5,000 reviews of productivity apps, observing that sentiment analysis can help spot sentence-level, feature-based comments.

Several studies have investigated why users like or dislike mobile apps with opinion mining approaches. Gu and Kim [GK15] proposed Software User Review Miner (SURMINER), a review summarization framework. SURMINER classifies reviews into five categories (aspect evaluation, praises, feature requests, bug reports, and others). Aspect-opinion pairs (*e.g.*, <background, nice>) are extracted from those reviews falling into the "aspect evaluation" category.

Using the same categories as Gu and Kim [GK15], Review Summary (REVSUM) proposed by Shah *et al.* [SSP19] considers not only aspect evaluation, but also feature requests and bug reports, for which REVSUM generates feature-level summaries.

Instead of general opinions, Fu *et al.* [FLL+13] focused on the negative reviews from users, as these reviews are more likely to help developers to improve their apps. Their tool, named WISCOM, applies topic modeling to the reviews associated with low ratings (1-star or 2-star) in order to extract keywords from the reviews and categories them into ten topics. As a result, many keywords in these topics exhibit clear reasons of dissatisfaction from users, such as "crashes" and "boring".

Other studies have attempted to understand which aspects of mobile apps draw the most concerns of users. Carreño *et al.* [CW13] presented a technique based on Aspect and Sentiment Unification Model (ASUM) to extract common topics (*e.g.*, updates, features) from app reviews and present users' opinions about those topics. Guzman *et al.* [GM14, GAB15] used SENTISTRENGTH to support a similar task. With their approach, a diverse sample of user reviews is automatically presented to developers with an overview of different opinions and experiences mentioned in the reviews. These studies allow developers to understand what users care about, which is critical in software design evolution.

Instead of directly presenting topics and their associated opinions to developers, many efforts have stepped back and focused on a more fundamental problem: how to correctly classify app reviews based on the type of information they provide. Indeed, given the huge amount of reviews available in app stores, how to efficiently identify the subset of reviews which interest developers remains a challenge.

Iacob and Harrison [IH13] proposed Mobile App Review Analyzer (MARA), which identifies feature requests from app reviews based on pre-defined linguistic rules. Panichella *et al.* [PSG+16] presented ARDOC, a tool which automatically classifies app reviews into five categories: information giving, information seeking, feature request, problem discovery, and other. Similarly, Maalej *et al.* [MKNS16] adopted a slightly different classification schema, in which reviews are categorized as bug reports, feature requests, user experiences, or text ratings. Chen *et al.* [CLH+14] used topic modeling to automatically group reviews into the ones reporting bugs, suggesting new features to implement, or not being informative (*i.e.*, not containing information useful for the app evolution). These studies enable developers to quickly focus on valid information and plan their next steps to evolve the software systems. Khan *et al.* [KXLW19] proposed Crowd-based Requirements Engineering approach by Argumentation (CROWDRE-ARG), an approach extracting users' opinions revtoward given features. As a running example, the authors retrieved discussions regarding a new Google-Map feature from Reddit online forum. CROWDRE-ARG classified the sentences from the discussions into three categories: 1) issues, 2) design alternatives or new features, and 3) supporting, attacking and neutral arguments or claims.

Ciurumelea *et al.* [CSPG17] takes the review classification to a more fine-grained level. Their approach User Request Referencer (URR) classifies reviews into six high level (*e.g.*, compatibility) and 12 low level categories (*e.g.*, device, android version, and hardware, which are all related to compatibility). Moreover, their approach recommends which relevant source code files need to be modified.

Besides app review classification, how to schedule the timeline to deal with these reviews has also been investigated. Scalabrino *et al.* [SBR+19] proposed Crowd Listener for releAse Planning (CLAP), an approach not only clustering related reviews into different categories (*e.g.*, functional bug report, suggestion for new feature, report of performance problems), but also prioritizing the clusters of reviews to be implemented. CLAP has been proved useful for planning the subsequent app release.

Besides app reviews, opinion mining has also been applied to classify tweets related to software projects [GAS17] with the similar goal of helping developers better understand user needs and providing important information for software evolution.

Opinion mining has also been involved in the bug fixing process. Antoniol *et al.* [AAP+18] built a classifier to identify whether an entry in the issue tracker is a bug or an enhancement. A precision between 64% and 98% and a recall between 33% and 97% were achieved when Alternating Decision Trees, Naïve Bayes Classifiers, and Logistic Regression are adopted.

Yang *et al.* [YZL18] proposed a novel bug severity-prediction approach by analyzing emotion similarity. The core idea behind their approach is comparing the emotion words in bug reports from the training set with those in the new bug report. The reliability of this approach for predicting bug severity has been verified on five open source projects. Similar studies were conducted by Umer *et al.* [ULS18] and Ramay *et al.* [RUY+19]. Differently from Yang *et al.* [YZL18], the authors used an adapted version of Naïve Bayes Multinomial as the classifier, Umer *et al.* [ULS18] adopted SVM, while Ramay *et al.* [RUY+19] adopted a deep neural network-based classifier.

Besides bug severity prediction, Goyal and Sardana [GS17] used a sentiment based model to predict the fixability of non-reproducible bugs. The authors found out that the reports of non-reproducible bugs contain more negative sentiment compared to those of reproducible bugs. Therefore, they incorporated the sentiment into the original meta-fields of bug reports and trained the classifier with various algorithms (Zero-R, Naïve Bayes, J48, random tree, and random forest) for fixability prediction. As a result, J48 and Naïve Bayes outperformed others when tested in Firefox and Eclipse projects, respectively.

2.3.4 Opinion Mining and Human Aspects of Software Development

Opinion mining techniques have also been used to study the human aspects of software development. Understanding developers' mental status and interaction behaviors can provide insights for better team management. Therefore, lots of studies have been dedicated to the analysis of developers' sentiment expressed during software development activities.

Werder [Wer18] inspected how emotions of development teams evolved over time in 1,121 GitHub projects. Their results indicated that the positive sentiment in teams gradually reduces over time in general. Lanovaz and Adams [LA19] compared the sentiment of users and developers in two R mailing lists: *R-help* and *R-devel*, which mainly target R users and developers, respectively. Their results suggested that developers tend to express more emotions. Moreover, the negative posts in *R-help* are more likely to receive no replies, while this does not hold for the *R-devel* mailing list.

Some researchers have specifically inspected the sentiment in commit comments. Guzman *et al.* [GAL14] analyzed the sentiment of over 60k commit comments on GitHub and provided evidence that projects which have more distributed teams tend to have a higher positive polarity in their emotional content. Moreover, comments written on Mondays are more likely to be negative. A similar study was conducted by Sinha *et al.* [SLS16]. By analyzing a much larger dataset (over 2.25 million commit comments), they observed that the negative sentiment was about 10% more than the positive sentiment. Interestingly, Tuesdays seem to have the most negative sentiment, which contradicts the findings of Guzman *et al.* [GAL14]. Singh and Singh [SS17a] performed another study concerning the sentiment polarity in commit messages. Instead of all commit messages, they focused on refactoring-related ones. After analyzing over 3k refactoring related commit messages from 60 GitHub projects, they found that developers tend to express more negative than positive sentiments. This result is consistent with that of Sinha *et al.* [SLS16]. The study by Pletea *et al.* [PVS14] compared the sentiment expressed in security-related and non-security related discussions around commits and pull requests on GitHub. Their study results provided evidence that developers tend to be more negative when discussing security-related topics.

In addition to commit comments, Claes *et al.* [CMF18] examined the use of emoticons in issue comments. In their study, 1.3 million and 4.5 million comments were extracted, respectively, from the issue tracking systems of Apache and Mozilla. After analyzing these comments, they found that Mozilla developers use much more emoticons than Apache developers, and Mozilla developers are more likely to express sadness and surprise with emoticons.

Paul *et al.* [PBS19] looked into the sentiment in code reviews from the perspective of gender differences. They mined the code reviews from six popular open source software projects, and compared the sentiment expressed by male and female developers. Their study disclosed that females tend to express less sentiments than males. Meanwhile, it is not uncommon that male developers express fewer positive encouragements to their female counterparts.

Given that many studies have answered what sentiments are embedded in software development activities, some have examined how these sentiments can impact the development activities. For example, researchers have investigated the relation between the sentiment in issue comments and the issue resolution process. Ortu *et al.* [OAD+15] analyzed the correlation between the sentiment in 560k JIRA comments and the time to fix a JIRA issue, finding that positive sentiment expressed in the issue description might reduce issue fixing time. Cheruvelil and da Silva [CdS19] analyzed the sentiment in issue comments and associated it to the issue reopening. They found that negative sentiment might lead to more issue reopenings, although the impact is not large.

Besides issue resolution, attention has also given to continuous integration builds. Souza and Silva [SS17b] analyzed the relation between developers' sentiment and builds performed by continuous integration servers. They found that negative sentiment both affects and is affected by the result of the build process. That is, the negative sentiment expressed in commits is more likely to result in broken builds, while broken builds can also lead to negative sentiment.

The impact of sentiment on code review process has also been investigated. Asri *et al.* [AKU+19] analyzed how the sentiment in developers' comments impacts the code review process outcome. By mining the historical data from four open source projects, they found that the code reviews with negative comments take longer to process.

The study by Garcia *et al.* [GZS13] instead focused on the impact of sentiment on developers' activeness in software projects. The authors analyzed the relation between the emotions and the activity of contributors in the Open Source Software project GENTOO. They found that contributors are more likely to become inactive when they express strong positive or negative emotions in the issue tracker, or when they deviate from the expected emotions in the mailing list.

While most studies mainly considers the impact of sentiment on software development activities, Freira *et al.* [SCON18] explored how feedback on GitHub can impact developers' mood. By analyzing 78k pull requests and 268k corresponding comments, they found that negative comments have a larger impact on developers' mood, compared to positive comments. The impact is more evident for first-time contributors, who might even refrain themselves from making further contributions to the repositories, especially in large software projects.

2.4 Discussion

While opinion mining has gained considerable popularity and its applications cover a wide range of SE tasks, we believe that there are still abundant opportunities to further improve the performance and maximize the value of opinion mining for software-related tasks.

Regarding the opinion mining techniques, while several approaches have been proposed and customized to the software context, they are often evaluated on a specific dataset (*e.g.,* issue reports). It remains unknown whether these tools can still achieve reliable performance when applied on other datasets (*e.g.,* Stack Overflow discussions). More investigations are required to understand their abilities. If limitations are spotted, it will be necessary to propose new approaches which better fit the context.

Regarding software requirements engineering, to recommend functional or non-functional requirements, most of the current approaches mine relevant knowledge from the documents or descriptions of similar software projects. It is also likely that no similar project can be found in the market, or that the requirements are scattered in many different projects. Therefore, adding external information sources like online discussions can be considered. Additionally, how to assemble the requirements collected from different projects still remains a challenge.

Regarding software design and implementation, while researchers have managed to use opinion mining to assist developers in choosing relevant APIs or techniques, some performance limitations still exist. For example, sentiment analysis tools not specifically tuned to software related contexts are used, which might lead to unreliable results. Besides, the quality attributes used to compare the APIs/techniques are often automatically generated with topic modeling, which sometimes can be arbitrary and not meaningful for developers. Additionally, when mining online resources to support development activities, researchers often only exploit one source of information, which is a very limited part of the available online discussions. Lots of valid information from other channels is ignored.

Regarding software maintenance and evolution, none of the studies have attempted to convert opinions into practical actions for software maintenance activities, such as bug fixing. As developers often discuss how to solve certain issues in both Q&A websites and issue tracking systems, these discussions can be mined to advise other developers.

Regarding human aspects of SE , while many studies provide valid insights with opinion mining (*e.g.,* relation between emotions and productivity), converting the provided information into practical actions is still a big challenge. Understanding what is happening is merely the first step. More studies should be conducted to leverage these insights to facilitate the development process, such as increasing productivity and promoting more inclusive environments.

In this dissertation, we mainly focus on addressing the following challenges. First, given the unreliable performance of existing sentiment polarity analysis tools when applied in SE , we investigate whether we can customize a state-of-the-art approach to obtain high accuracy for identifying sentiment polarity in software related texts (Chapter 3). Second, as automatically classifying online software related discussions often leads to arbitrary categories, we develop a new technique, which can produce both accurate and meaningful results (Chapter 4).

3

Sentiment Polarity Analysis in Software Engineering Contexts

The SE community has adopted sentiment analysis tools for various purposes (Section 2.3), such as assessing the polarity of mobile app reviews [GMBV12], and identifying distress or happiness in a development team *et al.* [TJA14]. Most of the prior works leverage sentiment analysis tools not designed to work on software-related textual documents. This "out-of-the-box" usage has been criticized due to the poor accuracy these tools achieved when applied in a context different from the one for which they have been designed and/or trained [TJA14, NCL15, JSDS17]. For example, the STANFORD CORENLP [SPW+13] opinion miner has been trained on movie reviews. In essence, *the key to make sentiment analysis successful when applied on SE datasets might be their customization to the specific context.*

Given the warning raised by previous work in our field (Section 2.2.1), there was the need for training and customizing the sentiment polarity analysis tool to the Stack Overflow context. Also, looking at the opinion mining literature, we decided to adapt STANFORD CORENLP, a state-of-the-art approach based on Recursive Neural Networks (RNNs). STANFORD CORENLP is able to compute the sentiment polarity of a sentence not by just summing up the sentiment of positive/negative terms, but by grammatically analyzing the way words compose the meaning of a sentence [SPW+13].

We built a training set by manually assigning a sentiment polarity score to a total of ~40k sentences/words extracted from Stack Overflow. Despite the considerable manual effort, the empirical evaluation we performed on our customized tool led to negative results, with unacceptable accuracy levels in classifying positive/negative opinions. Given this, we started a thorough empirical investigation aimed at assessing the actual performance of sentiment polarity analysis tools when applied on SE datasets with the goal of identifying a technique able to provide acceptable results. We experimented with all major techniques used in our community, by using them out-of-the-box as well as with customization designed to work in the SE context (*e.g.,* SENTISTRENGTH-SE [IZ17]). Also, we considered three different SE datasets: (i) our manually built dataset of Stack Overflow sentences, (ii) comments left on issue trackers [OMD+16], and (iii) reviews of mobile apps [VBR+16].

Our results show that none of the state-of-the-art tools provides a precise and reliable assessment of the sentiments expressed in the manually labeled Stack Overflow dataset we built (*e.g.*, all the approaches achieve recall and precision lower than 40% on negative sentences). Results are marginally better in the app reviews and in the issue tracker datasets, which however represent simpler usage scenarios for sentiment polarity analysis tools.

We share our experience and negative findings with the SE research community, showing the current difficulties in applying sentiment polarity analysis tools to software-related datasets, despite major efforts in tailoring them to the context of interest. Our results should also warn researchers to not simply use a (customized) sentiment polarity analysis tool *assuming* that it provides a reliable assessment of the sentiment polarities expressed in sentences, but to carefully evaluate its performance. Finally, we share our large training dataset as well as all the tools used in our experiments and the achieved results [LZB$^+$b], to foster replications and advances in this novel field.

Structure of the Chapter

Section 3.1 presents how we customized the state-of-the-art sentiment polarity analysis tool STANFORD CORENLP. Section 3.2 reports the negative results we obtained during evaluation. Section 3.3 reports the design and results of the study we performed to assess the performance of sentiment analysis tools on SE datasets, while Section 3.4 discusses the threats that could affect the validity of our results. Finally, after a discussion of lessons learned (Section 3.5), Section 3.6 concludes this chapter.

3.1   Customizing The State-Of-The-Art Sentiment Analysis Tool

In the section, we detail our work to customize the state-of-the-art sentiment polarity analysis tool STANFORD CORENLP with software related data. We report the **negative** results we achieved in Section 3.2.

3.1.1   Mining Opinions in SE Datasets

Previous work that attempted to mine opinions in SE datasets [TJA14, NCL15, JSDS17] offers a clear warning: *Using sentiment analysis/opinion mining techniques out-of-the-box on SE datasets is a recipe for negative results*. Indeed, these tools have been designed to work on user's reviews of products/movies and do not take into consideration domain-specific terms. For example, the word *robust* has a clear positive polarity when referred to a software product, while it does not express a specific sentiment in a movie review. This pushed researchers to create customized versions of these tools, enriching them with information about the sentiment of domain-specific terms (*e.g.*, SENTISTRENGTH-SE by Islam and Zibran [IZ17]).

Despite the effort done by some authors in developing customized tools, there is a second major limitation of the sentiment polarity analysis tools mostly used in SE (*e.g.*, SENTISTRENGTH [TBP$^+$10]). Such tools assess the sentiment of a sentence by looking at the single words in isolation, assigning positive/negative scores to the words and then summing these scores to obtain an overall sentiment for the sentence. Thus, the sentence composition is ignored. For example, a sentence such as "*I would not recommend this library, even though it is robust and fast*" would be assessed by these techniques as positive in polarity, given the presence of words having a positive score (*i.e.*, robust, fast). Such a limitation has been overcome by the STANFORD CORENLP [SPW$^+$13] approach used for the analysis of sentiment in movies' reviews. The approach is based on a Recursive Neural Network (RNN) computing the sentiment of a sentence based on how words compose the meaning of the sentence [SPW$^+$13]. Clearly, a more advanced approach comes at a cost: The effort required to build its training set. Indeed, it is not sufficient to simply provide the polarity for a vocabulary of words but, to learn how positive/negative sentences are grammatically built on top of positive/negative words, it needs to know the polarity of all intermediate nodes composing a sentence used in the training set.

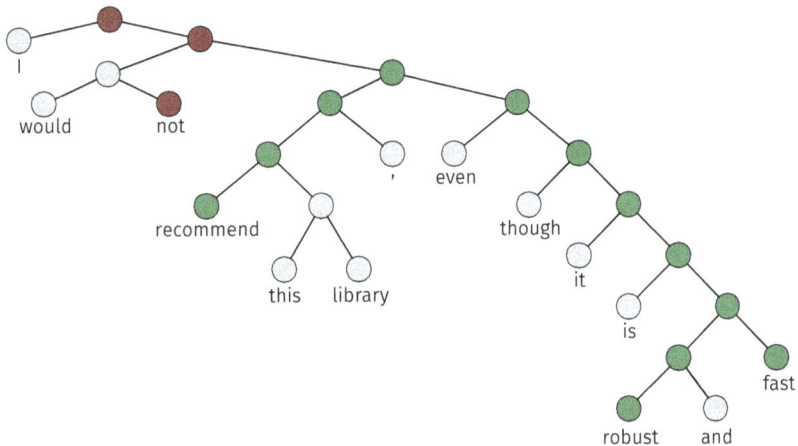

Figure 3.1. Example of the labeling needed to build the Stanford CoreNLP training set.

We discuss the example reported in Fig. 3.1. Gray nodes represent (sequences of) words having a *neutral* polarity, red ones indicate *negative* sentiment, green ones *positive* sentiment. Overall, the sentence has a negative sentiment (see the root of the tree in Fig. 3.1), despite the presence of several positive terms (the tree's leafs) and intermediate nodes. To use this sentence composed of 14 words in the training set of the RNN, we must provide the sentiment of all 27 nodes in the Penn Treebank-style phrase structure tree [SPW$^+$13], depicted in Fig. 3.1. This allows the RNN to learn that while "*it is robust and fast*" has a positive polarity if taken in isolation, the overall sentence is expressing a negative feeling about the API due to the "*I would not recommend this library*" sub-sentence.

Given the high context-specificity of our work to SE datasets (*i.e.,* Stack Overflow posts), we decided to adopt the STANFORD CORENLP tool [SPW$^+$13], and to invest a substantial effort in creating a customized training set for it. Indeed, as highlighted in previous work [TJA14, NCL15, JSDS17], it makes no sense to apply an approach trained on movie reviews on datasets in SE contexts.

Building a Training Set for Sentiment Polarity Analysis

We extracted from the latest available Stack Overflow dump (dated July 2017) the list of all discussions (i) tagged with Java, and (ii) containing one of the following words: *library/libraries, API(s)*. Given our original goal (*i.e.,* recommending Java APIs on the basis of crowdsourced opinions), we wanted to build a training set as domain-specific as possible for the RNN. By applying these filters, we collected 276,629 discussions from which we extracted 5,073,452 sentences by using the STANFORD CORENLP toolkit [MSB$^+$14]. We randomly selected 1,500 sentences and manually labeled them by assigning a sentiment polarity score to the whole sentence and to every node composing it.

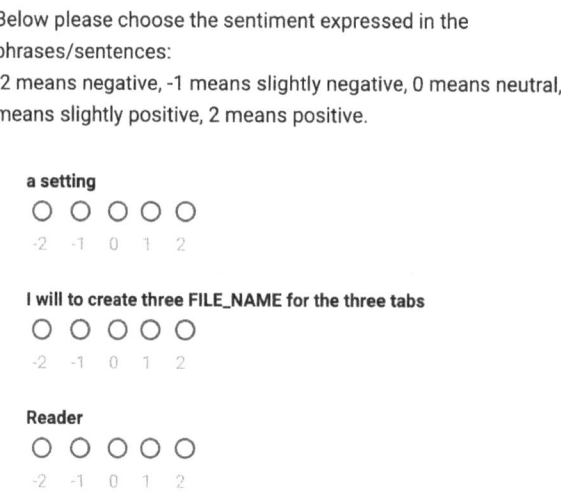

Figure 3.2. Web app used to label the sentiment polarity of the nodes extracted from Stack Overflow sentences.

The labeling process was performed by five evaluators and supported by a Web application we built (Fig. 3.2). The Web app showed to each evaluator a node (extracted from a sentence) to label with a sentiment polarity going from -2 to +2, with -2 indicating strong negative, -1 weak negative, 0 neutral, +1 weak positive, and +2 strong positive score. The choice of the five-levels sentiment polarity classification was not random, but driven by the observation of the movie reviews training set made publicly available by the authors of the STANFORD CORENLP [SPW$^+$13] sentiment analysis tool[1]. Note that a node to evaluate could be a whole sentence, an intermediate node (thus, a sub-sentence), or a leaf node (*i.e.,* a single word). To avoid any bias, the Web app did not show to the evaluator the complete sentence from which the node was extracted. Indeed, knowing the context in which a word/sentence is used could introduce a bias in the assessment of its sentiment polarity. Finally, the Web application made sure to have two evaluators for each node, thus reducing the subjectivity bias. This process, which took ~90 working hours of manual labeling, resulted in the total labeling of the sentiment polarity for 39,924 nodes (*i.e.,* 19,962 nodes extracted from the 1,500 sentences × 2 evaluators per node).

Once the labeling was completed, two of the evaluators worked on the resolution of conflicts (*i.e.,* cases in which two evaluator assigned a different sentiment polarity to the same node). All the 279 conflicts involving complete sentences (18.6% of the labeled sentences) were fixed. Indeed, it is of paramount importance to assign a consistent and double-checked sentiment polarity to the complete sentences, considering the fact that they will be used as a ground truth to evaluate our approach. Concerning the intermediate/leaf nodes, we had a total of 2,199 conflicts (11.9% of the labeled intermediate/leaf nodes). We decided to only manually solve 123 strong conflicts, meaning those for which there was a score difference ≥ 2 (*e.g.,* one of the evaluators gave 1, the other one -1), while we automatically process the 2,076 having a conflict of only one point. Indeed, slight variations of the assigned sentiment polarity (*e.g.,* one evaluator gave 1 and the other 2) are expected due to the subjectivity of the task. The final sentiment polarity score was s, in case there was agreement between the evaluators, while it was $round[(s_1 + s_2)/2]$ in case of unsolved conflict, where $round$ is the rounding function to the closest integer value and s_i is the sentiment polarity assigned by the ith evaluator.

3.2   Negative Results of Customization

We performed the assessment of the customized STANFORD CORENLP on the dataset of manually labeled 1,500 Stack Overflow sentences. Among those sentences, 178 are positive, 1,191 are neutral, and 131 are negative. We performed a ten-fold cross validation: We divided the 1,500 sentences into ten different sets, each one composed of 150 sentences. Then, we used a set as a *test set* (we only use the 150 complete sentences in the test set, and not all their intermediate/leaf nodes), while the remaining 1,350 sentences, with all their labeled intermediate/leaf nodes, were used for *training*[2]. Since we are mostly interested in discriminating between *negative*, *neutral*, and *positive* opinions, we discretized the sentiment polarity in the test set into these three levels. Sentences labeled with the sentiment polarity scores "-2" and "-1" are consid-

---

[1]https://nlp.stanford.edu/sentiment/trainDevTestTrees_PTB.zip

[2]The STANFORD CORENLP tool requires—during the training of the neural network—a so called *development* set to tune some internal parameters of the network. Among the 1,350 sentences with intermediate/leaf nodes in training set we randomly selected 300 sentences for composing the development set at each run.

ered negative (-1), those labeled with the score "0" as neutral (0), and those labeled with the scores "+1" and "+2" as positive (+1). We discretized the output of the RNN into the same three levels (*i.e.*, +1, 0, and +1). We assessed the accuracy of the opinion miner by computing recall and precision for each category. Computing the overall accuracy would not be effective, given the vast majority of *neutral* opinions in our dataset (*i.e.*, a constant *neutral* classifier would obtain a high accuracy, ignoring *negative* and *positive* opinions).

Table 3.1. Testing results of STANFORD CORENLP SO.

(a) Testing results of STANFORD CORENLP SO on all the sentences and neutral sentences.

Batch	# correct prediction	# neutral sentences	Neutral precision	Neutral recall
1	113	118	0.835	0.898
2	112	118	0.853	0.839
3	116	121	0.819	0.934
4	123	122	0.875	0.918
5	110	119	0.833	0.840
6	129	118	0.891	0.975
7	93	130	0.911	0.631
8	117	116	0.809	0.948
9	111	113	0.770	0.947
10	115	116	0.799	0.957
Overall	1139	1191	0.836	0.886

(b) Testing results of STANFORD CORENLP SO on positive sentences and negative sentences.

Batch	# positive sentences	Positive precision	Positive recall	# negative sentences	Negative precision	Negative recall
1	10	0.250	0.200	22	0.333	0.227
2	15	0.294	0.333	17	0.471	0.471
3	15	0.000	0.000	14	0.273	0.214
4	9	0.600	0.333	19	0.471	0.421
5	10	0.167	0.100	21	0.375	0.429
6	11	0.600	0.273	21	0.688	0.524
7	6	0.111	0.167	14	0.196	0.714
8	17	0.400	0.118	17	0.556	0.294
9	18	0.333	0.056	19	0.375	0.158
10	20	1.000	0.050	14	0.300	0.214
Overall	131	0.317	0.145	178	0.365	0.365

Table 3.1 reports the results achieved by STANFORD CORENLP SO[3] on Stack Overflow sentences. The table shows the number of correct predictions, the number of positive/neutral/negative sentences in the batch of testing sets and the corresponding precision/recall values, while the last row reports the overall performance on the whole dataset. Table 3.2 shows some concrete examples of sentiment polarity analysis with STANFORD CORENLP SO.

Table 3.2. Examples of sentiment polarity analysis results of Stanford CoreNLP SO.

Sentence	Oracle	Pred.
It even works on Android.	Pos.	Pos.
Hope that helps some of you with the same problem.	Pos.	Neg.
There is a central interface to access this API.	Neu.	Neu.
How is blocking performed?	Neu.	Neg.
I am not able to deploy my App Engine project locally.	Neg.	Neg.
Anyway, their current behavior does not allow what you want.	Neg.	Neu.

The results shown in Table 3.1 highlight that, despite the specific training, STANFORD CORENLP SO *does not achieve good performance in analyzing the sentiment polarity of Stack Overflow discussions.* Indeed, its precision and recall in detecting positive and negative sentiments are all below 40%, thus discouraging its usage in SE applications. Although STANFORD CORENLP SO can correctly identify more negative than positive sentences, only a small fraction of the sentences with positive/negative sentiment is identified. Also, there are more mistakenly than correctly identified sentences in both sets.

Based on the results we achieved, it is impracticable to build on the top of STANFORD CORENLP SO a reliable SE application: The high percentage of wrong sentiment polarity classification will likely result in unsatisfactory results. Thus, besides the huge effort we spent to train STANFORD CORENLP SO with a specific and large software dataset, we failed in achieving an effective sentiment analysis estimator. For this reason, we decided to shift our focus and perform a deeper analysis of the accuracy of sentiment analysis tools when used on software-related datasets. Specifically, we aim to understand whether (i) domain specific training data really helps in increasing the accuracy of sentiment polarity analysis tool; and whether (ii) other state-of-the-art sentiment polarity analysis tools are able to obtain good results on SE datasets, including our manually labeled Stack Overflow dataset. Understanding how these tools perform can also help us gain deeper insights into the current state of sentiment polarity analysis for SE.

---

[3]STANFORD CORENLP SO is the name of the tool with our new model trained with Stack Overflow discussions, while STANFORD CORENLP is the sentiment analysis component of STANFORD CORENLP with the default model trained using movie reviews.

3.3   Evaluating Sentiment Polarity Analysis for SE

Given the negative results we achieved in customizing the state-of-the-art sentiment polarity analysis tool STANFORD CORENLP with Stack Overflow data, we shift our focus to investigate how different contexts can impact the effectiveness of existing sentiment analysis tools. Therefore, we conducted a study to analyze the accuracy of these tools when applied to SE datasets. The *context* of this study consists of text extracted from three software-related datasets, namely Stack Overflow discussions, mobile app reviews, and JIRA issue comments.

3.3.1   Research Questions and Context

This study aims to answer the following research questions:

- **RQ$_1$**: *How does our* STANFORD CORENLP SO *perform compared to other sentiment polarity analysis tools?* We want to verify whether other state-of-the-art sentiment polarity analysis tools are able to achieve better accuracy on the Stack Overflow dataset we manually built, thus highlighting limitations of STANFORD CORENLP SO. Indeed, it could be that our choice of the STANFORD CORENLP and therefore of developing STANFORD CORENLP SO was not the most suitable one, and other existing tools already provide better performance.

- **RQ$_2$**: *Do different software-related datasets impact the performance of sentiment polarity analysis tools?* We want to investigate the extent to which, analyzing other kinds of SE datasets, *e.g.,* issue comments and app reviews, sentiment polarity analysis tools would achieve different performance than for Stack Overflow posts. For example, such sources might contain less neutral sentences and, the app reviews in particular, be more similar to the typical training sets of sentiment polarity analysis tools.

The context of the study consists of textual documents from three different software repositories, *i.e.,* (i) Q&A forums, *i.e.,* Stack Overflow discussions, (ii) app stores, *i.e.,* users' reviews on mobile apps, and (iii) issue trackers, *i.e.,* JIRA issue comments. We chose these types of textual documents as they have been studied by SE researchers, also in the context of sentiment polarity analysis [PSG⁺15, OAD⁺15, CLN17, UK17b]. As our goal is to evaluate the accuracy of different sentiment polarity analysis tools on these three datasets, we need to define the ground truth sentiment polarity for each of the sentences/texts they contain. The following process was adopted to collect the three datasets and define their ground truth:

- **Stack Overflow discussions.** We reuse the ground truth for the 1,500 sentences used to evaluate STANFORD CORENLP SO .

- **Mobile app reviews.** We randomly selected 341 reviews from the dataset of 3k reviews provided by Villarroel *et al.* [VBR⁺16], which contains manually-labeled reviews classified on the basis of the main information they contain.

Four categories are considered: *bug reporting, suggestion for new feature, request for improving non-functional requirements* (*e.g.,* performance of the app), and *other* (meaning, reviews not belonging to any of the previous categories). When performing the random selection, we made sure to respect the proportion of reviews belonging to the four categories in the original population in our sample (*e.g.,* if 50% of the 3k reviews belonged to the "other" category, we randomly selected 50% of our sample from that category).

Once selected, we manually labeled the sentiment polarity of each review. The labeling process was performed by two evaluators. The evaluators had to decide where the text is positive, neutral, or negative. A third evaluator was involved to solve 51 conflict cases.

- **JIRA issue comments.** We use the dataset collected by Ortu *et al.* [OMD$^+$16], containing 4k sentences labeled by three raters with respect to four emotions: *love, joy, anger,* and *sadness*. This dataset has been used in several studies as the "golden set" for evaluating sentiment analysis tools [JSDS17, IZ17]. During the original labeling process, each sentence was labeled with one of six emotions: *love, joy, surprise, anger, sadness, fear*. Among these six emotions, *love, joy, anger,* and *sadness* are mostly expressed. As also done by Jongeling *et al.* [JSDS17], we map the sentences with the label *love* or *joy* into positive sentences, and those with label *anger* or *sadness* into negative sentences.

The new datasets are used for testing only, and they are not involved in the tool training process. Table 3.3 reports for each dataset (i) the number of sentences extracted, and (ii) the number of positive, neutral, negative sentences.

Table 3.3. Dataset used for evaluating sentiment polarity analysis tools in SE

Dataset	# sentences	# positive	# neutral	# negative
Stack Overflow	1,500	178	1,191	131
App reviews	341	186	25	130
JIRA issue	926	290	0	636

3.3.2 Data Collection and Analysis

On the three datasets described above we experimented with the following tools, which are popular in the SE research community:

- SENTISTRENGTH. SENTISTRENGTH does not directly give the text sentiment polarity, instead, it reports two sentiment strength scores: one score for the negative sentiment expressed in the text from -1 (not negative) to -5 (extremely negative), the other for the positive sentiment expressed from 1 (not positive) to 5 (extremely positive). We sum these two scores, and map the sum of over 0, 0, and below 0 into positive, neutral, and negative, respectively.

- **NLTK.** Based on VADER SENTIMENT ANALYSIS, NLTK reports four sentiment strength scores for the text analyzed: "negative", "neutral", "positive", and "compound". The scores for "negative", "neutral", and "positive" range from 0 to 1, while the "compound" score is normalized to be between -1 (most extreme negative) and +1 (most extreme positive). As suggested by the author of the VADER component[4], we use the following thresholds to identify the sentiment of the text analyzed: $score \geq 0.5$: positive; $-0.5 < score < 0.5$: neutral; $score \leq -0.5$: negative.

- **STANFORD CORENLP.** By default, STANFORD CORENLP reports the sentiment polarity of the text on a five-value scale: very negative, negative, neutral, positive, and very positive. Since we are only interested in discriminating between negative, neutral, and positive opinions, we merged very negative into negative, and very positive into positive.

- **SENTISTRENGTH-SE.** As it is a tool based on SENTISTRENGTH, and uses the same format of reported results, we interpret its sentiment score by adopting the same approach we used for SENTISTRENGTH.

- **STANFORD CORENLP SO.** Similarly, we use the same approach adopted for STANFORD CORENLP to convert five-scale values into three-scale values. To examine the performance on app reviews and JIRA issue comments, we used the Stack Overflow labeled sentences (including internal nodes) as training set[5].

We assess the accuracy of the tools by computing recall and precision for each of the three considered sentiment categories (*i.e.,* positive, neutral, negative) in each dataset.

3.3.3 Results

Table 3.4 reports the results we achieved by applying the five sentiment polarity analysis approaches on the three different SE datasets. The table reports the number of correct predictions made by the tools, and precision/recall for predicting sentiment of positive/neutral/negative sentences. For each dataset/metric, the best achieved results are highlighted in **bold**. In the following we discuss the achieved results aiming at answering our research questions.

---

[4]https://github.com/cjhutto/vaderSentiment
[5]In this case, 20% of the training set was used as development set.

Table 3.4. Evaluation results for sentiment analysis tools applied in SE domain. In bold the best results.

(a) Evaluation results for the whole dataset and neutral sentences.

Dataset	Tool	# correct prediction	Neutral precision	Neutral recall
Stack Overflow	SENTISTRENGTH	1,043	0.858	0.772
	NLTK	1,168	0.815	**0.941**
	STANFORD CORENLP	604	**0.884**	0.344
	SENTISTRENGTH-SE	**1,170**	0.826	0.930
	STANFORD CORENLP SO	1,139	0.836	0.886
App reviews	SENTISTRENGTH	213	0.113	0.320
	NLTK	184	0.093	**0.440**
	STANFORD CORENLP	**237**	**0.176**	0.240
	SENTISTRENGTH-SE	201	0.106	0.400
	STANFORD CORENLP SO	142	0.084	0.320
JIRA issues	SENTISTRENGTH	**714**	-	-
	NLTK	276	-	-
	STANFORD CORENLP	626	-	-
	SENTISTRENGTH-SE	704	-	-
	STANFORD CORENLP SO	333	-	-

(b) Evaluation results for the whole positive and negative sentences.

Dataset	Tool	Positive precision	Positive recall	Negative precision	Negative recall
Stack Overflow	SENTISTRENGTH	0.200	**0.359**	0.397	0.433
	NLTK	**0.317**	0.244	**0.625**	0.084
	STANFORD CORENLP	0.231	0.344	0.177	**0.837**
	SENTISTRENGTH-SE	0.312	0.221	0.500	0.185
	STANFORD CORENLP SO	**0.317**	0.145	0.365	0.365
App reviews	SENTISTRENGTH	0.745	**0.866**	0.815	0.338
	NLTK	0.751	0.812	**1.000**	0.169
	STANFORD CORENLP	**0.831**	0.715	0.667	**0.754**
	SENTISTRENGTH-SE	0.741	0.817	0.929	0.300
	STANFORD CORENLP SO	0.770	0.253	0.470	0.669
JIRA issues	SENTISTRENGTH	0.850	**0.921**	0.993	0.703
	NLTK	0.840	0.362	**1.000**	0.269
	STANFORD CORENLP	0.726	0.621	0.945	0.701
	SENTISTRENGTH-SE	**0.948**	0.883	0.996	**0.704**
	STANFORD CORENLP SO	0.635	0.252	0.724	0.409

RQ$_1$: How does our Stanford CoreNLP SO perform as compared to other sentiment polarity analysis tools?

To answer RQ$_1$, we analyze the results achieved by the five tools on the Stack Overflow dataset we built.

As for the comparison of STANFORD CORENLP SO with the original model of STANFORD CORENLP, the results show that on neutral sentences STANFORD CORENLP SO achieves a better recall while keeping almost the same level of precision. Also, on positive and negative sentences STANFORD CORENLP SO is still able to provide a good increment of the precision.

However, in this case the increment of precision has a price to pay: STANFORD CORENLP SO provides levels of recall lower than STANFORD CORENLP. The comparison between STANFORD CORENLP and STANFORD CORENLP SO should be read taking into account that the original STANFORD CORENLP model is trained on over 10k labeled sentences (*i.e.,* >215k nodes). STANFORD CORENLP SO is trained on a smaller training set. Thus, it is possible that a larger training set could improve the performance of STANFORD CORENLP SO. However, as of now, this is a mere conjecture.

When looking at other tools, the analysis of the results reveal that all the experimented tools achieve comparable results and—more important—none of the experimented tools is able to reliably assess the sentiment expressed in a Stack Overflow sentence. Indeed, while all the tools are able to obtain good results when predicting neutral sentences, their accuracy falls when working on positive and negative sentences. For example, even considering the tool having the highest recall for identifying positive sentences (*i.e.,* SENTISTRENGTH) (i) there is only 35.9% chance that it can correctly spot a positive sentence and (ii) four out of five sentences that it will label as positive will be actually false positives (precision=20%). The recall is almost the same as randomly guessing which has 33.3% chance of success. These results reveal that there is still a long way to go before researchers and practitioners can use state-of-the-art sentiment polarity analysis tools to identify the sentiment expressed in Stack Overflow discussions.

RQ$_1$ main findings: (i) the training of STANFORD CORENLP on Stack Overflow discussions does not provide a significant improvement as compared to the original model trained on movie reviews; (ii) the prediction accuracy of all tools are biased toward the majority class (neutral) for which a very good precision and recall is almost always achieved; and (iii) all tools achieve similar performance and it is impossible to identify among them a clear winner or, in any case, a tool ensuring sufficient sentiment assessment of sentences from Stack Overflow discussions.

RQ$_2$: Do different software-related datasets impact the performance of sentiment analysis tools?

To answer RQ$_2$, we compare the accuracy of all tools on the three datasets considered in our study. When we look at results for app reviews, we can see that, differently from what observed in the Stack Overflow dataset, most tools can predict positive texts with reasonable precision/recall values. Even for negative reviews, the results are in general much better. It is worth noting that STANFORD CORENLP is competitive for identifying positive and negative sentiment as compared to other tools. Indeed, compared to other texts in SE datasets, such as Stack Overflow discussions and JIRA issues, app reviews can be less technical and relatively more similar to movie reviews, with which the original model of STANFORD CORENLP is trained. However, when identifying neutral app reviews, all tools exhibit poor accuracy. This is likely due to the fact that, while positive and negative app reviews could be easily identified by the presence/absence of some "marker terms" (*e.g.,* the presence of the *bug* term is likely related to negative reviews), this is not the case for the neutral set of reviews, in which a wider and more variegate vocabulary might be used.

When inspecting results for JIRA issue comments, we find that the tools STAN-FORD CORENLP and SENTISTRENGTH-SE have better accuracy than others. However, SENTISTRENGTH-SE provides a better precision-recall balance across the two categories of sentiment (*i.e.,* positive and negative). Despite the mostly good results achieved by the experimented tools on the JIRA dataset, there are some important issues in the evaluations performed on this dataset.

First, the absence of neutral sentences does not provide a clear and complete assessment of the accuracy of the tools. Indeed, as shown in the app reviews, neutral texts might be, in some datasets, the most difficult to identify, likely due to the fact that they represent that "grey zone" close to both positive and negative sentiment.

Second, the JIRA dataset is built by mapping emotions expressed in the comments (*e.g.,* joy or love) into sentiment polarities (*e.g.,* positive). However, such a mapping does not always hold. For instance, positive comments in issue tracker does not always express joy or love (*e.g., thanks for the updated patch*), thus allowing to obtain a very partial view of the accuracy of sentiment polarity analysis tools.

To highlight the importance of *neutral* items in the evaluation of a sentiment polarity analysis tool, Table 3.5 shows the confusion matrices obtained by the five different sentiment polarity analysis tools on the Stack Overflow dataset (see Table 3.3). In the matrices, each row represents the actual sentiment polarity, while each column represents the predicted sentiment polarity using corresponding tools.

All tools are effective in discriminating between positive and negative items. For example, our STANFORD CORENLP SO only misclassified two negative sentences as positive, and 16 positive sentences as negative. NLTK only misclassifies five negative sentences as positive, and three positive sentences as negative. The errors are mostly due to negative/positive sentences classified as neutral and *vice versa*. This confirms the issues found by Tourani *et al.* [TJA14] when using SENTISTRENGTH on SE data, and this is why evaluating sentiment polarity analysis tools on datasets not containing neutral sentences introduces a considerable bias. Similar observations hold for the app reviews dataset, in which the performance in classifying neutral reviews is, as shown in Table 3.4, extremely poor.

Table 3.5. Confusion matrices on the Stack Overflow dataset.

SENTISTRENGTH			
	Positive	Neutral	Negative
Positive	47	66	18
Neutral	173	919	99
Negative	15	86	77

NLTK			
	Positive	Neutral	Negative
Positive	32	96	3
Neutral	64	1121	6
Negative	5	158	15

STANFORD CORENLP			
	Positive	Neutral	Negative
Positive	45	30	56
Neutral	145	410	636
Negative	5	24	149

SENTISTRENGTH-SE			
	Positive	Neutral	Negative
Positive	29	93	9
Neutral	59	1108	24
Negative	5	140	33

STANFORD CORENLP SO			
	Positive	Neutral	Negative
Positive	19	96	16
Neutral	39	1055	97
Negative	2	111	65

RQ$_2$ main findings: The accuracy of sentiment polarity analysis tools is, in general, poor on SE datasets. We found no tool able to reliably discriminating between positive/negative and neutral items. Indeed, while the accuracy on the app reviews and JIRA datasets are acceptable, (i) in the app reviews dataset the accuracy in identifying neutral items is very low, and (ii) the data obtained with the JIRA dataset can not be considered as reliable due to the discussed issues.

3.4   Threats to Validity

Threats to *construct validity* concern the relation between theory and observation. The first concern is related to our manual sentiment labeling. Sentiment expressed in the text might be misinterpreted by people. The labeling might also be impacted by evaluators' subjective opinions. Although we adopted an additional conflict resolving process, it is not guaranteed that the manually assigned sentiment is always correct.

Another threat is the sentiment score mapping, *i.e.*, mapping five-scale sentiment to three-scale sentiment. Indeed, sentiment expressed in the text have different degrees. Predicting slightly negative sentence as neutral should be considered a smaller mistake than predicting a very negative sentence as neutral, since the threshold to draw a line between the neutral and the negative sentiment can be more subjective.

Threats to *internal validity* concern internal factors we did not consider that could affect the variables and the relations being investigated. In our study, they are mainly due to the configuration of sentiment analysis tools/approaches we used. In most cases, we use the default or suggested parameters, for example, the threshold for NLTK. However, some parameters might be further tuned to increase the sentiment prediction performance.

Threats to *conclusion validity* concern the relation between the treatment and the outcome. During our study, we randomly selected sentences from Stack Overflow discussions and app reviews from an existing dataset [VBR$^+$16]. While we considered statistically significant samples, we cannot guarantee that our samples are representative of the whole population.

Threats to *external validity* concern the generalizability of our findings. While the evaluation has considered the most commonly used sentiment analysis tools in SE, some less popular tools might have been ignored. Constantly there are lots of new ideas and approaches popping up in the NLP domain, but few of them have been examined and verified in the SE context. Since our goal is to seek a good sentiment polarity analysis tool for software-related texts, in this chapter we only select the tools already used in previous SE studies. Our datasets are limited to three frequently mined SE repositories, while texts in other contexts, such mailing list and IRC chats, are not considered.

3.5   Lessons Learned

The results of our study provided us with a number of lessons learned.

No tool is ready for real usage of identifying sentiment polarity expressed in SE related discussions yet. No tool, including those specifically customized for certain SE tasks, can provide precision and recall levels sufficient to entail the tool adoption for a task such as identifying the sentiment of Stack Overflow posts. By relying on such tools, we would generate wrong predictions. Our results warn the research community: Sentiment polarity analysis tools should always be carefully evaluated in the specific context of usage before building something on top of them.

Specific re-training is required, but does not represent a silver bullet for improving the accuracy. Previous literature has pointed our that sentiment polarity analysis tools cannot be used out-of-the-box for SE tasks [JSDS17, TJA14, NCL15, IZ17]. In some cases, tools have introduced a data preprocessing or a re-training to cope with the specific SE lexicon, in which there are positive or negative words/sub-sentences that are not positive or negative in other contexts, or *vice versa* (*e.g.,* the word *bug* generally carries a negative sentiment when referred to an API, while it can be considered neutral in movie reviews). However, as results have shown, this might still be insufficient to guarantee good accuracy in terms of both precision and recall on all polarity levels. Also, customization is very dataset specific, and therefore applying the tool on different datasets would require a new training. In other words, customizing a sentiment analysis tool for JIRA does not make it ready for Stack Overflow and *vice versa*. Finally, some algorithms, such as recursive neural networks, require costly re-training. In our case, the training performed with 1,500 sentences (which turned into labeling almost 40k nodes) revealed to be insufficient for a clear improvement of the STANFORD CORENLP accuracy.

Some SE applications make sentiment polarity analysis easier than others. Sentiment analysis tools perform better on app reviews. App reviews contain sentences that, in most cases, clearly express the opinion of a user, who wants to reward an app or penalize it, by pointing out a nice feature or a serious problem. Hence, the context is very similar to what those sentiment tools are familiar with. Still, as observed, the tools' performance on the *neutral* category is very poor. Looking at the issue tracker data, besides the lack of neutral sentences in the JIRA dataset (which *per se* makes the life of the sentiment analysis tools much easier), again the predominance of problem-reporting sentences may (slightly) play in favor of such tools. Stack Overflow is a different beast. Posts mostly contain discussions on how to use a piece of technology, and between the lines somebody points out whether an API or a code pattern is good or less optimal. In many cases, without even expressing strong opinions. This definitely makes the applicability of sentiment analysis much more difficult.

Should we expect 100% accuracy from sentiment polarity analysis tools? No, we should not. In our manual evaluation, out of the 1,500 Stack Overflow sentences we manually labeled, there were 279 cases of disagreement (18.6%). This means that even humans are not able to agree about the sentiment expressed in a given sentence. This is also in line with findings of Murgia *et al.* [MTAO14] on emotion mining: Except when a sentence expresses clear emotions of love, joy and sadness, even for humans it is hard to agree. Hence, it is hard to expect that an automated tool can do any better. Having said that, advances are still needed to make sentiment analysis tools usable in the SE domain.

Text reporting positive and negative sentiment is not sufficient to evaluate sentiment polarity analysis tools. As discussed, the most difficult task for sentiment analysis tools is to discriminate between positive/negative *vs* neutral sentiment, while they are quite effective in discriminating between positive and negative sentiment. This is why datasets such as the JIRA one that we, and others, used in previous work [JSDS17, IZ17], is not sufficient to evaluate sentiment polarity analysis tools. We hope that releasing our dataset [LZB+b] will help in more robust evaluations of sentiment polarity analysis tools.

3.6 Conclusion

In this chapter, we trained a new model to identify the sentiment polarity of software-related texts on a set of 40k manually labeled sentences/words extracted from Stack Overflow discussions. We also compared the performance of STANFORD NLP based on our new model with other state-of-the-art sentiment analysis tools commonly used in SE studies. Our results suggest that no tool is ready for practical use in SE applications yet, and further investigations on how to leverage domain-specific features of texts for sentiment analysis are necessary.

Some say that the road to hell is paved with good intentions. Our work started out with what we consider a promising idea: We wanted to customize a state-of-the-art sentiment polarity analysis approach for the SE domain. To do so, we wanted to leverage the large body of knowledge that is stored in Q&A websites like Stack Overflow. The approach was going to exploit opinion mining using deep learning through RNN. However, as we finalized our work we noticed that it simply did not work, because of the unacceptable performance.

The reason for the failure is manifold. Firstly, it highlights how machine learning, even in its most advanced forms, is and remains a black box, and it is not completely clear what happens in that black box. To this one can add the design principle "*garbage in, garbage out*": No matter how advanced a technique, if the input is not appropriate, it is improbable that an acceptable output can be produced. In the specific case one might argue that Stack Overflow is not really the place where emotions run high: It is a place where developers discuss technicalities. Therefore it is rather obvious that opinion mining will have a hard time. While this might be true, our study revealed that also in datasets where emotions are more evident, like app reviews and issue trackers, there is an intrinsic problem with the accuracy of current state-of-the-art sentiment analysis tools.

Our negative experience indicates that simple customization of existing sentiment polarity analysis tools might not be enough for obtaining satisfactory accuracy in sentiment polarity detection for SE tasks. Instead, we need a novel approach essentially different from the existing ones. Therefore, we decided to adopt a pattern matching-based solution, which is introduced in Chapter 4.

4

Mining Opinions from Q&A Sites to Support Software Design Decisions

Our previous work in Chapter 3 has shown that out-of-the-box, customized or re-trained sentiment polarity analysis tools are particularly unreliable (and very often in disagreement) when applied to SE corpora. Therefore, it is very unlikely to obtain satisfactory results when applying these tools in SE tasks. We have to propose an alternative approach to accurately identify the sentiment polarity in online discussions. Meanwhile, we also need to consider how we can leverage the sentiment information for providing correct and insightful opinions to developers.

A recent work by Uddin and Khomh [UK17c] dealt with API opinion mining by relying on an SVM-based aspect classification approach and a customized Sentiment Orientation algorithm [HL04]. Stemming from the positive and negative results highlighted in previous attempt to automatically mine API opinions and from the seminal work by Uddin and Khomh [UK17c] in this field, we propose a novel approach named Pattern-based Opinion MinEr (POME), which leverages linguistic patterns contained in Stack Overflow sentences referring to APIs, and classify whether (i) a sentence refers to a particular API aspect (functional, documentation, community, compatibility, performance, reliability, or usability), and (ii) it has a positive or negative polarity.

We first link sentences in Stack Overflow discussions to APIs using a modified version of the approach by Treude and Robillard [TR16]. Then, we parse the sentences using the spaCy [spa] and identify whether a sentence matches a pattern among 157 manually defined ones. Each pattern consists of a natural language parse tree where each leaf can either be a generic part-of-speech (*e.g.*, a noun) or, in some cases, a specific part-of-speech (taken from a thesaurus we have built), characterizing an aspect positively or negatively. We have evaluated our approach along three dimensions:

1. We assess the precision and recall of POME in identifying API-related opinions in Stack Overflow on a manually labeled dataset of 1,662 sentences. We compare different variants of POME based on simple pattern matching as well as on machine learning algorithms, finding that its best configuration achieves a precision ranging between 0.61 and 1.00 and a recall ranging between 0.13 and 0.44, depending on the quality aspect subject of the opinion.

2. We compare the performance of the opinion polarity assessment when using pattern matching with six sentiment analysis tools, finding that the defined 157 patterns help in achieving higher values of precision/recall both for positive (0.92 precision and 0.99 recall) and for negative (0.94 precision and 0.73 recall) opinions.

3. We conducted a survey with 24 Computer Science students and professional developers to collect their assessment about the precision of the opinions mined by POME and by the state-of-the-art opinion mining tool OPINER [UK17c] for four popular APIs. The achieved results show that, for most of the quality aspect categories (*e.g.,* usability), POME is able to mine opinions with a higher precision than OPINER.

4. We release POME's source code, the Web app used to label patterns, and the list of patterns we manually defined and all the data used in our evaluations in a replication package [LZB⁺a].

Structure of the Chapter

Section 4.1 presents our proposal of a rationale-based API recommender system. Section 4.2 thoroughly describes the technical details of POME, the core technique behind the system. Section 4.3 reports the design of the study we performed to assess the performance of POME on sentiment polarity identification and quality aspect categorization, and Section 4.4 presents the corresponding results. Finally, after the discussion of threats to validity (Section 3.5), Section 4.6 concludes this chapter.

4.1 Rationale-Based Software API Recommender: A Proposal

In this section, we present our proposal to build a rationale-based software API recommender. We describe our motivation, outline the architecture, and present the most relevant and the state-of-the-art tool. We also discuss why we need a novel approach for system implementation.

4.1.1 Motivation

Online discussions among software developers on various communication channels — *e.g.,* mailing lists, issue trackers, and Question & Answer (Q&A) forums such as Stack Overflow — are playing a major and increasingly important role in software development. Such sources bring various pieces of information, including examples of how to use programming language constructs, application programming interfaces (APIs) or frameworks, and discussions about design choices or algorithmic solutions to certain development problems. To cope with the limited search capabilities of Q&A forums and other sources, and to alleviate developers' burden of manually searching for relevant information, researchers have proposed a wide variety of recommender systems. Such systems can for example link Stack Overflow discussions to code snippets [RR13], produce documentation [WYT13], enhance existing documentation by mining Stack Overflow discussions [SIH14], or identify insights about APIs [TR16].

Naturally, developers' discussions contain opinions, *e.g.,* whether a certain API is suitable for solving a given problem, or what the pros and cons of a given framework are. For example, some developers might recommend an API for its rich functionality, while others may warn about its performance. Recommenders could therefore exploit such opinions — *i.e.,* perform *opinion mining* — and suggest APIs that best satisfy the developers' needs, which can be better functionality, better performance, increased compatibility, ease of use, etc.

Given the potentially valuable information in these online discussions, we propose to design and implement a system to recommend software APIs to developers with rationales (*i.e.,* what the benefits and the drawbacks to adopt a specific API are). Our goal is to assist developers in assessing the quality of software APIs exploiting crowdsourced knowledge by mining developers' opinions on Stack Overflow.

4.1.2 System Architecture

In our perspective of a rationale-based software API recommender, the system should take as input a short description of a task at hand (*i.e.,* functional requirements), and then suggest which APIs developers can use, and what the pros and cons of adopting those APIs are. The basic idea is to leverage crowdsourced knowledge by mining opinions posted by developers while discussing on Q&A websites such as Stack Overflow.

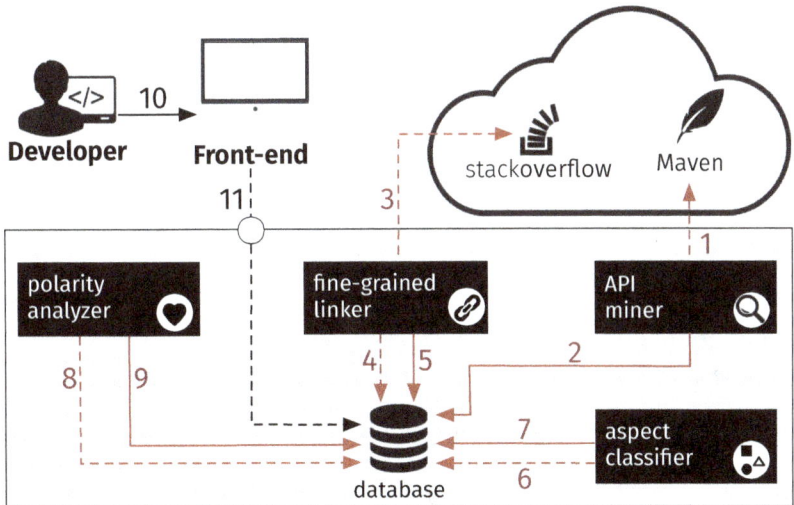

Figure 4.1. Our vision of the rationale-based software API recommender system.

The overall idea is depicted in Fig. 4.1. The dashed arrows represent dependencies (*e.g.,* ① and ③), while the full arrows indicate flows of information pushed from one component to another. Arrows depicted in red (*i.e.,* those numbered from ① to ⑨) indicate operations performed only once with the goal of storing crowdsourced opinions about software APIs in a database; the black ones represent instead actions triggered by a request for recommendations about the software API to use made by the developer using the front-end.

The *API miner* mines from the maven central repository[1] all available Java APIs (① in Fig. 4.1). The relevant information about these APIs is then extracted and stored into our database ②.

The *fine-grained linker* mines Stack Overflow discussions to establish links between the APIs stored in the database ④ and relevant sentences in Stack Overflow discussions ③. For example, the sentence *"Apache commons-io is the straightforward solution to programmatically copy files"* is linked to the commons-io library.

Knowing the sentences related to an API, the *aspect classifier* categorizes each sentence based on the non-functional requirements it refers to (*e.g.,* usability, performance, security, etc.) ⑥, and adds this information to the database ⑦. The sentences not classified as "none" (*i.e.,* those discussing quality aspects relevant to mined opinions about APIs) are then analyzed by the *polarity analyzer* ⑧, that identifies the sentiment they express and consequently their polarity, *i.e., positive* or *negative* (we ignore sentences with a *neutral* sentiment since they are not of interest when mining opinions), and stores this information in the database ⑨.

Finally, a developer interested in accessing opinions about an API can submit a textual query through the Web-based front-end ⑩. She can search for a specific API or, if she does not know which API to use, the query can be used to describe the task she wants to perform (*e.g.,* reading JSON files in Java). This information is provided to a Web service ⑪ to identify the most relevant APIs for the given query and provide as output the opinions mined for them.

4.1.3   Opiner: The Most Relevant and the State-Of-The-Art Tool

The closest work to our proposed API recommender system is OPINER [UK19][2], an online API review search and summarization engine we discussed in Section 2.3.2. To grasp a better understanding of how OPINER works, we illustrate with an example.

As it can be seen from Fig. 4.2, users can find an API in three different means:

- *Search API.* Users can search with the API names to locate a specific API.

- *Search API Aspect.* Users can search with the keyword representing an aspect (*e.g.,* Usability). OPINER will present the list of the most popular APIs based on the aspect. Meanwhile, the lists of APIs with the most positive and the most negative reviews regarding this aspect are also returned.

---

[1] http://central.maven.org/maven2/maven/
[2] The online app can be found at http://opiner.polymtl.ca/.

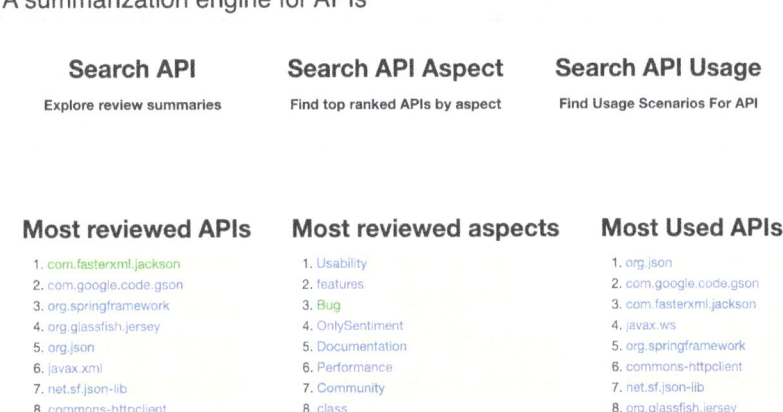

Figure 4.2. The homepage of OPINER.

- *Search API Usage.* Users can search with the API name to see how the API is used in code fragments. A brief summary of the API is also given.

To understand how OPINER classifies API-related discussions into different categories and sentiment polarities, the most reviewed API "com.fasterxml.jackson" was taken as an example (Fig. 4.3). OPINER adopted both a pre-defined list of static aspects (*e.g.,* performance, security) and dynamically inferred aspects for specific APIs (*e.g.,* the aspect "implementation" for the API "com.fasterxml.jackson"). The discussions on API are categorized into static aspects with a classifier based on SVM, while the dynamic aspect identification is done with the help of a text summarization technique TextRank [MT04]. Each aspect is ranked with up to five stars to indicate how positive the relevant discussions are by assessing the sentiment polarity in the texts.

OPINER was evaluated by recruiting professional software engineers to pick the right API for two development tasks. Their results indicate that with the help of OPINER, developers can make the right decision more accurately and quickly.

Coincidentally, we were working on our approach for the proposed rationale-based API recommender system at the same time when Uddin and Khomh were crafting OPINER. In fact, Uddin and Khomh opted for a customized version of the Sentiment Orientation algorithm [HL04] to detect the sentiment polarity of sentences related to APIs. Given our experience reported in Chapter 3 regarding the performance of state-of-the-art sentiment polarity analysis approaches, we adopted an entirely different solution based on pattern matching. We show in Section 4.4 the detailed comparison between the two tools.

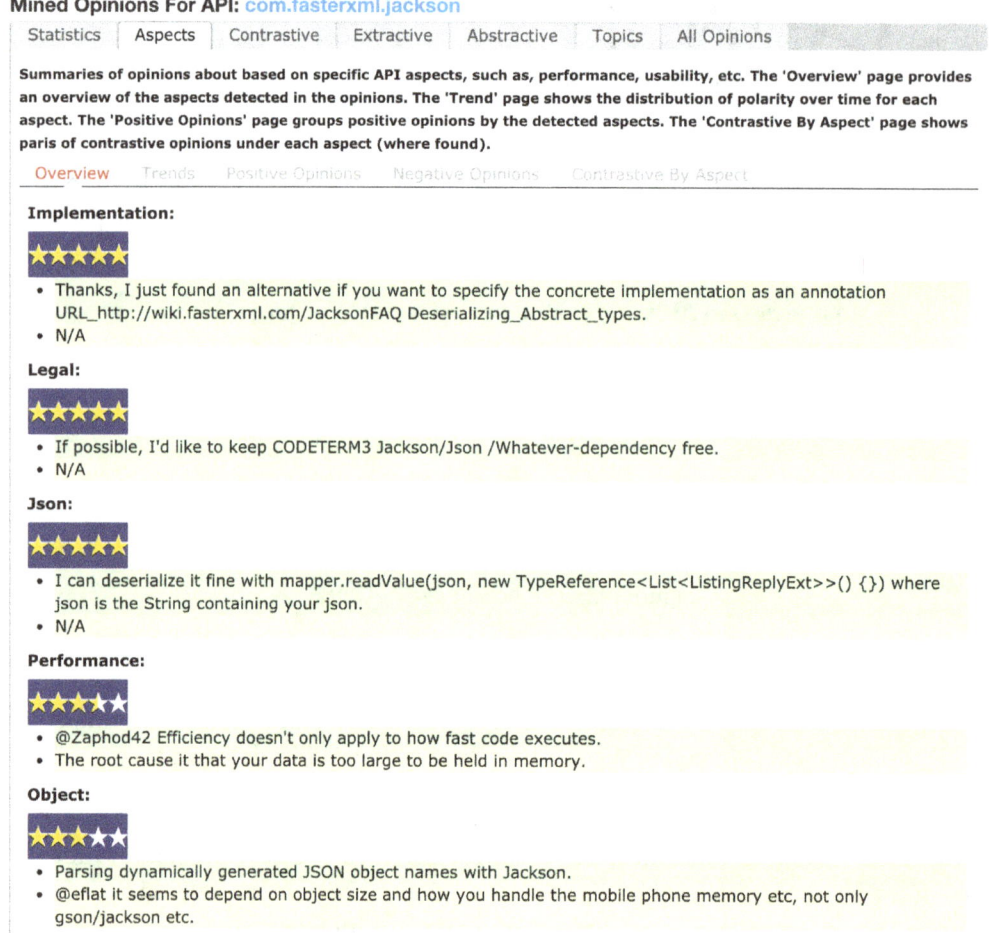

Figure 4.3. Screenshot of the "Aspects" page of the most reviewed API from OPINER.

While tools like OPINER can already classify API-related opinions into different aspects and sentiment polarity, it is pre-assumed that developers know which APIs can be used to implement certain functionalities. This is however not always the case when a developer encounters a new task in an unfamiliar domain. Meanwhile, as discussed in Section 2.2.1, previous studies have already warned us the necessity to carefully verify the reliability of opinion mining tools before they are applied in software related contexts. Indeed, the amount of online discussions related to APIs is huge. We need to make sure that developers can get correct information without too much noise. Therefore, a technique with a high precision is desired. To reach this goal, we decided to customize a state-of-the-art approach for our specific application.

4.2   POME: Pattern-based Opinion MinEr

As introduced in Section 4.1.2, our proposed rationale-based API recommender system consists of four main components: 1) an API miner, 2) a fine-grained linker, 3) a polarity analyzer, and 4) an aspect classifier. In the following, we detail the design of these main components in our novel approach Pattern-based Opinion MinEr (POME).

4.2.1   API Miner

The *API miner* is implemented as a Web scraper for extracting all available Java APIs from the Maven central repository [mav]. We record for each API its: (i) name, (ii) description, (iii) link to the jar file of the latest version, and (iv) release date of the jar file. We collected this information for a total of 116,318 APIs, between May and June 2017, storing it in our database.

Table 4.1. Regular expressions for extracting API-related sentences in Stack Overflow answers.

No	Regular expression	Case sensitive?
1	$(?i). * \backslash bPackageName\backslash.TypeName\backslash b.*$ **Description**: Fully-qualified API type [TR16]	
2	$.*(|[a\text{-}z]+ |[\backslash.!?] |[\backslash(<])TypeName)([> \backslash)\backslash., !?\$] |[a\text{-}z]+).*$ **Description**: Non-qualified API type [TR16]	✓
3	$.* < a.*href.*PackageName/TypeName\backslash.html.* > .* < /a > .*$ **Description**: Link to the API official documentation [TR16]	✓
4	$. * ClassName\backslash.MethodName[\backslash(\_]$ **Description**: Reference to a method of a specific class	✓

4.2.2   Fine-Grained Linker

This component retrieves sentences from Stack Overflow posts related to a given API. Given an API (*e.g.,* Google Gson), we use the information collected by the API miner to download its jar file. Using Java Reflection we extract the complete list of its classes and methods. We then link sentences in Stack Overflow discussions to APIs, using a reimplementation of the linker by Treude and Robillard [TR16]. There are two differences between our approach and the one by Treude and Robillard [TR16]. First, while they use the Stack Overflow API to retrieve the Stack Overflow discussions, we rely on the December 2017 official Stack Overflow data dump to avoid issues related to usage limitations of the API. Second, they use the first three regular expressions reported in Table 4.1 to identify sentences including (i) the fully-qualified API type (*e.g.,* com.google.code.gson); (ii) the non-qualified

API type (*e.g.,* Gson); and (iii) the link to the official API documentation (*e.g.,* `https://sites.google.com/site/gson/gson-user-guide`). In our approach, we also retrieve Stack Overflow sentences matching the fourth regular expression shown in Table 4.1. We decided to include this fourth regular expression since we observed that many sentences on Stack Overflow discuss issues related to APIs by referring to specific APIs rather than to the API type (*i.e.,* name) or to its documentation. While this additional regular expression might introduce false positives, matching both the class name and the method name mitigates this risk. We discuss the precision of this additional regular expression in Section 4.5.

We use the *fine-grained linker* to identify all relevant sentences for a given API only from Stack Overflow answers (*i.e.,* we do not consider questions), because opinions are unlikely to reside in the questions, where users mostly ask for help. Also, we discard sentences belonging to questions posted before the release date of the API jar file under analysis, to reduce the risk of mining opinions referring to old releases of the API. The sentences identified by the *fine-grained linker*, along with the link to the respective API, are stored in the POME's database for all previously mined APIs.

4.2.3 Aspect Classifier

The *aspect classifier* analyzes the stored sentences to identify the quality aspect(s) discussed in them. In the following, we discuss different ways to perform this task, while in Section 4.3 we explain how we identified the best solution.

Pattern matching-based approach

The conjecture is that users providing opinions about APIs on Stack Overflow tend to use repetitive discourse patterns that can be encoded to capture both the quality aspect(s) and the sentiment of the opinion (thus, pattern matching can be used in the context of the *polarity analyzer*). To identify the patterns, we manually analyzed 4,346 Stack Overflow sentences identified by the *fine-grained linker* as related to APIs belonging to the six categories of popular APIs (provided by Maven central) reported in Table 4.2.

Table 4.2 reports the name of the category, the number of API-related sentences extracted from Stack Overflow discussions, the number of sentences we manually analyzed, and the link to Maven central listing the APIs belonging to the specific category. From each category, we only extracted sentences related to the five most used APIs listed on `https://mvnrepository.com/`. For categories having more than 1,000 linked sentences, we manually analyzed only a randomly selected subset to avoid bias in the definition of the patterns (*i.e.,* extract patterns that are very specific to one predominant API category in our dataset).

The 4,346 sentences have been manually analyzed by four evaluators (authors of this study), with the support of a Web app (Fig. 4.4), to categorize each one as expressing or not an opinion about the linked API. Each sentence was randomly assigned to two of the four evaluators, resulting in $\simeq$2,180 sentences per evaluator. In

Table 4.2. Dataset used for patterns' definition and training of the machine learning algorithms.

Category	# sentences linked	# sentences validated	URL
Bytecode APIs	2,645	999	goo.gl/rzoqc7
Embedded SQL DB	622	622	goo.gl/kknzvD
HTTP Clients	1,714	999	goo.gl/b8vgQN
JSON APIs	4,764	999	goo.gl/9cas1C
Reflection APIs	481	481	goo.gl/6935xc
SSH APIs	246	246	goo.gl/2ih4h6
Overall	**10,481**	**4,346**	-

Table 4.3. Numbers of sentences identified for each of the aspects during manual analysis.

Quality aspect	# Opinions	
	Negative	Positive
Community	2	8
Compatibility	21	10
Documentation	3	29
Functional	13	153
Performance	12	26
Reliability	18	10
Usability	9	74
None	*3,958*	

case a sentence did not report any opinion, we assigned the *"none"* label. If an opinion was identified, the evaluator firstly selected the part of the sentence reporting the opinion. Then, she classified the selected part of the sentence in terms of the quality aspect(s) the opinion refers to (*e.g., compatibility*). No predefined list of quality aspects was provided. However, every time the evaluator had to analyze a sentence, the Web application showed the list of quality aspects created so far, allowing the evaluator to select one of the already defined aspects. In a context like the one encountered in this work, where the number of possible quality aspects might be large, such a choice helps using consistent naming without introducing a substantial bias. The list of aspects obtained during the labeling process is as follows, and Table 4.3 presents the number of sentences identified for each of the aspects.

- Sentences related to the *community* aspect talk about the activities of the community maintaining the API (*e.g.,* is the API actively maintained?).

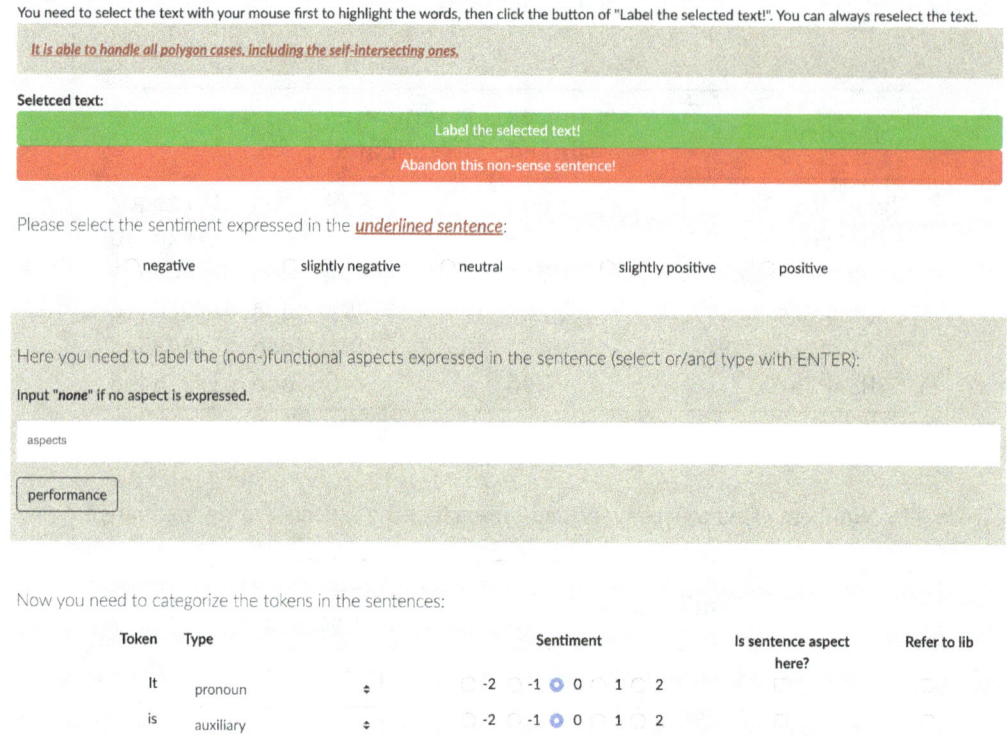

Figure 4.4. Web app used to label the opinions expressed in sentences.

- Sentences related to the *compatibility* aspect talk about the compatibility of the API with respect to specific platforms, programming languages, or other APIs.

- Sentences related to the *documentation* aspect talk about the content/quality of the API documentation.

- Sentences related to the *functional* aspect talk about the features offered/not offered by the API.

- Sentences related to the *performance* aspect talk about the performance of the API (*e.g.,* speed, memory footprint).

- Sentences related to the *reliability* aspect talk about the reliability of the API (*e.g.,* whether it is buggy or not).

- Sentences related to the *usability* aspect talk about the usability of the API, in terms of how easy is to use/adapt it and evolve/maintain the code using it.

The evaluator also assigned a *negative* or *positive* sentiment to the reported opinion (this information is used in the context of the *polarity analyzer*) and, finally, she identified in the selected part of the sentence the Parts-of-Speech (POS) referring to the linked API and the quality aspect(s), *i.e.,* noun, adjective, etc. To better understand the process, let us discuss an example of manual analysis. Consider the sentence: *"Based on my personal experience, Gson is the fastest library out there"*. First, the evaluator selects the part reporting the opinion, in this case: *"Gson is the fastest library"*. Then, she assigns the *performance* quality aspect and a *positive* sentiment to it. Finally, she marks "Gson" as a proper noun referring to the library, and "fastest" as an adjective related to the quality aspect assigned to the opinion (*i.e., performance*).

Once each sentence was manually analyzed by any two of the evaluators, we collected all the conflicts and solved them by adding a third evaluator who was not previously involved in the analysis of that sentence. A conflict could be related to (i) the part of the sentence selected as opinion, (ii) the sentiment polarity assigned to the opinion, and (iii) the quality aspect(s) identified.

The output includes 388 sentences classified as reporting an opinion and referring to seven different quality aspects (and 3,958 discarded as not discussing quality aspects). Table 4.3 reports the number of positive and negative opinions identified for each of them. About 9% of the linked sentences (388/4,346) explicitly report negative or positive opinions related to one of the quality aspects. While the percentage might look low, if we consider the number of posts on Stack Overflow (~50M at the date of the writing), the amount of opinions is still impressive.

The 388 manually annotated API-related sentences were exploited to identify recurrent patterns used in Stack Overflow discussions for expressing opinions about APIs. With "patterns" we refer to lexical rules that capture the syntax and semantics of the opinionated sentences. One of the evaluators conducted a pilot study using API-related sentences including opinions about *performance*. Since we wanted to define patterns considering both the syntax and the semantic of API-related sentences, the evaluator working on the patterns' extraction not only had the quality aspect and the sentiment assigned to each sentence as information, but also the parts of speech related to each token (*i.e.,* noun, verb, adverb, etc.) and their syntactic dependencies.

To reduce the number of patterns belonging to the same quality aspect, the evaluator could also create a bag of words related to verbs, adjectives and adverbs and use them for defining patterns. A positive pattern of the *performance* category is shown in Fig. 4.5. The *Pos_Adjective_Performance* includes positive adjectives linkable to performance, such as *fastest, performant*, etc.

Once the pilot study was completed, the evaluator trained other three evaluators in a 30-minute session that involved discussing the results and some ambiguous sentences. The API-related sentences belonging to the other six quality aspects were randomly distributed among the four evaluators. For each quality aspect, all the API-related sentences were coded by the same evaluator. The same API-related sentence can fall into more than one quality aspect. For this reason, it is possible to infer more than one pattern from the same sentence. At the end of the patterns' extraction, all the evaluators created a catalog of inferred patterns to merge similar patterns into a more general pattern. Each decision taken at this stage was representative of the opinion of all evaluators.

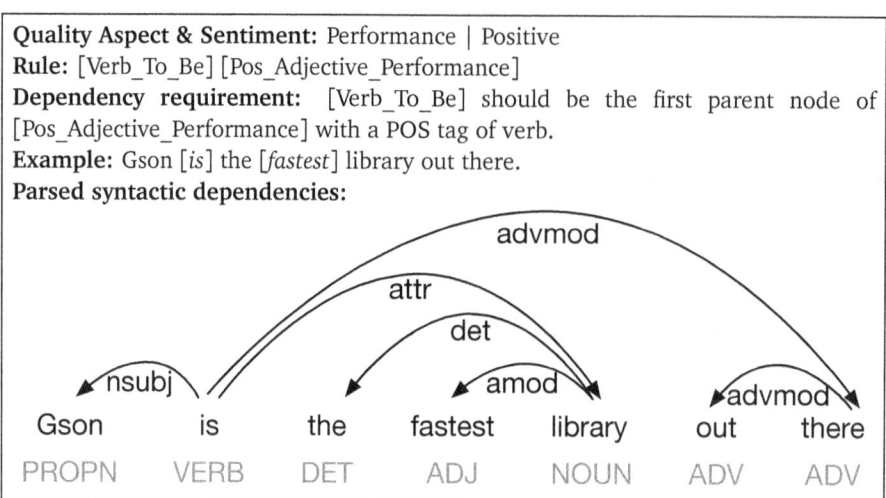

Quality Aspect & Sentiment: Performance | Positive
Rule: [Verb_To_Be] [Pos_Adjective_Performance]
Dependency requirement: [Verb_To_Be] should be the first parent node of [Pos_Adjective_Performance] with a POS tag of verb.
Example: Gson [*is*] the [*fastest*] library out there.
Parsed syntactic dependencies:

Figure 4.5. An example of a positive pattern belonging to the performance category.

In the end, we obtained a list of 157 patterns, each one representative of a specific quality aspect expressing a specific sentiment. Given a sentence S as input, the *aspect classifier* can then be used to check whether S matches one of the defined patterns. To do this, the *aspect classifier* uses the spaCy [spa] NLP library to build a dependency tree of S. The tree reports (i) the POS in S, and (ii) the dependency relations between the tokens composing S. This allows to (i) easily verify whether S matches a given pattern, and (ii) identify negated terms, needed to correctly assess the sentiment polarity of the matched pattern (*e.g.*, if a positive pattern for performance is matched but a positive performance adjective is negated, then the sentiment polarity is inverted to negative).

Machine learning-based approach

Another possibility to implement the *aspect classifier* is to use a machine learning algorithm trained on a set of manually labeled sentences.

We exploit previously labeled sentences (Table 4.2) to train machine learners to classify a given sentence into eight categories: the seven quality aspects we consider plus "none". Specifically, we used all the sentences with opinions and randomly selected same amount of sentences without opinions for training to avoid bias. We used the scikit-learn [PVG+11] Python library to experiment with 10 different machine learners. As predictor variables, we used the terms contained in the sentences. For preprocessing we remove stop words and punctuations, and performed word stemming. We considered each term as a predictor variable. Besides analyzing the single words contained in each sentence, we extract the set of *n-grams* composing it, considering $n \in [2\ldots3]$.

We consider as features for the machine learner the presence/absence of the 157 patterns, *i.e.*, whether a sentence matches each of the patterns we previously defined. There is a key difference between the pattern matching approach and employing patterns as a feature of a machine learner. In the first case, patterns are used as rules, and sentences matching a given pattern are automatically classified into an aspect and sentiment polarity. In the second case, the presence of a pattern, may (or may not) contribute toward a classification along with other features. We experimented each machine learner with seven different combinations of features: (i) BOW-only (Bag Of Words), only considering single terms, (ii) n-grams-only, (iii) patterns-only, (iv) BOW+n-grams, (v) BOW+patterns, (vi) n-grams+patterns, and (vii) BOW+n-grams+patterns. A possible problem is that some categories are rarer than others. A machine learning algorithm tends to assign sentences to more frequent categories, because an error in under-represented categories is more acceptable than an error in other categories to achieve a better overall accuracy. To prevent this, we re-balanced our training set using Synthetic Minority Over-sampling TEchnique (SMOTE) [CBHK02], an oversampling method which creates synthetic samples from the minor class. We experimented each algorithm both with and without SMOTE.

4.2.4 Polarity Analyzer

The *polarity analyzer* analyzes the sentences classified as relevant by the *aspect classifier* to identify the sentiment polarity of the opinions. We investigated two different options for the implementation of the *polarity analyzer*, and we evaluate their performance to pick the best one (see Section 4.3).

Pattern matching-based approach

The set of 157 patterns we extracted for the *aspect classifier* can be also used to assess the sentiment polarity of the opinions.

Indeed, each pattern is related to an aspect and to a sentiment polarity. Thus, the first possibility is to use pattern matching to identify the sentiment of opinions.

Sentiment polarity analysis tools

A second possibility to determine a sentence's sentiment polarity is to exploit one of the many sentiment analysis tools existing in the literature. We experimented with six of them with their default settings: SENTISTRENGTH [TBP+10], SENTISTRENGTH-SE [IZ17], NLTK [HG14], SENTICR [ABIR17], SENTI4SD [CLMN18], and STANFORD CORENLP [SPW+13].

4.2.5 POME in Action

We implemented POME as an online application. POME implements a Java API search engine. A developer who needs to parse JSON files without prior knowledge of any relevant API, can search with a query "parse JSON". POME uses Information Retrieval (IR) techniques to list the APIs in the database having a textual description relevant

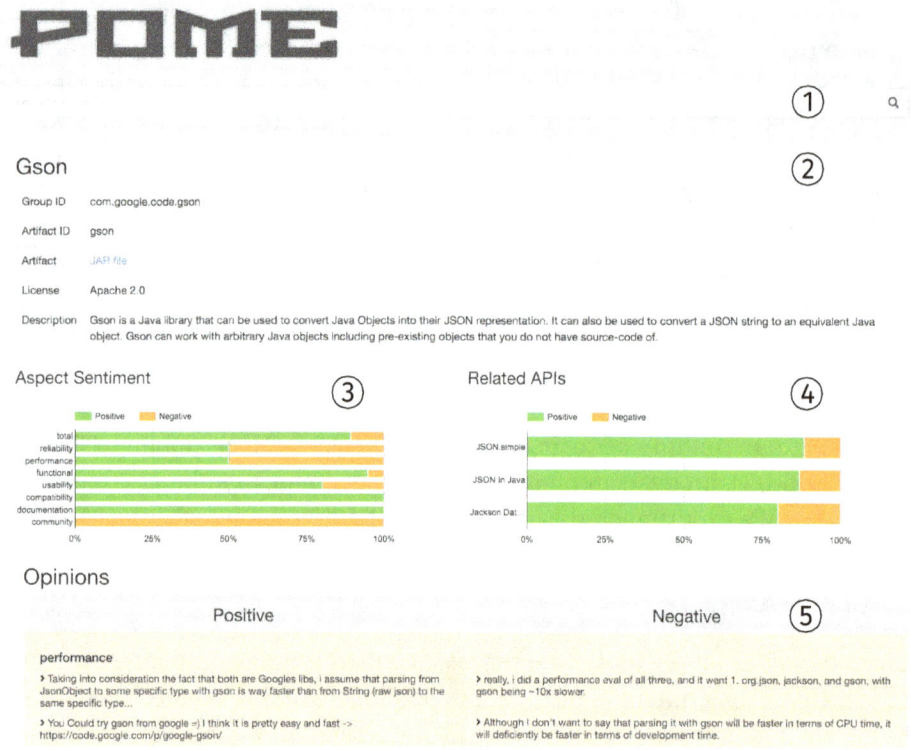

Figure 4.6. Information and opinions about the "Gson" API presented by POME.

for the query. The developer can select an API, for example "Gson", to assess what the users' opinions about this API are. POME will then present relevant information about "Gson" as shown in Fig. 4.6, and including:

1. **Basic information.** The API group ID, artifact ID, link to the `jar` file, license, and description ②.

2. **Opinions on the API classified by aspect.** POME analyzes the polarity of the mined opinions and presents the results with a bar chart ③, where the green and orange depict the percentages of positive and negative opinions, respectively. Each bar in the chart stands for one aspect, while the top bar summarizes the overall polarity of all opinions, that are listed in the table below ⑤. By clicking a bar in the chart, POME only shows in the table opinions related to the aspect of interest.

3. **Opinions on related APIs.** POME also presents a bar chart ④ summarizing opinions of related APIs, *i.e.,* same/similar functionality, identified as the ones having a high textual similarity in terms of description or belonging to same categories in Maven. Each bar stands for one API, and bars are ordered by decreasing ratio of positive opinions. Users can open the information pages of related APIs by clicking the bars.

Table 4.4. Dataset used to answer RQ1 & RQ2.

Category	# APIs	# sentences	URL
Configuration APIs	20	67	goo.gl/gnQr51
Mocking	37	199	goo.gl/6iTVeQ
Validation Frameworks	40	171	goo.gl/sQ15rp
XML Processing	34	468	goo.gl/TwPtgD
JDBC Pools	5	757	goo.gl/yDuWq1
Overall	**136**	**1,662**	-

4.3 Evaluating the Performance of POME

As we have implemented the novel approach POME for our rationale-based API recommender system, we need to evaluate the accuracy of POME in mining opinions from Stack Overflow discussions and classifying these opinions according to the quality aspects they refer to (*e.g.,* performance, usability, compatibility) and their sentiment polarity (*i.e.,* negative or positive). Therefore, in this study, we collected 2,075 sentences extracted from Stack Overflow discussions related to 136 APIs from the Maven central repository [mav]. The material used in this evaluation along with its working dataset is available in our replication package [LZB+a].

4.3.1 Research Questions

We aim at answering the following research questions (RQs):

RQ1: *How does a rule-based aspect classifier for Stack Overflow perform, compared to machine learning approaches?* This RQ compares the performance of different implementations of the *aspect classifier, i.e.,* the pattern matching approach and the machine learning approaches.

RQ2: *How does the rule-based polarity analyzer perform, compared to state-of-the-art sentiment analysis tools?* This RQ evaluates the accuracy of the *polarity analyzer* when using (i) a pattern matching approach, or (ii) six state-of-the-art sentiment analysis tools.

RQ3: *How does* POME *perform compared to* OPINER, *a state-of-the-art tool for mining opinions from Stack Overflow?* This RQ compares POME with OPINER [UK17c].

4.3.2 Context Selection & Data Collection

Table 4.4 and Table 4.5 present the datasets we used.

Table 4.5. Dataset used to answer RQ3

Aspect	POME opinions			OPINER opinions		
	# pos	# neg	# sum	# pos	# neg	# sum
community	1	0	1	2	0	2
compatibility	6	5	11	3	0	3
documentation	16	0	16	9	4	13
functional	123	10	133	19	13	32
performance	11	8	19	5	2	7
reliability	3	4	7	2	22	24
usability	16	2	18	92	35	127
Total	176	29	205	132	76	208

Study context for RQ$_1$ and RQ$_2$

We considered a set of sentences from Stack Overflow discussions, mined from the official Stack Overflow dump dated Dec 2017, identified using our *fine-grained linker* as relevant to one of the 136 APIs belonging to the five popular categories of APIs from Maven central listed in Table 4.4. 1,662 sentences were mined as relevant to at least one of the 136 subject APIs. The 136 APIs used in the context of RQ$_1$ and RQ$_2$ have not been used to define the patterns exploited by our approach for the opinions detection and classification. We performed a manual analysis to categorize each of the 1,662 sentences as expressing or not an opinion about the linked API. In case the sentence did not report any opinion, we assigned it to a *"no opinion"* label. Instead, if an opinion was identified, the sentence was further classified in terms of the quality aspect(s) the opinion refers to (*i.e.,* one or more among *community, compatibility, documentation, functional, performance, reliability,* and *usability*). Finally, the sentiment of the reported opinions was manually assessed by assigning a value between *negative* and *positive*.

The manual analysis was performed by three evaluators and supported by a Web application ensuring that two evaluators were assigned to each sentence. All 1,662 sentences were labeled by two evaluators. The Cohen's kappa coefficient is 0.6492 for sentiment and is 0.6494 for aspect, which demonstrates a substantial agreement. A fourth evaluation not involved in the manual analysis then solved conflicts. A conflict can concern the sentiment of a sentence as well as the quality aspects assigned to it. Overall, 523 sentences (31%) were classified as reporting opinions (505 related to one aspect, 18 to two aspects): *community* (10), *compatibility* (73), *documentation* (41), *functional* (246), *performance* (30), *reliability* (56), and *usability* (85). This manual process was performed before the definition of the patterns' catalog to avoid the evaluators being influenced during the process. Also, in **RQ$_3$** we involved external evaluators in the judgment of the opinions mined by POME (and by OPINER [UK17c]), to have an external and unbiased view on the quality of the mined opinions.

To answer RQ_1, we ran different POME implementations on the dataset of 1,662 sentences to assess their accuracy in identifying opinion aspects. The implementations include the pattern matching approach and machine learning approaches in all variations (Section 4.2).

Concerning RQ_2, we compared the accuracy of POME in assessing the sentiment of opinions with the six sentiment analysis tools mentioned in the previous section. We only conducted the comparison on the subset of 523 sentences for which the best configuration of the *aspect classifier* (output of RQ_1) can detect the existence of opinions. Indeed, when envisioning POME as a tool deployed to mine opinions and assign a polarity to them, our priority was to identify the *polarity analyzer* implementation better suited for the sentences identified by the *aspect classifier* as opinions, since the discarded ones are not shown to the POME user.

Study context for RQ_3

To compare with OPINER [UK17c], we collected the opinions mined by the two tools for four APIs including "`springframework`", "`glassfish.jersey`", "`mongodb`", and "`google.gwt`", and asked developers and CS students to assess their accuracy. Those APIs are listed in the top-ten "most reviewed APIs" in OPINER [UK] and were not used in the POME's pattern definition nor in RQ_1 and RQ_2. Once the best *aspect classifier* (RQ_1) and *polarity analyzer* (RQ_2) were identified, we ran POME on the Stack Overflow data dump to identify opinionated sentences related to the four APIs, collecting in total 205 opinions.

To compare with OPINER we performed the following steps[3]. First, we collected the opinions mined by OPINER for the subject APIs from the original implementation of the authors [UK]. Second, we only considered the opinions mined by OPINER for the same APIs that are related to the same aspects used in POME. Third, OPINER uses a set of heuristics to link Stack Overflow sentences onto APIs. One of the heuristics it uses is the explicit mention of the library in the sentence (similar to what we also do). Other heuristics focus on increasing the number of collected opinions (*i.e.,* higher recall) at the expense of precision. For example, the "same conversation association" links an opinionated sentence to the nearest library mentioned in a Stack Overflow conversation. Since in RQ_3 we evaluate the precision of the mined opinions, we did not want to penalize OPINER by considering for POME sentences linked with an approach designed to ensure high precision (like the one implemented in our *fine-grained linker*) and for OPINER sentences linked with heuristics possibly introducing imprecisions. Therefore, among all opinionated sentences mined by OPINER, we only considered those explicitly mentioning the subject library. Finally, since OPINER identified more sentences than POME, we tried to balance the number of sentences to be evaluated by participants for the two tools: if the number of sentences identified by OPINER for a specific aspect was lower or equal than 10, we kept all sentences related to that aspect. This applied to *community, compatibility,* and *performance*. Other-

---

[3]The comparison was conducted in May 2018.

wise, for a given aspect A_i, we compute the percentage p_{A_i} of sentences identified by OPINER for A_i (e.g., if 10 out of 100 overall opinions mined by OPINER are related to A_i, then such a percentage is 10%). Then, we randomly select $p_{A_i} \times n_{pome}$, where n_{pome} is the total number of opinions identified by POME, among those identified by OPINER for A_i.

We invited 11 developers, 12 Computer Science (CS) students (BSc, MSc, PhD), and 1 postdoc to evaluate the accuracy of the opinions mined by POME and by OPINER for the subject APIs. Participants had an average of 7.5 years of Java development (median=6). Each participant was asked to use a Web app to label the aspect and sentiment polarity (positive, neutral, negative) expressed in the sentences. While the tools automatically classify the sentiment polarity into positive or negative, we gave to the annotators the option to select neutral, to identify false positives in the sentiment identification. The sentences were randomly selected from the considered APIs, and shown in random order. Participants were not aware that the opinions were extracted from different tools to avoid any type of bias. Each sentence was labeled by two participants, and participants were required to label at least 30 sentences. On average, participants labeled 48.5 sentences (median=36).

Each sentence was firstly labeled by two participants. If two participants did not agree with each other on either aspect or sentiment, a third participant would be asked to solve conflicts related to the aspect classification and to the sentiment polarity again through the Web app. For 18 sentences identified by OPINER, the participants solving the conflict were not able to assign an aspect/sentiment with a high confidence. Thus, we preferred to exclude these 18 sentences from our dataset, as they are characterized by a high degree of subjectivity (three humans were not able to agree on the aspect and or sentiment polarity). The final number of opinions evaluated in RQ3 for each tool is reported in Table 4.5.

4.3.3   Data Analysis

To answer RQ_1 we compare the precision and recall of each experimented approach in classifying sentences (as belonging or not to one of the seven aspects) for the dataset of 1,662 sentences. To answer RQ_2 we compare the precision and recall of the sentiment analysis classification performed by the pattern matching approach and the six sentiment analysis tools. To answer RQ_3 we compare the precision of the opinions mined by POME and OPINER both in terms of aspects they identify and sentiment assigned to the opinions. We report the percentage of correctly identified aspects and sentiment for both tools. To compare the precision of POME and OPINER we use Fisher's exact test [Fis22], which statistically compare proportions. Since we perform multiple comparisons (one for each aspect) we adjust p-values using Holm's correction [Hol79]. We also report, for the overall dataset, the Odds Ratio (OR) i.e., the ratio between the chance (odd) POME has to correctly classify aspect and sentiment v.s. odd achieved by OPINER.

Table 4.6. Performance of the best Machine Learning approach using seven different set of features and the Pattern matching approach.

(a) Performance for the aspects "community", "compatibility", and "documentation".

	Community		Compatibility		Documentation	
	Pr	Rc	Pr	Rc	Pr	Rc
BOW-only	0.00	0.00	0.39	0.10	0.21	0.71
BOW+n-grams	0.00	0.00	0.38	0.07	0.34	0.45
patterns-only	0.00	0.00	0.75	0.12	1.00	0.21
BOW+patterns	0.00	0.00	0.76	0.30	0.60	0.36
n-grams+patterns	0.00	0.00	0.75	0.12	1.00	0.21
BOW+n-grams+patterns	0.00	0.00	0.87	0.27	1.00	0.24
Patternd matching	1.00	0.20	0.86	0.33	0.95	0.44

(b) Performance for the aspects "functional" and "performance".

	Functional		Performance	
	Pr	Rc	Pr	Rc
BOW-only	0.33	0.03	0.75	0.10
BOW+n-grams	0.26	0.11	0.67	0.07
patterns-only	0.63	0.10	1.00	0.37
BOW+patterns	0.66	0.16	1.00	0.37
n-grams+patterns	0.63	0.10	1.00	0.37
BOW+n-grams+patterns	0.63	0.13	1.00	0.37
Pattern matching	0.61	0.30	1.00	0.40

(c) Performance for the aspects "reliability" and "usability".

	Reliability		Usability	
	Pr	Rc	Pr	Rc
BOW-only	0.21	0.09	0.88	0.08
BOW+n-grams	1.00	0.02	1.00	0.08
patterns-only	0.00	0.00	1.00	0.13
BOW+patterns	0.00	0.00	1.00	0.13
n-grams+patterns	0.00	0.00	1.00	0.13
BOW+n-grams+patterns	0.00	0.00	1.00	0.13
Pattern matching	0.78	0.13	1.00	0.32

4.4   Results Discussion

RQ$_1$: *How does a rule-based aspect classifier for Stack Overflow perform, compared to machine learning approaches?* Table 4.6 reports the precision and recall in detecting each of the seven quality aspects discussed in API-related sentences. Table 4.6 compares the performance obtained using the *pattern matching* approach (bottom row) and the best performing machine learner, *i.e.,* LINEARSVM. We show the results when using SMOTE to balance the training set, since it often ensured a boost in performance. Also, we do not show the results when using n-grams only, as this approach obtained poor accuracy. The complete results including all machine learning approaches are in the replication package [LZB+a].

While a reasonable recall is useful to get enough recommendations, in the context of opinion mining a high precision is preferable to avoid misleading recommendations. Using BOW for training the machine learner guarantees a relatively high precision for two of the seven quality aspects, namely *usability* (0.88) and *performance* (0.75), with a recall floating around 0.10. Adding n-grams does not significantly improve the performance of POME with respect to BOW-only. The only exception is for *reliability* for which the LINEARSVM is able to reach a precision equals to 1, but with a very low recall (0.02). The limited contribution of n-grams is in line with the findings of Uddin and Khomh [UK17a].

When patterns are included as features (from the third to the sixth rows in Table 4.6), the performance substantially improves, especially for precision. Training the LINEARSVM with patterns only is sufficient to obtain the similar performance ensured by the combination of all features (BOW+n-grams+patterns). This confirms the pivotal role of patterns in the classification.

Finally, the last row of Table 4.6 reports results obtained using the patterns as rules (*i.e.*, plain pattern matching) without any learning algorithm. The precision for all aspect categories is comparable to the one obtained using patterns as features for training LINEARSVM, with the exception that other approaches failed to detect sentences with *community* aspect. It is worth noting that the recall is significantly higher. The approach using pattern-matching is able to obtain, for each quality aspect, a precision varying in the range [0.61-1.00] with a recall varying in [0.13-0.44]. The API-related sentences belonging to *documentation* or *performance* are the ones better identified in terms of both precision (0.95 and 1.00) and recall (0.44 and 0.40). For both *reliability* and *community*, the precision is high (0.78 and 1.00) with a low recall (0.13 and 0.20). Given the above results, our decision was to implement the aspect classifier of POME using the pattern matching approach, given its simplicity and performance.

RQ$_2$: *How does the rule-based polarity analyzer perform, compared to state-of-the-art sentiment analysis tools?* To answer RQ$_2$, we use the 186 API-related sentences identified as containing opinions when running the implementation of the aspect classifier chosen in RQ$_1$. Table 4.7 reports the precision and recall, of (i) six state-of-the-art sentiment analysis tools and (ii) the pattern-based approach, in identifying the sentiment expressed in the sentences. As also highlighted in previous literature [LZB+18], sentiment analysis tools show poor performance in identifying the sentiment (positive or negative) reported in SE datasets. Our results tend to confirm the above statement and, most importantly, underline how the pattern-based approach outperforms the state-of-the-art tools for both positive and negative opinions. This is expected since (i) the patterns have been properly determined looking at API-related sentences mined from Stack Overflow, and (ii) the sentences considered

Table 4.7. Evaluation results for sentiment analysis tools.

Tool	# correct	Positive precision	Positive recall	Negative precision	Negative recall
SentiStrength	48	0.73	0.23	0.35	0.34
SentiStrength-SE	11	0.78	0.05	0.44	0.09
NLTK	30	0.83	0.17	0.67	0.14
SentiCR	8	0.00	0.00	0.80	0.18
Senti4SD	21	0.72	0.09	0.57	0.18
Stanford CoreNLP	63	1.00	0.15	0.29	0.93
Pattern matching	166	0.92	0.99	0.94	0.73

for evaluation have been selected using the approach that verifies the presence of at least one of the 157 patterns. Specifically, for both positive and negative opinions, the pattern-based approach has a precision ≥ 0.90. The recall is higher for positive opinions than for negative ones (0.99 and 0.64 respectively).

To sum up, the pattern-based approach has good performance in terms of both precision and recall, while for sentiment analysis tools a high precision comes at the expense of low recall. The only exception to this trend is STANDFORD CORENLP that, however, exhibit a very low precision for the negative opinions. Looking more in-depth at the low recall of sentiment analysis tools, it is possible to state that the big challenge resides in the presence of many sentences wrongly classified as neutral.

As an example, when a sentence clearly reports that the API provides some useful features (*"the Commons Configuration project from Apache will do the job; it will allow you to write and read Properties files"*) the pattern-based approach is able to correctly identify it as a positive opinion, while all the sentiment polarity analysis tools label it as neutral. The same happens for the sentence *"as already stated above there is a compatibility issue with mockito-all"*, in which the pattern-based approach is able to recognize the presence of a negative feeling from the compatibility point of view, while the sentiment analysis tools classify the sentence as neutral. Note that this is a limitation of these tools in the specific context in which we are using them. However, this does not mean that they do not achieve satisfactory performance when assessing the sentiment polarity in other contexts (*e.g.,* users' happiness on Stack Overflow).

Given the above results, in POME we rely on the pattern-matching approach to identify sentiment polarity, rather than using existing sentiment analysis tools.

RQ$_3$ *How does* POME *perform compared to* OPINER, *a state-of-the-art tool for mining opinions from Stack Overflow?* To answer RQ3, we compare the results of both aspect detection and sentiment analysis achieved by POME and OPINER on the sentences they extracted from Stack Overflow.

Results shown in Table 4.8 indicate that POME achieves an overall better precision. That is, when POME identifies an aspect from a discussion, the chance of it being correct is higher than that identified by OPINER (0.72 *vs* 0.28).

Table 4.8. Precision for POME and OPINER in aspect & sentiment prediction.

Predicted aspect	Aspect prediction		Sentiment prediction	
	POME	OPINER	POME	OPINER
Community	1.00	0.00	1.00	0.50
Compatibility	0.36	0.33	0.45	0.33
Documentation	0.75	0.54	0.69	0.54
Functional	0.75	0.16	0.76	0.16
Performance	0.79	0.58	0.68	0.43
Reliability	0.57	0.46	0.57	0.42
Usability	0.67	0.24	0.78	0.41
Overall	**0.72**	**0.28**	**0.73**	**0.38**

According to Fisher's exact test, the difference is statistically significant (p-value< 0.001) with an OR=6.6, *i.e.,* POME has 6.6 times more chances of providing a correct aspect classification than OPINER. The same trend holds for each aspect except "compatibility", where both OPINER and POME exhibit low performance. One example of misclassification by POME in this category is *"it did not work for me with my spring-boot version"*, classified by POME as compatibility-related (due to the pattern "did not work [...] [proper noun] version"). The study participants labeled the sentence as not reporting any opinion, probably because it is not clear whether the problem experienced by the user is an actual compatibility issue (as opposed, *e.g.,* to a misuse of the API by the user).

POME significantly outperforms OPINER when identifying opinions related to "usability" and "functional" aspects, with the Fisher's exact test indicating that differences are statistically significant (adjusted p-value< 0.001). In other cases differences are not statistically significant on single categories because of the small number of samples. However, the ORs are always in favor of POME, ranging from 1.1 for "compatibility" to 16.0 for "functional". We can conclude that POME performs better than OPINER in aspect identification. Since for most aspects POME can achieve a precision greater than 0.6, we can say that the opinions mined by POME are generally reliable, considering that a random assignment of aspect would result in a precision of 1/8 (0.125).

We qualitatively discuss some examples related to functional-related sentences, in which POME obtains a 0.75 precision as compared to the 0.16 achieved by OPINER. Examples of sentences correctly classified in this aspect by POME are *"you can do most of this config using application.properties if you are using spring-boot"*, and *"the Guava library has an Ordering.greatestOf method that returns the greatest K elements from an Iterable [...]"*. Concerning the misclassifications related to the functional aspects, one of the POME's patterns causing false positives is "[with|use] [library] [pronoun] [helping verb] [verb]" (see [LZB⁺a] for an explanation of this pattern) that matches, for example, the sentence *"if you are **using mongo-java-driver** then **you can have** a* *look at this SO answer*". This pattern was responsible for 7 out of the 33 false positives in the functional aspect. However, it also helped in identifying 8 true positives, thus posing the usual recall *vs* precision dilemma. As for OPINER, its precision in identifying opinions about functional aspects is quite low. The misclassifications include "*I am working on a jersey web service*" and "*an important architectural difference is that GWT-RPC operates at a more functional level*". Probably, this is due to the features (words) used by the machine learner to classify the aspects. Indeed, "service" and "functional" are likely to be keywords characterizing feature-related sentences.

When comparing the results of sentiment prediction, POME almost doubles the precision of OPINER (0.73 *vs* 0.38), and performs better in all categories. Fisher's exact test indicates that the observed differences are, again, statistically significant for "functional" and "usability" (adjusted p-value< 0.001 in both cases). In other cases the test did not report significant differences, again because of the limited number of samples. The ORs are always in favor of POME, ranging from 1.6 of "*compatibility*" to 16.7 of "*functional*". On the overall dataset, we have a statistically significant difference (p-value< 0.001) and an OR$=4.3$, *i.e.*, POME has four times more chances of OPINER in indicating the correct sentiment polarity. Also for what concerns the sentiment prediction the strongest difference between the two approaches is observed in the functional-related sentences. Since we already discussed this category for the aspect identification, we focus our qualitative analysis on the compatibility-related sentences, the ones exhibiting the smaller difference in sentiment prediction precision among the two approaches (0.45 *vs* 0.33). Here, the POME's misclassifications are mostly due to the wrong handling of negations, often caused by misspelling/typing issues. For example, POME misclassifies as positive the sentiment of the sentence "*the problem is that FrameLayout.LayoutParams constructor doesn`t support another FrameLayout as a parameter until the api 19.*" due to the use of the backtick instead of an apostrophe, which caused the negation handling failure. Other examples are typos like "*cann't*" instead of "*can't*". Integrating a spell checker could solve the problem, although it must cope with having source code words not being correct English words.

Concerning OPINER, the main problem is represented by sentences considered by the participants as do not actually reporting an opinion and, thus, being neutral in terms of sentiment while classified as positive/negative by the tool. This is the case for "*BTW, I'm working with Spring MVC*", classified as a positive compatibility sentence by OPINER and as non-opinionated by participants.

Despite the better results achieved by POME, **OPINER identifies a higher number of opinions for these APIs (4 times higher than that identified by POME), thus very likely exhibiting a higher recall**. POME has been designed to favor precision over recall, and in RQ$_3$ we are only focusing on the precision of the mined opinions, since assessing the recall would require the analysis of the entire Stack Overflow. The precision reported in RQ$_3$ is not as high as for the other RQs. This might depend on the specific dataset and/or on whom performed the labeling. The datasets used in the previous RQs have been created by the authors, having a deeper knowledge of the problem. Also, they discussed cases where there was a disagreement, while this did not happen for RQ_3 participants. Although instructions were given for evaluators of RQ_3, the annotation task remains highly subjective. In spite of these concerns, POME advances the current state-of-the-art in aspect and sentiment identification. Also, the difficulty annotators had in their task highlights once more that grasping API opinions from Stack Overflow sentences is not an easy task, and therefore recommenders such as POME and OPINER are valuable.

4.5   Threats to Validity

Construct validity. This affects the creation of the labeled dataset used in RQ1 and RQ2. The threat has been mitigated by having multiple evaluators classifying aspects and sentiments. As for the slightly modified approach by Treude and Robillard [TR16], we manually validated all the sentences extracted with the fourth regular expressions introduced by us in order to discriminate between sentences referring to APIs. Among the 10,481 sentences extracted by our *Fine-grained linker*, 360 have been identified using the fourth rule in Table 4.1. One evaluator manually analyzed all of them, classifying 74% of the sentences correctly linked to the API [LZB+a].

Internal validity. It is possible that a different calibration of the machine learners produce better results. Therefore, results reported in Table 4.6 and Table 4.5 represent a lower-bound for the different configurations of POME.

Conclusion validity. Where needed we supported our claims through appropriate statistical procedures. As for the aspect-specific comparison, it is possible that Type-II errors occurred (failed to reject hypothesis due to limited sample), however we showed how the differences were statistically significant on the overall dataset.

External validity. While we have validated POME, and compared it with OPINER, on unseen data, it is possible that a different dataset would exhibit different results. Also, another dataset could exhibit different distributions of the identified aspects, and, possibly, further aspects we did not consider. However, this still makes the approach applicable, possibly by augmenting the set of identified patterns. POME is suitable for popular APIs, due to the large availability of opinions to mine. However, this applies to any recommender based on (historical) data mining.

4.6   Conclusion

Given the fact that existing approaches as well as their customized versions cannot achieve satisfactory performance in identifying sentiment polarity in software related data, we propose POME, an approach that leverages natural language parsing and pattern-matching to determine their polarity (positive vs negative). At the same time, POME also classifies Stack Overflow sentences referring to APIs according to seven aspects (e.g., performance, usability). Our empirical studies indicate that POME can achieve a high accuracy in identifying both quality aspects and sentiment polarity.

POME also outperforms a state-of-the-art tool (OPINER [UK17c]). POME aids developers to quickly gain understandings of the overall quality, pros, and cons of APIs. Our design and implementation of POME has successfully proved the possibility of mining opinions from online resources to support software design decisions (*i.e.,* choosing suitable APIs). As opinions are embedded in many other kinds of sources, and they can be related to many other development activities, our future work is given.

5

Conclusions and Future Work

We strongly believe that mining opinions from online resources can allow developers to easily access peers' expertise. By extracting knowledge from these opinions and convert it into actionable items, we can facilitate software development activities.

We presented the current state of the art in opinion mining and their applications within SE contexts. Meanwhile, we highlighted the limitations of current studies regarding the lack of performance verification and the under-exploited value of opinion mining for software-related tasks.

Given that existing approaches often lead to unsatisfactory accuracy when applied to SE, we first attempted to re-train the state-of-the-art technique STANFORD CORENLP with software related data. The re-training was performed on a set of 40k manually labeled sentences/words extracted from Stack Overflow. Despite such an effort- and time-consuming training process, the results were negative. That is, there was no significant performance improvement for our customized version of STANFORD CORENLP. We then changed our focus and performed a thorough investigation of the accuracy of commonly used tools to identify the sentiment polarity of SE related texts. The results showed that none of these state-of-the-art tools achieved a reliable assessment of the sentiment polarities expressed in our manually labeled dataset. Meanwhile, we also studied the impact of datasets on tool performance, and found that the performance varies on different datasets. Our study alarmed the research community about the strong limitations of current sentiment polarity analysis tools.

Given these negative results achieved, we proposed another approach, Pattern-based Opinion MinEr (POME), which leverages natural language parsing and pattern-matching to classify not only sentiment polarity (positive v.s. negative), but also seven aspects related to quality aspects of APIs (*e.g.,* performance, usability). The patterns have been inferred by manually analyzing 4,346 sentences from Stack Overflow linked to a total of 30 APIs. Based on this approach, we have investigated how online resources can be leveraged to help developers take decisions during software implementation. More specifically, we implemented a rationale-based software API recommender system, which takes as input the textual description of a certain functionality and recommends to developers suitable APIs with rationales (*i.e.,* what the pros and cons are to adopt a specific API).

We evaluated POME by (i) comparing our pattern-matching approach with machine learners leveraging the patterns themselves and n-grams extracted from Stack Overflow posts; (ii) assessing the ability of POME to detect the polarity of sentences, as compared to sentiment analysis tools; (iii) comparing POME with the state-of-the-art Stack Overflow opinion mining approach, OPINER, through a study involving 24 human evaluators. Our study showed that POME exhibits a higher precision than a state-of-the-art technique (OPINER), in terms of both opinion aspect identification and polarity assessment.

Given the high accuracy achieved by POME, we demonstrated the possibility of mining opinions from Q&A sites to assist developers in decision making when they need to compare and choose APIs for completing programming tasks.

5.1 Limitations

While we have achieved promising results for mining opinions from online discussions to support software design decisions, we foresee several limitations of our study, mainly concerning four aspects: 1) the customization of STANFORD CORENLP can be further improved; 2) the performance of our proposed approach POME can be further improved, especially the recall; 3) we only leveraged the discussions on Stack Overflow, while there are much more data available online; and 4) we only focused on mining opinions to support design decisions, while there are many other software development activities where opinion mining can be beneficial.

5.1.1 Customization of Stanford CoreNLP

In our study, we labeled 1,500 Stack Overflow sentences and their 20k internal nodes to customize STANFORD CORENLP. For RNN-based approach, we would expect that if we feed in more reliable labeled data, the performance can be improved.

5.1.2 Performance Improvement of pome

Although our proposed approach POME achieved a high precision, the recall was still not comparably promising. For popular APIs, this might not be a big issue, as there are abundant opinions available online. However, for APIs which are not widely discussed, failing to extract relevant information might significantly reduce the usefulness of our approach. Therefore, more effort should be devoted to further improving the performance of the current opinion mining techniques.

5.1.3 Various Available Data Online

In our study, we mainly focused on Stack Overflow. In fact, developers share their opinions and knowledge in various communication channels under modern software development practices, such as email lists, IRC, and GitHub. Scarce relevant discussions can also be found on social media, such as Twitter and Facebook.

However, to maximize the value of all these data, there are still some open challenges to address. First, the linking between different information sources might be missing and needs to be re-discovered. For example, when developers try to find a solution to fix an issue raised on issue tracking systems, they might ask for help on Stack Overflow. How to link the questions on Stack Overflow back to the issues is not trivial. Second, these online communication channels might have very different structures, which requires researchers designing specific approaches for each information source, resulting in a substantial effort.

5.1.4 Opinion Mining in Different Software Development Activities

In our study, we mainly discussed how to support software design decisions using opinion mining. In fact, the opinions online can also assist in many different software development activities, with some of them illustrated in Section 2.3.

5.2 Future Work

Given the limitations of our study, we foresee the following directions as our future work.

5.2.1 Improvement of Opinion Mining Techniques

To improve the performance of opinion mining techniques, there are several directions we can potentially investigate:

1. *Addressing the ambiguity of technical terms.* As discussed before, one major reason of the unsatisfactory performance of opinion mining techniques is that these approaches can often "misunderstand" the technical terms. This concerns two aspects. First, proper nouns such as API names may hinder the correct interpretation of part-of-speech. For example, "Spark", a well known cluster-computing framework, is often parsed as a verb, especially when it is not correctly capitalized. Second, the same term might have different sentiment in different contexts. For instance, the word "issue" is considered expressing neutral sentiment in the sentence "This issue report is well-written", while it can also express negative sentiment in sentences like "This is definitely an issue". One possible solution is to leverage domain specific vocabularies and to consider the grammatical position of the technical terms at the same time.

2. *Training or tuning the approach with more data.* When we train or tune our approach, the more reliable data we feed in, the better performance we can achieve. While it is an expensive process to manually label the data, we believe the benefits it brings can justify these efforts. At the same time, it is worth investigating whether incorporating data from other relevant domains to the training set can contribute to performance improvement.

5.2.2   Support for Different Software Development Activities

While opinion mining can be applied to various software development activities, below we give two examples related to software maintenance and documentation.

Opinion Mining in Software Maintenance

In online Q&A websites like Stack Overflow, developers often suggest several different solutions to an implementation related question. In these solutions, developers sometimes provide not only their preferences based on personal experience, but also concrete tests and experiments. This information can be leveraged to help developers refactor their own implementation by replacing it with a more efficient one verified by other developers. In a more practical scenario, we can foresee an intelligent IDE able to indicate which parts of source code can be refactored by mining opinions on similar code from Stack Overflow.

The challenges for this research direction mainly come from two aspects: 1) the discussion often involves several different entities (*e.g.,* implementation approaches) at the same time, and it is not trivial to extract the corresponding pieces of information for each entity; 2) the dimensions involved can be much wider and more fine-grained than the aspects we have identified in our previous work POME.

Opinion Mining in Software Documentation

Another interesting direction to investigate is mining opinions to support software documentation. Since developers usually have limited time to complete software components and they are often unwilling to document their code, lots of software projects lack proper documentation, which results in difficulties when maintaining existing code. If we can mine developers' internal discussions to automatically generate or augment software documentation, it will be valuable for maintainers to better and more quickly understand the software systems.

Indeed, it is common for developers to reason about their implementation on communication channels to get their code changes accepted. This makes it possible to extract the rationale behind developers' code implementation, and injects it in the documentation. This problem is not trivial due to several factors: 1) discussions might be long, 2) several developers might voice their opinions, 3) and some opinions may not be adopted in the end. Therefore, it is necessary to accurately retrieve the relevant piece of information and summarize it.

5.3   Closing Words

In this dissertation, we showed that mining opinions from online discussions can efficiently support design decisions during software development. We highlighted the intrinsic problem regarding the accuracy of current state-of-the-art opinion mining tools, and the necessity of carefully verifying the performance of opinion mining techniques when applying them in the SE domain. We also pointed out that simply customizing existing opinion mining approaches with software related data does not necessarily guarantee performance improvement. In fact, there are no universally reliable opinion mining tools for SE tasks. Instead, when researchers attempt to choose the tool to mine opinions from software related texts, they will sometimes need to re-design or customize an approach exclusively for that specific task.

We urge that researchers should think twice when using off-the-shelf opinion mining tools designed outside the SE field. While this increases the difficulty of conducting relevant studies, this extra effort of understanding and tailoring methodologies can advance our field. Indeed, given the vast amount of valuable information online and the potential benefits developers might receive from that, the hard work will eventually pay off.

Appendices

On the Uniqueness of Code Redundancies

Code redundancy widely occurs in software projects. Researchers have investigated the existence, causes, and impacts of code redundancy, showing that it can be put to good use, for example in the context of code completion. When analyzing source code redundancy, previous studies considered software projects as sequences of tokens, neglecting the role of the syntactic structures enforced by programming languages. However, differences in the redundancy of such structures may jeopardize the performance of applications leveraging code redundancy.

We present a study of the redundancy of several types of code constructs in a large-scale dataset of active Java projects mined from GitHub, unveiling that redundancy is not uniform and mainly resides in specific code constructs. We further investigate the implications of the locality of redundancy by analyzing the performance of language models when applied to code completion. Our study discloses the perils of exploiting code redundancy without taking into account its strong locality in specific code constructs.

This study is based on the following publication [LPM+17]:

On the Uniqueness of Code Redundancies

Bin Lin, Luca Ponzanelli, Andrea Mocci, Gabriele Bavota, Michele Lanza. In *Proceedings of the 25th International Conference on Program Comprehension (ICPC 2017) – Technical Research Track*, pp. 121–131, 2017

A.1   Introduction

Code redundancy, namely identical parts of code occurring multiple times, is common in software projects [DRD99], and manifests itself in different forms. At a coarse-grained level, developers may explicitly duplicate code snippets with different intentions, for example to break through given programming language limitations, or to construct reusable coding templates [KBLN04]. While literature often suggests that this kind of redundant code, called *code clones*, is to be avoided as it can lead to code bloat, not all code redundancies are harmful [KG06a]. Moreover, numerous practical applications leveraging code redundancy have been implemented for different purposes, such as locating bugs [LLMZ06], supporting refactoring operations [BMD⁺00], detecting plagiarism [BTZ07], and supporting code completion [HBS⁺12].

A particular kind of redundancy, considering code at the token level, has been the subject of recent studies, and proven to be effective for numerous applications. To understand how redundant software is, at the token level, Gabel and Su [GS10] fragmented source code into fixed-length sequences (*i.e.,* token-level n-grams) and measured uniqueness of software by quantifying the sequence redundancy. The authors examined 6,000 projects and found that software is highly repetitive when the sequences are short, *e.g.,* given sequences of six tokens, more than half of the code is redundant. Also, Tu *et al.* [TSD14] reported on the *localness* of software, showing that code exhibits repetitive forms in local contexts at the file level, *i.e.,* repetitions of a specific n-gram localized in few files.

Hindle *et al.* [HBS⁺12] showed that source code is "natural", which means it is highly repetitive and predictable, even more than natural language.

This does not come as surprise: Unlike natural language, programming languages are more constrained by syntax, and these constraints are likely to correlate with repetitiveness. Moreover, Ray *et al.* [RHG⁺16] studied a large set of bug fix commits from 10 Java projects, and investigated the relationship between buggy code and code "naturalness". As a result, they found that buggy code is less "natural".

However, some constructs (*e.g.,* method and class declarations) are more constrained than others (*e.g.,* sequences of method calls) and thus one might wonder if every part of the source code is equally redundant. Currently, there is no detailed analysis regarding this particular matter. Understanding where code redundancy resides is important as it might improve the performance of applications that leverage code redundancy.

Hindle *et al.* [HBS⁺12] developed a simple code completion engine for Java based on an n-gram language model and examined their engine on five Apache projects: Ant, Maven, Log4J, Xalan, and Xerces. For each project, they trained a trigram model from the corpus of the tokenized source code, and used two tokens to predict the next token. They combined this approach with the default Eclipse code recommendation engine, and the results suggested that an n-gram language model can effectively improve the performance of the recommendation engine. Since different parts of source code might have different levels of redundancy, we are interested in investigating whether the n-gram model based completion performs equally well in different parts of code, from which we can further infer whether unevenly distributed redundant code impacts the applications leveraging code redundancy.

We address this problem with two different studies performed on a large-scale dataset composed of 2,640 Java project repositories. First, we analyze the overall redundancy rate of the source code and then compare it with the redundancy rates of 12 source code constructs (*e.g.,* import and class declarations, catch blocks, etc.). Our results suggest that although code redundancy is common in software, it is very localized in specific code constructs (*e.g.,* in package declarations). Then, we explore the influence of the significantly different code redundancy rates observed for the code constructs on the performance of the language model based code completion. We find that while the language model is very accurate when recommending code tokens belonging to typically redundant constructs, its performance strongly decreases when suggesting tokens related to poorly redundant code constructs. In essence, our findings highlight the importance of considering the strong locality of code redundancy when exploiting it.

Structure of the Chapter

We describe our problem context in Section A.2. Section A.3 explores the redundancy of different code constructs, and Section A.4 focuses on an application, *i.e.,* the language model based code completion, to analyze the impact of the unequal code redundancy. We discuss the threats that affect the validity of our studies in Section A.5. Finally, Section A.6 illustrates the related work and Section A.7 outlines the conclusions.

A.2   Study Context

Table A.1 summarizes the dataset used for our studies.

Table A.1. Dataset Statistics

	Overall	Per project		
		Mean	Median	St. deviation
Java files	1,461,290	554	237	1,123
Tokens	1,079,112,838	4,087,549	152,873	970,681
ELOC	146,886,573	55,639	20,892	125,762
Forks	314,594	119	25	412
Stars	864,227	327	50	1,194
% Java code	-	91.5	92.4	5.6

The *study context* consists of 2,640 open source Java projects hosted on GitHub, mined on Nov 21, 2016 using the following constraints:

- **Programming language.** Projects need to have at least 80% of their effective lines of code (ELOC, lines of code without comments and empty lines) [DRD99] written in Java. Java is the reference language for the infrastructure used in this study.

- **Activity level.** To exclude inactive projects, they need to have at least one commit in the three months preceding the data collection.

- **Popularity.** The number of forks[1] and stars[2] of a repository are two proxies for its popularity on GitHub. Forking a repository means getting a copy of the repository to implement changes not affecting the original project. Starring a repository allows GitHub users to express their appreciation for the project. Projects with less than ten stars and no forks are excluded from the dataset, to avoid the inclusion of likely irrelevant projects.

- **Size.** Projects must have at least 50 files and 5,000 ELOC. Again, the goal is to filter out irrelevant projects.

2,714 projects satisfy these constraints. We removed 74 projects that could not be correctly parsed by the tools we use (*e.g.,* ANTLR, SRCML). Table A.1 reports descriptive statistics for size and popularity of the selected projects, showing a high degree of diversity of the dataset in terms of both these attributes. The complete list of projects considered in the studies is available in our replication package[LPM+].

A.3 Study I: Source Code Redundancy

The *goal* of the study is to assess to what extent source code is redundant both when considering it as a whole (*i.e.,* the complete code base of a software project) as well as when focusing on specific code constructs (*e.g.,* when considering import declarations). The *context* of the study consists of the 2,640 Java projects detailed in Section A.2. While previous research already investigated the source code redundancy phenomenon [GS10, HBS+12, AS14], to the best of our knowledge there are no studies (i) run on such a scale[3], and (ii) analyzing the redundancy rate of different code constructs.

A.3.1 Research Questions

We aim at answering the following research questions (RQ):

RQ$_1$: *How redundant is source code?* This RQ aims at assessing to what extent source code is redundant. In the context of RQ$_1$ we analyze the code redundancy

---

[1]https://help.github.com/articles/fork-a-repo/

[2]https://help.github.com/articles/about-stars/

[3]The study by Gabel and Su [GS10] is run on 6,000 projects. However, they sample a limited number of tokens (~1,500) from each project, while we analyze all tokens from each project (on average, 432,290 tokens per project).

when considering the complete code base of a software project. RQ_1 will corrobo-rate/confute the findings of previous studies reporting the high redundancy of source code [GS10, HBS$^+$12, AS14]. Moreover, the results of RQ_1 serve as a reference for RQ_2, in which we assess the redundancy rate of different code constructs.

RQ_2: *To what extent are different code constructs redundant?* This RQ sheds light on the redundancy rate of different code constructs, missing in the current literature. Knowing the redundancy rate of different constructs is necessary to design techniques and tools assuming the high repetitiveness of code, *e.g.,* language models support-ing code completion [HBS$^+$12]. While these techniques work fairly well in general, they might perform poorly when dealing with specific parts of the code being always unique or rarely repetitive.

A.3.2   Data Extraction

To answer our research questions and measure code redundancy we adopt a method-ology similar to the one used by Gabel and Su [GS10]. In particular, for each project P_i in our dataset, we perform the following steps:

Code sequencing. We tokenize the P_i's source code and extract tokens' sequences of length l (*i.e.,* token-level l-grams). The sequences extraction is performed in each P_i's Java file starting from its first token (*e.g.,*`package`) and using a sliding window of length l advancing at steps of one token. For example, assuming $l = 9$, from the code statement `for(i=0; i<n; i++)` the following sequences are extracted: "`for(i=0; i<n`", "`(i=0; i<n;`", "`i=0; i<n; i`", "`=0; i<n; i++`", "`0; i<n; i++)`". We analyze code redundancy for sequences of different lengths by varying l from 3 to 60 in steps of 3 (*i.e.,* 3, 6, 9, etc.). This process resulted in the extraction of over 1 billion tokens and around 1 billion sequences. Also, we tokenize each sequence at two different abstraction levels: *no abstraction* and *token type only*. For the *no abstraction* approach, the sequence `if (a > b)` is tokenized into the list of tokens "`if, (, a, >, b, )`". For token types only, the same sequence is tokenized into a list of lexical classes "`IF, LB` (left bracket), `ID` (identifier), `GT` (greater than), `ID, RB` (right bracket)". Token types are generated with ANTLR4 [Par13].

Sequence redundancy detection. We mark each of the extracted sequences as either "redundant" (*i.e.,* there exists at least one repetition of the sequence in P_i) or "not redundant" (*i.e.,* the sequence is unique in P_i). Differently from Gabel and Su [GS10], we look at code redundancy within the scope of each single project: We do not consider a sequence $s_j \in P_i$ as redundant if it also appears in another project P_k. This choice is dictated by the fact that some "practical" applications of code redun-dancy make more sense when only considering the code from a single project.

For example, regarding the language model used to support code completion [HBS$^+$12], the authors built a different model for each system. This is needed as each project has its own domain and thus its own vocabulary. Since in our second study we investigate if and how the differences in the redundancy rate of different code constructs impact the performance of such techniques, we decided to focus on the code redundancy within each single project.

Linking tokens to code constructs. To address RQ_2 we need to identify the code construct to whom the analyzed tokens belong. To this aim, we parse the source code by relying on the SRCML infrastructure [CDM13] and assign each token to one of the twelve code constructs listed in Table A.2 (in **bold** the tokens belonging to the specific code construct). We extract matched code constructs without considering whether they contain other constructs or not. For example, the code sequence "`for(int i=0; i<n; i++)`" is classified as a "for control" construct, although it contains a variable declaration "`int i=0;`".

Table A.2. Identified code constructs

Construct	Example
package	`package com.abc;`
import	`import java.io.*;`
if condition	`if(a == b) {...}`
while condition	`while(a > n) {...}`
for control	`for(int i=0; i<n; i++) {...}`
class declaration	`class Square extends Shape {...}`
method declaration	`public int getX {...}`
method call	`System.out.println("Hello!");`
method body	`public int getX { return x; }`
variable declaration	`int x = 0;`
catch parameter	`catch (Exception e) {...}`
catch block	`catch (Exception e) {break;}`

While other code constructs could be extracted, we maintain that the number and diversity of constructs considered in our study to be sufficient to observe differences in the redundancy rate of different parts of the source code.

A.3.3 Data Analysis

We answer RQ_1 by reporting box plots depicting the *redundancy rate* of tokens belonging to sequences (i) tokenized by using both the *no abstraction* and the *token type only* representation and (ii) having different lengths l. The redundancy rate is computed as the number of tokens belonging to sequences marked as "redundant" divided by the total number of tokens in the analyzed sequences [GS10].

To answer RQ_2, we compare via box plots the redundancy rate of tokens belonging to different code constructs. We also statistically compare the redundancy rate of the different constructs by exploiting the Mann-Whitney test [Con99] with results intended as statistically significant at $\alpha = 0.05$.

To control the impact of multiple pairwise comparisons (*e.g.,* the redundancy of tokens belonging to the `package` construct is compared against the redundancy of tokens belonging to the *if condition*, the *while condition*, etc.), we adjust p-values using the Holm's correction [Hol79]. We also estimate the magnitude of the differences by using the Cliff's Delta (d), a non-parametric effect size measure [GK05] for ordinal data. We follow well-established guidelines to interpret the effect size: negligible for $|d| < 0.10$, small for $0.10 \leq |d| < 0.33$, medium for $0.33 \leq |d| < 0.474$, and large for $|d| \geq 0.474$ [GK05].

A.3.4 Results

We discuss the achieved results according to the two RQs.

1) RQ$_1$: How redundant is source code? Fig. A.1 shows the boxplots depicting the tokens' redundancy rate for sequences having increasing lengths, both when *no abstraction* is used as well as when considering only the *token type*.

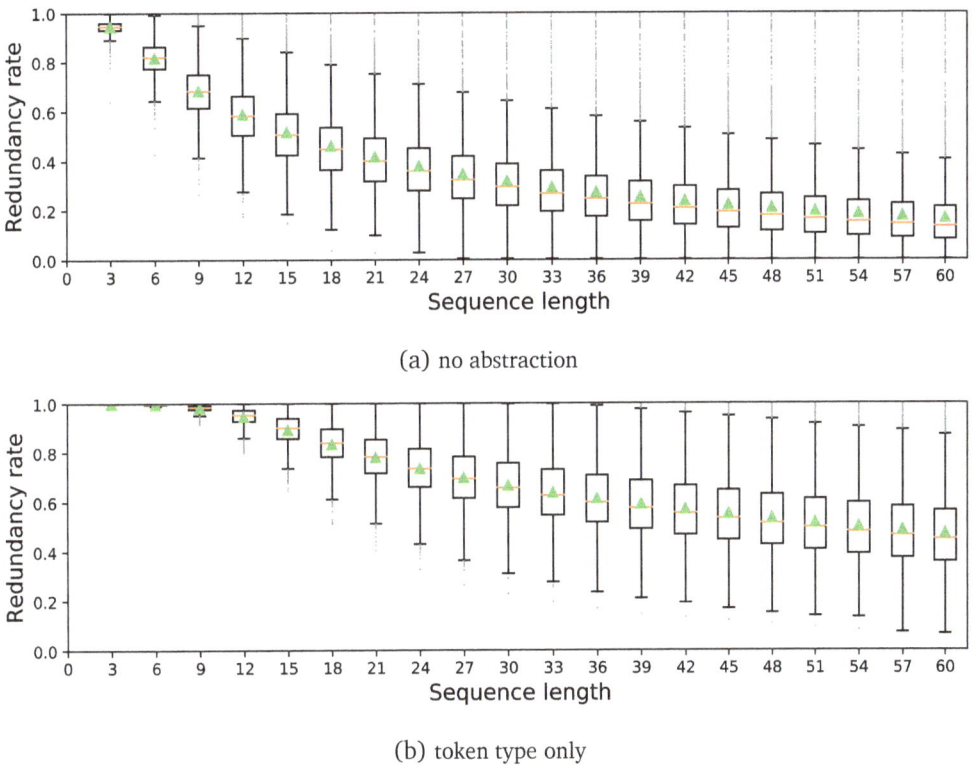

(a) no abstraction

(b) token type only

Figure A.1. Redundancy rate for sequences having different lengths

The red square in each boxplot represents the mean value of the distribution. We draw three main conclusions:

1. **When considering the project's code as a whole, source code is highly redundant**. For tokens belonging to sequences of length 3, the redundancy rate is very high, also without abstraction (*i.e.*, when considering exact copies of the 3 tokens), with a median of 0.95. High redundancy rates (> 0.5) are generally observed for sequences of length up to 15.

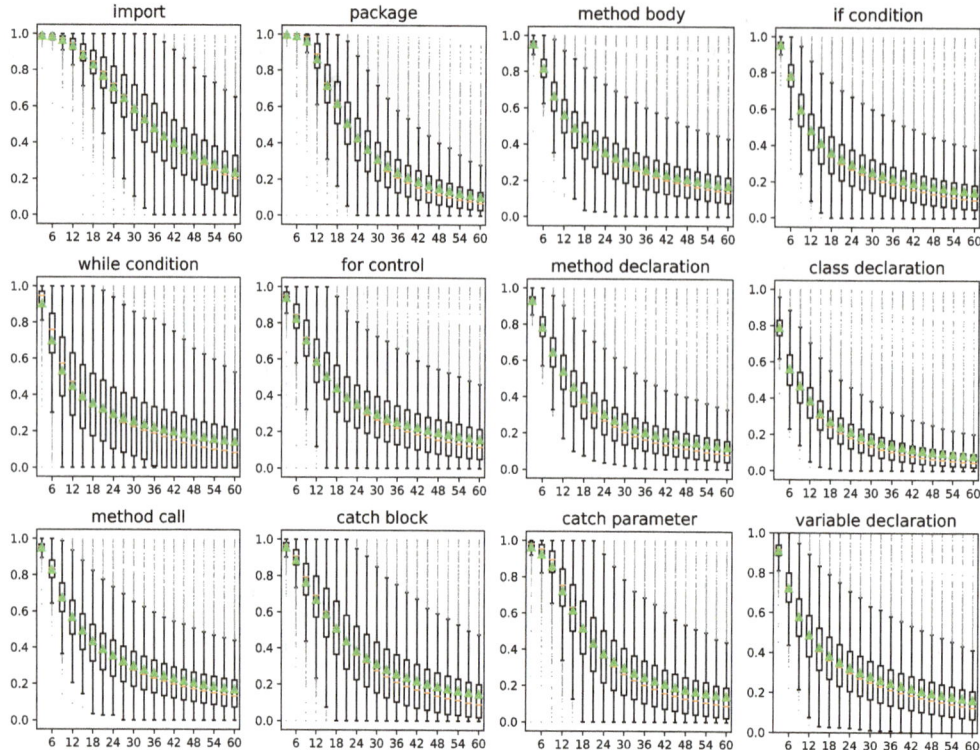

Figure A.2. Redundancy rate for different types of code constructs when no abstraction is applied.

2. **The longer the sequences the lower the redundancy rate.** The trend depicted in Fig. A.1 is clear, and highlights a sort of logarithmically decreasing function when observing the median values of the boxplots from left (short sequences) to right (long sequences).

   This is to be expected, since it is much less likely to find duplications of long sequences as compared to shorter ones.

3. **When only considering the token type, the redundancy rate substantially increases.** Again, this is an expected results, considering the abstraction level introduced when only looking for token types. For example, while the two sequences if(a > b) and if(c > d) are considered as different in the *no abstraction* approach, they are considered as redundant from the *token type only* perspective.

Our findings thus corroborate the observations by Gabel and Su [GS10], and confirm the high redundancy of source code. Our next RQ investigates *where* the redundancy is, when looking more closely at the source code.

2) RQ$_2$: To what extent are different code constructs redundant? Fig. A.2 shows the boxplots depicting the redundancy rate for different types of code constructs when considering sequences of different lengths without applying abstraction[4]. Concerning the impact of the sequence length on the redundancy rate, all code constructs follow the same trend previously observed for the whole project. However, it is evident that tokens belonging to different types of code constructs do not exhibit the same redundancy rate.

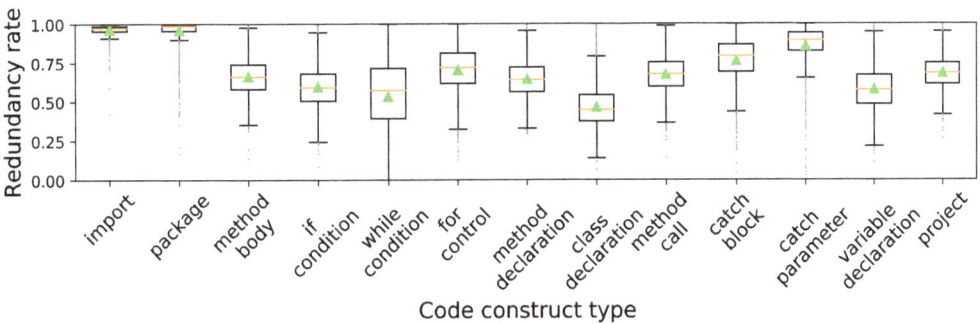

Figure A.3. Redundancy rate of different code constructs when no abstraction is applied and the sequence length is 9.

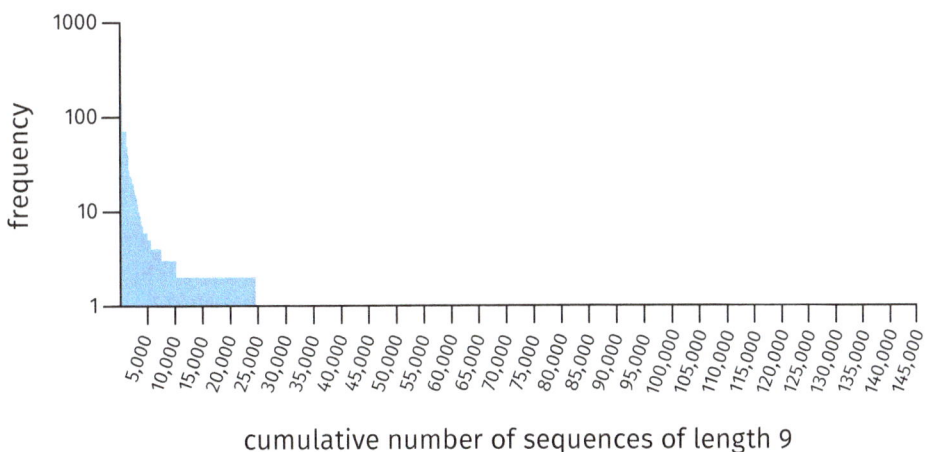

Figure A.4. Microsoft Thrifty: Cumulative frequency for sequences of length 9.

---

[4]Results for the *token type only* approach is in our replication package[LPM+]

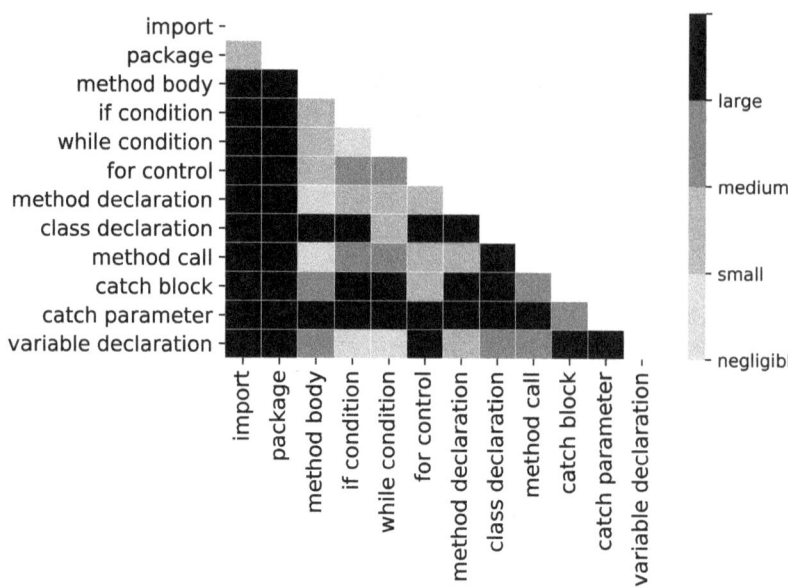

Figure A.5. Statistical comparisons for the redundancy rates of different types of code constructs for sequences of length 9.

Fig. A.3 compares the redundancy rate of code constructs when the sequence length is 9. The redundancy rate of the whole project is also shown in Fig. A.3 (boxplot on the right), serving as a baseline for comparison. The main message highlighted by Fig. A.3 is that the redundancy rate of different code constructs significantly differs. This is clear, for example, when comparing `import` declarations (median=0.97) and `while` conditions (median=0.57). Such strong differences are confirmed by the statistical analysis in Fig. A.5[5].

In the heatmap in Fig. A.5, a white block indicates that the difference in terms of redundancy rates of two code constructs is not statistically significant (adjusted p-value ≥ 0.05). Blocks with four different grayscale values from light to dark represent a significant difference accompanied by a negligible, small, medium and large effect size, respectively. Confirming what can previously observed, `import`, `package`, and `catch` parameter constructs are significantly more redundant than other constructs. All of the statistical comparisons result in a significant difference, and 74% of the cases have medium or large effect sizes. Thus, the statistical analysis confirms the high variability of redundancy rate for different types of code constructs.

Up to now we considered as redundant a token from a sequence repeated at least once [GS10]. We also investigated the frequency of redundant sequences (*i.e.*, how many times sequences are repeated in the code). Indeed, the frequency with which a sequence is repeated in the code impacts techniques leveraging code redundancy, like language models that need to learn what the likely sequences of code tokens are.

---

[5]Results for sequences of different lengths are in our replication package[LPM+]

The analysis being computationally expensive, we performed it on 30 randomly selected projects. Fig. A.4 shows, using a logarithmic scale, the frequency of the 144,494 unique tokens sequences of length 9 extracted from Microsoft Thrifty.

While the code redundancy, measured as explained in Section A.3.2, is quite high for this system (0.80)—indicating that most of tokens belong to redundant sequences—the median frequency of the redundant sequences is just 2, with a third quartile of 4. This means that at least 75% of the redundant sequences in this system are repeated at most 4 times in the code, while there are very few sequences repeated hundreds of times (leading to the long tailed distribution in Fig. A.4). The most redundant sequence is (`org.apache.thrift.protocol.`, generally used in `catch` statements (*e.g.,* `catch (org.apache.thrift.protocol.TProtocolException)`). This sequence is repeated 743 times. Other very frequent sequences are those related to `import` statements (*e.g.,* `import com.microsoft.thrifty.schema.`—161 times).

When looking at the frequency of redundant sequences, most of the code redundancy is in very specific parts of the code. Indeed, we observed a long tailed frequency distribution shown in Fig. A.4 for all the 30 selected systems[6]. Such a characteristic of code redundancy can strongly impact approaches leveraging it. This is the focus of our second study.

A.4   Study II: Language Models & Code Completion

The *goal* of this study is to investigate the performance of an n-gram language model aimed at recommending the next code token to write (*i.e.,* the nth token) given $n-1$ written tokens. Basically, we assess the accuracy of the language model proposed by Hindle *et al.* [HBS+12] for code completion both overall (*i.e.,* when used in any part of the source code) as well as when focusing on specific code constructs.

A language model is a probability distribution that estimates how often a sentence occurs in a textual dataset. Language models are widely employed in many domains such as speech recognition and code completion. The n-gram model is one of the most commonly used language models and it determines the probability of having a word w_i given the previous n-1 words. Such a probability is denoted by $p(w_i|w_{i-1}, w_{i-2}, \ldots, w_{i-n+1})$, where $w_{i-n+1}, \ldots, w_{i-1}, w_i$ are n continuous words. The probability that w_i follows $w_{i-n+1}, \ldots, w_{i-2}$, w_{i-1} is estimated by training the language model on a training test, composed of textual documents. When applying the language model to software-related tasks, the training set is composed of code documents.

The most common way to evaluate the performance of a n-gram model is instead to run it on an previously unseen set of test documents (again, code documents in the case of software-related tasks) known as the test set, and assess its ability to predict the actual word w_i following a sequence of $n-1$ consecutive words extracted from the test set (this process is repeated for many sequences) [CG96]. Our conjecture is that

---

[6]Results available in our replication package [LPM+].

the substantially different redundancy rates observed in Study I for the different code constructs might influence the performance of the language model and suggest its applicability only to specific parts of the code (*i.e.,* the ones having high redundancy).

A.4.1   Research Questions

The study aims at answering the following RQs:

RQ₃: *How effective is the language model in supporting code completion?* This RQ assesses the performance of the n-gram language model when applied to code completion. The evaluation approach followed in this study is similar to the one of Hindle *et al.* [HBS+12], where they evaluated the a 3-gram language model on five systems. We (i) run a much larger evaluation involving 2,640 subject systems, and (ii) study the impact of the n parameter on the model performance.

RQ₄: *How effective is the language model in supporting code completion for different code constructs?* This RQ investigates whether and how the predictive performance of the n-gram language model varies on different code constructs (*i.e.,* the same 12 constructs considered in Study I). To the best of our knowledge, this is the first study running such an analysis. RQ₄'s findings will shed some light on the importance of considering the strong locality of code redundancy.

A.4.2   Data Extraction

To answer our research questions we perform the following steps for each project P_i in our dataset:

1. Create training and test sets. We randomly split the P_i's Java files into a training set accounting for 90 % of P_i's ELOC, and a test set composed by the remaining 10%. Our training/testing strategy is different with respect to the one adopted by Hindle *et al.* [HBS+12]. They randomly selected 200 files from each subject system, using 160 for training and 40 for testing. Such an approach does not consider the whole project's code base, and does not provide a clear indication of the "amount of code", intended as ELOC, actually used for training and testing; indeed, this strongly depends on the size of the specific files selected for training and testing.

2. N-grams extraction. As in Study I, we tokenize the P_i's Java code in both training and test set. Note that *no abstraction* is used in this study, since we want to support code completion by recommending to the developer the exact token to write given the previous $n-1$ tokens (as done in [HBS+12]). We vary n from 3 (the original value used in [HBS+12]) to 15 at steps of one (*i.e.,* 3, 4, etc.).

3. Linking tokens to code constructs. As done in Study I, we map each token to one of the code constructs listed in Table A.2. This allows us to answer RQ₄, by reporting the performance of the language model when predicting tokens belonging to different code constructs.

After collecting this data, for each project P_i and for each considered value of n, we train the language model on the n-grams extracted from the P_i's training set, obtaining a model $M_{P_i,n}$. Then, we run $M_{P_i,n}$ on the n-grams extracted from the P_i's test set, trying to predict for each n-gram the nth token given the $n-1$ continuous tokens preceding it. Overall, this resulted in the testing of the language model on a minimum of 104,953,587 n-grams (for $n = 15$) and a maximum of 106,726,166 (for $n = 3$).

A.4.3 Data Analysis

We answer RQ$_3$ by showing boxplots reporting the percentage of tokens correctly predicted by the language model (*i.e.,* its accuracy) for each of the experimented n values. Since the language model provides a ranked list of tokens likely following the provided $n-1$ tokens (with the most likely on top), we compute the model accuracy when considering the top t recommendations it generates, varying t from 1 to 10 at steps of one. For example, when considering $t = 1$, we consider a recommendation as correct only if the correct token appears in the first position of the ranked list, while for $t = 10$ the recommendation is tagged as correct if the correct token appears in the top-10.

Concerning RQ$_4$, we compare the accuracy of the language model when predicting tokens belonging to different code constructs. This is done via boxplots and statistical tests, following the same procedure adopted in RQ$_2$.

A.4.4 Results

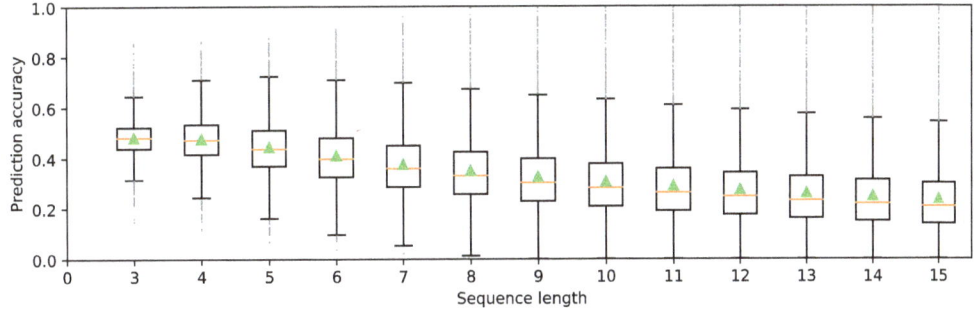

Figure A.6. Prediction accuracy rates of the language model when supporting code completion (top 1 recommendation).

1) RQ$_3$: How effective is the language model in supporting code completion? Fig. A.6 shows the accuracy of the n-gram language model when used to support code completion. In particular, Fig. A.6 reports the accuracy achieved when only considering the top ranked suggestion (*i.e.,* the token having the highest probability of following the $n-1$ tokens) when varying n between 3 and 15.

The language model achieves its maximum accuracy (median = 0.48) when $n = 3$, and its performance regularly decreases with the increasing of n (worst accuracy achieved at $n = 15$). Such a finding might seem counterintuitive. Indeed, one would

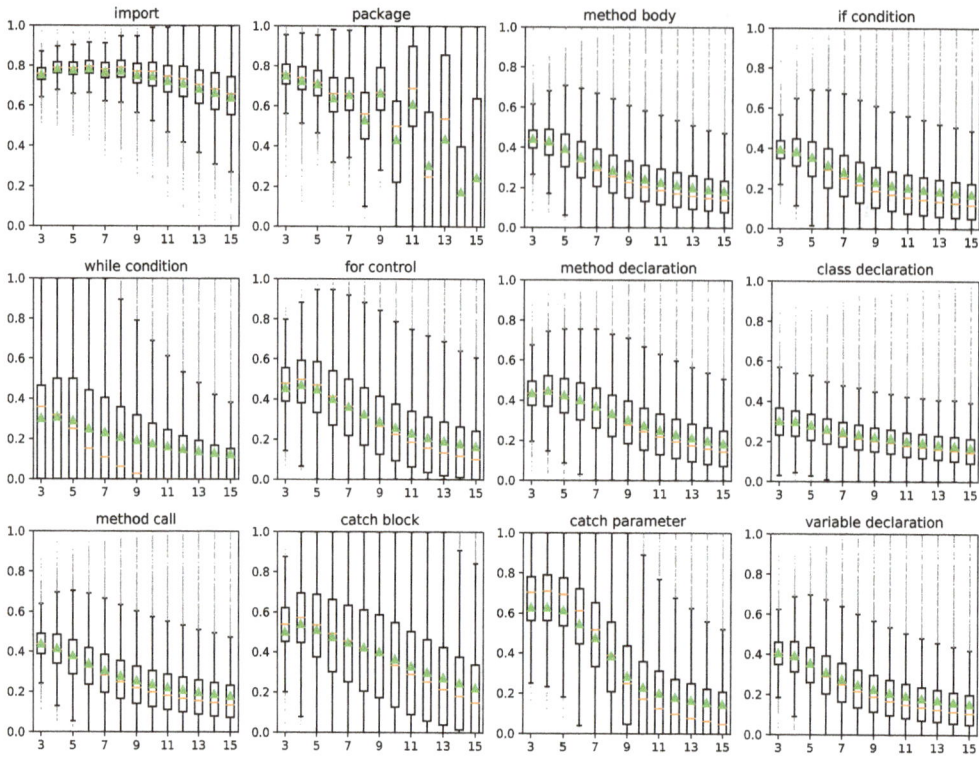

Figure A.7. Accuracy of the language model when supporting code completion on different constructs (top-1 recommendation)

expect that the more information is fed into the language model, *i.e.*, the higher the number of $n-1$ subsequent tokens provided to the model, the easier is for the model to guess the nth following token. Increasing the number of tokens fed into the model does also (i) increases the possible noise provided to it, and (ii) reduces to "locality" of the n-1 fed tokens (*i.e.*, increases the likelihood of having tokens belonging to different statements). Let us discuss this using the following example statements:

```
import org.program_comprehension.*;
import java.io.*;
public static void main ...
```

Considering our experimental design, when using $n=3$, we start reading the first two tokens (`import org`) and ask the language model to recommend the third one (`.`). Then, we feed the following two tokens (`org.`) and again ask the language model to suggest the third token (`program_comprehension`). This process is continued until we reach the last token in the file. As we can see, for low values of n we provide very *localized* sequences of $n-1$ tokens to predict the nth one. In other words, the $n-1$ tokens are generally part of the same code statement and narrow down the possible tokens that can follow them.

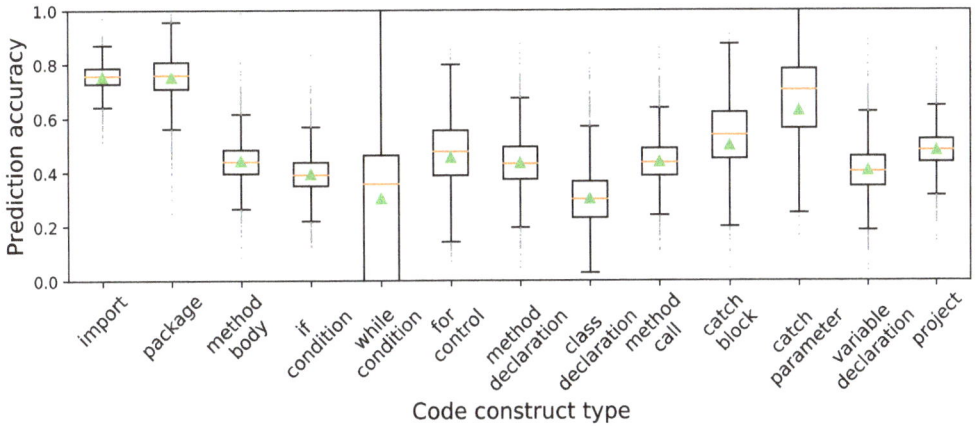

Figure A.8. Accuracy of the 3-gram model when supporting code completion on different constructs (top-1 recommendation)

When $n = 15$, in the example above we provide as input to the language model the whole first two import statements (for a total of 14 tokens), asking the language model to predict the 15th token (*i.e.,* public). In this case it is challenging for the language model to guess the correct token, due to the poor localization of the fed information (the 14 input tokens belong to statements unrelated with the one in which we ask the language model to support the auto completion).

Our results support the findings by Bruch *et al.* [BMM09] and Nguyen *et al.* [NNN+12], and highlight the importance of exploiting contextual information when supporting code completion. The accuracy obtained when considering the top t recommendations with t going from 2 to 10 is available in our replication package [LPM+] and is consistent with the same observations.

RQ$_4$: How effective is the language model in supporting code completion for different code constructs?

Fig. A.7 shows the accuracy of the n-gram language model (for different values of n) when used to support code completion on different code constructs (again, when the top recommendation is considered, other results in [LPM+]). Overall, the trend is the same previously observed for the whole project: The model performs better for small n values.

What heavily varies is the performance of the language model when applied to the different types of code constructs. To zoom into this analysis, Fig. A.8 and A.9 compare the performance of the 3-gram language model on the different constructs via boxplots and statistical tests, respectively. Hereafter, we discuss the results for $n = 3$ as in the original paper by Hindle *et al.* [HBS+12], while results for other values of n are available in the replication package [LPM+]. The achieved results highlight that:

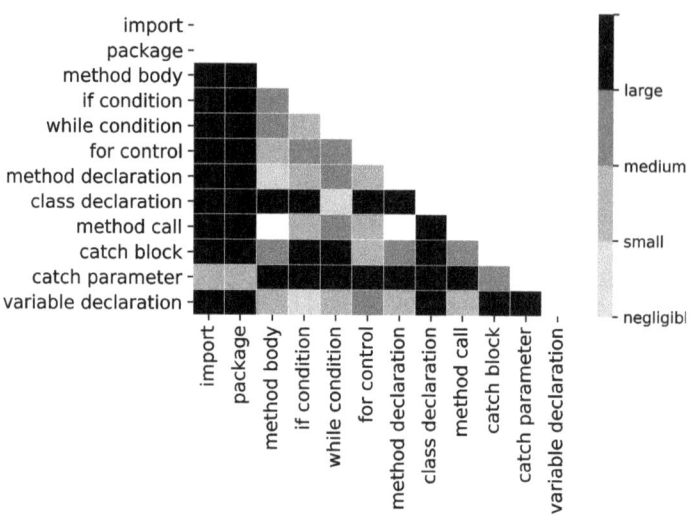

Figure A.9. Statistical comparisons for the accuracy of the 3-gram language model on different code constructs

- **The performance of the language model varies a lot across different types of code constructs.** This is clear both in the boxplots (Fig. A.8) as well as from the results of the statistical analysis (Fig. A.9), in which several significant differences accompanied by a medium/large effect size are observed. For example, the performance of the language model is very good when supporting code completion for import and package statements (median=0.76), while it strongly drops when working on while conditions (median=0.36).

- **There is a clear correlation between the redundancy rate of code constructs, and the performance of the language model when applied on them.** While this is evident when putting together the results of our two studies, we also compute the correlation between the redundancy rate of code constructs and the accuracy of the language model in predicting tokens belonging to them by using the Spearman rank correlation analysis [Coh13]. We obtained a correlation coefficient of $\rho = 0.71$, highlighting a *strong* correlation on the basis of the guidelines provided by Cohen [Coh13].

We further dig into the results by looking for the code tokens correctly predicted by the language model when setting $n = 3$ on the same 30 randomly selected systems used in Study I. We discuss in detail the results for Microsoft Thrifty, on which 13,176 out of 29,763 tokens have been correctly predicted (44% accuracy).

The top ten correctly predicted tokens on this system are: ".", "(", ")", ";", "}", "{", "public", "thrift", "apache", "=", accounting for a total of 9,494 (72%) of the correctly predicted tokens. Only two of the top-10 correctly predicted tokens are project specific (*i.e.*, "thrift" and "apache") and they are correctly predicted since, as shown in Study I, frequently used in `catch` statements. In addition, 1,073 correctly predicted tokens (a further 8%) is represented by Java keywords. The results obtained from other 29 systems are in line with these findings and confirm that most of the correctly predicted tokens are not project specific.

We believe that these findings are of paramount importance when considering the use of language models for supporting code completion. Indeed, while the performance of the language model could be overall acceptable (*e.g.,* 44% accuracy on Microsoft Thrifty), it is mostly effective in recommending tokens (i) belonging to very specific parts of the code (*e.g.,* `import` and `catch` statements), and (ii) mainly representing syntactic sugar of the programming language.

Our results indicate that language models alone cannot effectively support code completion and that, as proposed by Hindle *et al.* [HBS+12], they can only *complement* recommendations generated by other techniques. Also, our findings clearly highlight the strong impact that unevenly redundancy rates of code constructs can have on applications assuming the high redundancy of source code.

A.5   Threats to Validity

Threats to *construct validity* concern the relation between theory and observation. In this work they are mainly due to the measurements we performed.

In Study II, we assess the performance of the language model presented by Hindle *et al.* [HBS+12] in supporting code completion by using their same experimental design. In particular, given a project P_i, we train the language model on a set of P_i's files and test it on all the n-grams (we experimented with different values of n) extracted from files belonging to the test set. As done in [HBS+12], each file in the test set was scanned from the beginning to the end to extract all its n-grams on which the language model was then evaluated.

Such an approach aims at simulating the code writing by the developer: She writes the first $n-1$ tokens, and uses the code completion to recommend the nth token, then she writes other $n-1$ tokens, and again uses code completion to suggest the next token, etc. Clearly, developers do not write code by following such a linear approach from the beginning to the end, and we acknowledge such a threat.

Note that the performance we report for the language model cannot be directly compared with the one reported in the original paper by Hindle *et al.* [HBS+12]. Indeed, while we report the raw accuracy of the language model when used to support code completion, in [HBS+12] the authors show the gain in terms of accuracy obtained over the Eclipse built-in code completion module. Since our primary goal was to show how the different redundancy rates of code constructs impact the performance of techniques exploiting such a redundancy, we preferred to report the language model accuracy by itself.

Threats to *internal validity* concern external factors we did not consider that could affect the variables and the relations being investigated. In Study I, when assessing software redundancy, we did not experiment with all possible sequence lengths, but we limited our analysis to sequences going from 3 to 60 tokens at steps of 3. Still, the trend observed in the achieved result is quite clear, and shows that, as expected, the redundancy rate decreases with the increase of the sequence length (see Fig. A.2). We do not expect to observe anything different by further increasing the sequence length. In both our studies, we did not consider all possible code constructs that can be extracted from Java systems. However, the number and diversity of the considered constructs have been sufficient to observe differences in the redundancy rate and in the accuracy of the language model.

Threats to *conclusion validity* concern the relation between the treatment and the outcome. Although this is mainly an observational study, wherever possible we used an appropriate support of statistical procedures, integrated with effect size measures that, besides the significance of the differences found, highlight the magnitude of such differences.

Threats to *external validity* concern the generalizability of our findings. While our studies have been performed on a large code base including 2,640 projects, we are aware that (i) all subject projects are written in Java, thus calling for the need of analyzing software projects in other programming languages, and (ii) we limited our analysis to open source projects ignoring industrial systems.

A.6   Related Work

A.6.1   Code Redundancy

Code clones, *i.e.*, code fragments similar to other ones by some given definition of similarity [RCK09], are a common form of code redundancy, and have been widely studied. We limit our discussion to few of the works focusing on clones. Baker [Bak95] inspected two systems and tried to find maximal sections of code over a certain length which are exactly the same or only differ in parameter names. Their results indicate that around 20% of the code is (near-)duplicated. Roy and Cordy [RC08] examined 15 Java and C systems, and reported that ∼15% of the Java methods and 2.5% of the C functions are exact clones. Kapser and Godfrey [KG04] conducted two case studies and reported that 50% of the clones were related to function clones. With another case study on the Apache web server, they later showed the existence of "cloning hotspots": 17% of the code contained 38% of the clones [KG06b].

Mockus [Moc07] analyzed 13.2 million source code files from open source projects, and reported that over 50% of files were reused across projects. While our work is naturally related to code clones, we focus on the code redundancy phenomenon at a lower granularity level, with the goal of investigating (i) how it varies in code constructs, and (ii) how this variations impacts the performance of techniques leveraging code redundancy.

Other studies have explored code redundancy from a different perspective. Barr *et al.* [BBD+14] found that 42% of the code changes can be largely reconstituted from existing code. Nguyen *et al.* [NNN16] reported that 12.1% of the routines (*i.e.*, a portion of code that performs a specific task, such as methods) are repeated between 2 and 7 times in projects. Finally, the study by Gabel and Su [GS10] is certainly the most related to our work. Indeed, Study I represents a *differentiated replication* of the investigation presented in [GS10], featuring a different and larger code base and investigating at a fine-grained level how code redundancy changes across code constructs.

A.6.2 Code Completion

Code completion is one of the killer features of modern IDEs, and researchers have proposed different methods to improve code completion accuracy. Again, due to the lack of space we focus our discussion on a few representative works.

By mining existing code, Bruch *et al.* [BMM09] (i) filter out candidates from the list of tokens recommended by the IDE that are not relevant to the current working context and (ii) rank candidates based on how relevant to the context they are. These features help in substantially improve the standard IDE code completion engine.

Nguyen *et al.* [NNN+12] exploited context-sensitive information in their GraPacc, showing its effectiveness in code completion. GraPacc models API usage patterns by relying on a graph representation, where nodes represent actions (*e.g.,* method calls) and controls (*e.g.,* while) points, and edges represent control and data flow dependencies between nodes. Context information such as the relation between API and other code elements is considered for ranking most fitted API usage patterns.

Raychev *et al.* [RVY14] extracted sequences of method calls from a large codebase and trained a language model on them. They applied this model to support the auto-completion of method calls, achieving an accuracy of 90% when considering the top three results. We experimented in Study II the previously discussed language model proposed by Hindle *et al.* [HBS+12], showing that its performance substantially varies when applied to constructs characterized by different redundancy.

The language model proposed by Hindle *et al.* was improved by Nguyen *et al.* [NNNN13, NNN16] and by Tu *et al.* [TSD14]. Nguyen *et al.* [NNNN13] presented a statistical semantic language model for source code extending the standard language model by annotating each token with its type and semantic role. Also, they exploit a more advanced *n*-gram topic model to support code completion. In a related work of the authors, they also proposed the use of an AST-based language model instead of the *n*-gram language model to recommend the next valid syntactic template and detect common syntactic templates [NNN16].

Tu *et al.* [TSD14] enriched the language model with a cache exploiting a specific *localness* of software, *i.e.,* repetitions of a specific n-gram localized in few files. Other approaches [TSD14, NNNN13, NNN16] achieve improvements over the language model proposed by Hindle *et al.* [HBS+12].

In our study we chose to adopt the simplest approach (*i.e.,* Hindle *et al.* [HBS+12]) since our goal was not to experiment with the best code completion tool available, but to show that approaches leveraging code redundancy should consider its strong locality in specific code constructs.

A.7   Conclusion

We examined the redundancy of code constructs, and investigated the impact of its inequality on an application leveraging code redundancy, namely n-gram based code completion.

Our results indicate that while software is quite redundant when considered as a whole, the redundancy is localized in specific code constructs. Such a characteristic of code redundancy strongly impacts the performance of application exploiting code redundancy, like n-gram based completion.

Our future work will focus on the definition of smarter code completion tools leveraging our findings, and on customizing the use of the language model on the basis of the specific code constructs on which it is applied.

On the Impact of Refactoring Operations on Code Naturalness

Recent studies have demonstrated that software is natural, that is, its source code is highly repetitive and predictable like human languages. Also, previous studies suggested the existence of a relationship between code quality and its naturalness, presenting empirical evidence showing that buggy code is "less natural" than non-buggy code. We conjecture that this quality-naturalness relationship could be exploited to support refactoring activities (*e.g.,* to locate source code areas in need of refactoring). We perform a first step in this direction by analyzing whether refactoring can improve the naturalness of code.

We use state-of-the-art tools to mine a large dataset of refactoring operations performed in open source systems. Then, we investigate the impact of different types of refactoring operations on the naturalness of the impacted code. We found that (i) code refactoring does not necessarily increase the naturalness of the refactored code; and (ii) the impact on the code naturalness strongly depends on the type of refactoring operations.

This study is based on the following publication [LNBL19]:

On the Impact of Refactoring Operations on Code Naturalness

Bin Lin, Csaba Nagy, Gabriele Bavota, Michele Lanza. In *26th IEEE International Conference on Software Analysis, Evolution and Reengineering (SANER 2019) - Early Research Achievements Track*, pp. 594–598, 2019

B.1   Introduction

Software is not unique. Researchers have discovered that for sequences of six tokens extracted from the source code, the probability of finding the same sequence in other software projects is higher than 50% [GS10]. Based on this finding, Hindle *et al.* [HBS+12] introduced the concept of source code "naturalness", to indicate that source code is highly repetitive and predictable, just like a text written in human language. They showed that this characteristic can be captured by statistical language models and can be leveraged for different SE tasks, such as code completion [TSD14] and fault localization [RHG+16]. The latter application proposed by Ray *et al.* was possible thanks to the finding that buggy code is less natural (*i.e.,* less predictable) than correct code [RHG+16].

One interesting unanswered question is whether software refactoring (*i.e.,* the activity of improving code quality without modifying the system's external behavior) can be seen as a process implicitly aiming at improving code naturalness. Intuitively, we might think the source code is easier to maintain if it is more natural, as there are fewer "surprising" and "unfamiliar" code fragments for developers. Thus, it can be conjectured that developers focus their refactoring attentions on code exhibiting low naturalness. If such a conjecture is confirmed, information about the naturalness of code components could be leveraged to support refactoring operations (*e.g.,* by identifying code components in need of refactoring).

We perform a first step in that direction by investigating whether refactoring operations applied by software developers result in an improvement of the code naturalness.

We use RMINER [TME+18], a state-of-the-art refactoring miner, to mine 1,448 refactoring operations performed by developers in 619 open source projects. These operations cover 10 different refactoring types (*e.g.,* move method, extract class). Once these operations are collected, we employ the statistical language model proposed by Tu *et al.* [TSD14] to measure the naturalness of the code components before and after the refactoring. This allows us to verify whether different types of refactoring operations improve the code naturalness. Our results show that the impact on the code naturalness strongly depends on the specific type of refactoring operation. For example, "Extract Method" refactoring is more likely to increase the code naturalness, while "Pull Up Method" refactoring often leads to lower naturalness. These results suggest that leveraging code naturalness for identification of refactoring opportunities is far from trivial, and highlight the need for additional investigations in this direction.

Structure of the Chapter

We illustrate the related work in Section B.2 and describe the design of our study in Section B.3. Section B.4 presents our preliminary results. The threats that affect the validity of our studies are discussed in Section B.5. In the end, Section B.6 outlines the conclusions and future work.

B.2   Related Work

The naturalness of software has received considerable attention in the SE research community. After the seminal work by Hindle *et al.* [HBS+12], several studies have investigated the code naturalness from different perspectives. Tu *et al.* [TSD14] found that the distribution of repetitive code is highly skewed in the source code. Lin *et al.* [LSM+17] disclosed that different parts of source code are not equally repetitive.

Researchers have also studied the relation between naturalness and software defects. Campbell *et al.* [CHA14] found that syntax errors are less natural than other code, and this fact can be used to augment compilers' ability to locate missing and extra tokens. Ray *et al.* [RHG+16] evaluated the naturalness of buggy code and the corresponding fixes by analyzing over 8,000 fix commits from 10 Java projects. Their results showed that buggy code is less natural, and the naturalness increases once the bug is fixed. They also showed that focusing on unnatural code is cost-effective in finding bugs compared to other state-of-the-art static bug finders.

The most relevant work is the study conducted by Arima *et al.* [AHK18], which uses code naturalness as a metric to evaluate whether a refactoring operation is effective. With the assumption that appropriate refactoring should raise the code naturalness, the authors constructed a gold set of 28 refactoring operations extracted from JUnit4[1] by searching for the keywords "refactor" and "clean" in commit logs and manually filtering out those commits containing more than one refactoring. As a result, the code naturalness increases after 19 out of the 28 refactorings, which indicates that naturalness might be a potential valid metric for evaluating the quality of refactoring. Our study, while having a similar objective (*i.e.,* studying the impact of refactoring operations on code naturalness) is performed on a much larger dataset composed of 1,448 refactorings extracted from 619 systems. We also investigate the impact of refactoring operations on the code naturalness by considering the type of implemented refactoring (*e.g.,* move method) as an independent variable to study (possibly having an effect on the "naturalness" dependent variable).

B.3   Study Design

Our *goal* is to investigate whether refactoring operations increase the naturalness of the refactored code. We assess how the code naturalness is impacted (i) overall, meaning when considering all types of refactoring operations together, and (ii) by specific types of refactoring.

B.3.1   Research Question

Our study aims at answering the following Research Question (RQ):

RQ: *How does refactoring impact the naturalness of source code?* This RQ assesses how the naturalness of source code changes after refactoring operations. We also

---

[1]https://github.com/junit-team/junit4

investigate whether there is an observable difference for the change in naturalness for different kinds of refactorings. To the best of our knowledge, this is the first study running such an analysis on a large dataset while considering specific refactoring types.

The findings of this RQ will shed light on the possibility of using code naturalness to support the identification of code components in need of refactoring.

B.3.2 Study Context

The *study context* consists of 619 Java projects on GitHub[2], mined on Nov. 6, 2018, using the following selection criteria:

- **Activity level.** To exclude inactive projects, the projects must have at least one commit in the three months preceding the data collection.

- **Popularity.** Projects need to have at least 100 forks[3] and 100 stars[4], to avoid the inclusion of likely "toy-projects". Forks and stars serve as two proxies for the popularity of software repositories on GitHub.

We found 2,663 projects satisfying these constraints. However, due to the computational cost of our experimental design that requires retraining the statistical language models assessing the naturalness several times (details follow), we selected from this set a random subset of 1,500 projects for our study. We believe that 1,500 projects still ensure a good generalizability of our results. After mining refactoring from these repositories, we found 619 projects containing at least one of the refactoring operations we study (discussed in Section B.3.3). These 619 projects compose our study context.

B.3.3 Data Collection

To answer our research question, we first mine refactoring operations from the collected projects, and then assess the naturalness of the impacted code components before and after each refactoring commit.

Refactoring Mining

We use RMINER [TME+18] to mine the refactoring operations in the randomly selected 1,500 projects. RMINER extracts refactoring operations by inspecting two adjacent commits using an AST-based statement matching algorithm. RMINER is reported to have a precision of over 0.95 for most refactoring types, except "Change Package" (0.85) and "Move Field" (0.884). The recall achieved by RMINER is also fairly high: 0.80 for most refactoring types, except "Rename Class" (0.711), "Extract & Move

---

[2]https://github.com/
[3]https://help.github.com/articles/fork-a-repo/
[4]https://help.github.com/articles/about-stars/

Method" (0.412), and "Move Method" (0.764). Thus, adopting RMINER allows us to obtain different types of refactorings with considerable accuracy. While RMINER can detect various types of refactorings, in this study we only consider those do not requiring the creation of new source code files (*e.g.,* we exclude "Extract Class" refactoring), since this avoids the introduction of confounding factors in the computation of the code naturalness (*i.e.,* the naturalness of the same files before/after refactoring is compared). Table B.1 reports the types of refactoring operations considered in our study.

Table B.1. Considered Refactorings in Our Study

Level	Refactorings considered
Method	Extract Method, Inline Method, Pull Up Method, Push Down Method, Rename Method, Move Method, Extract and Move Method
Field	Pull Up Field, Push Down Field, Move Field

After obtaining all the commits with refactoring operations, we filtered out commits in which more than one refactoring type was applied, again to better isolate and study the effect of a single type of refactoring operation on the code naturalness. In the end, we obtained 1,448 refactoring operations from 619 projects, while no relevant refactorings were detected in the other 881 projects.

Naturalness Measurement

Like the work by Tu *et al.* [TSD14] and Ray *et al.* [RHG+16], we use *cross-entropy* to assess the naturalness of code components. The idea behind *cross-entropy* is that if a code snippet is more natural, it will be more likely to appear in the training corpus. The *cross-entropy* of a code snippet S composed by tokens $t_1...t_n$ of length N is calculated as

$$H_M(S) = -\frac{1}{N}\log_2 P_M(S) = -\frac{1}{N}\sum_1^N \log_2 P(t_i|h) \qquad \text{(B.1)}$$

where $P_M(S)$ and $P(t_i|h)$ are the probabilities estimated by the language model M, t_i is the token to be predicted, and h is the preceding tokens followed by t_i. In our study, we adopted the cache language model proposed by Tu *et al.* [TSD14]. This model combines a traditional n-gram language model and an added "cache" component to exploit the localness property of source code. Like other statistical language models, it learns from a corpus of source code, and then predicts the probability P of occurrence for each token in the new file. In practice, a low *cross-entropy* indicates high *naturalness*.

To understand how naturalness changes due to refactoring, we measure the naturalness for every commit that has a refactoring operation. For each operation, we construct a training corpus, composed of all the files in the commit before the refactoring, excluding the files being refactored. This corpus is used to compute the *cross-entropy* of the excluded files and their corresponding refactored version.

B.3.4   Data Analysis

We compare the *cross-entropy* change caused by each type of refactoring operation via violin plots. The comparison of *cross-entropy* of files before and after refactoring is also performed via statistical tests by using the Wilcoxon signed-rank test [Wil45], with results intended as statistically significant at $p \leq 0.05$. We also estimate the magnitude of the differences by using the effect size r, which can be used for the Wilcoxon signed-rank test [Fie13]. We follow well-established guidelines to interpret the effect size: negligible for $|r| < 0.10$, small for $0.10 \leq |r| < 0.3$, medium for $0.3 \leq |r| < 0.5$, and large for $|r| \geq 0.5$ [Coh92].

B.4   Preliminary Results

We first provide an overview of how code naturalness changes after refactoring with statistical analysis, and then give concrete examples of refactoring activities that had a positive/negative effect on code naturalness. Finally, we compare our results with those achieved by Arima *et al.* [AHK18].

B.4.1   Statistical Analysis of Results

Table B.2 reports the impact of the 1,448 detected refactoring operations on the cross-entropy of the involved code components. Despite the quite large set of refactoring operations considered in our study, it is worth noticing that the mined refactorings are not equally distributed regarding their refactoring type. Indeed, "Extract Method" and "Rename Method" account for 66.0% of the total refactorings. Among all refactoring types, "Push Down Method" and "Push Down Field" are the least performed, and account only for 1.0% of the overall dataset. In the following analyses, these two types of refactorings are excluded due to the low number of occurrences.

For all these refactorings, we calculated the cross-entropy change (*i.e.,* the difference between the cross-entropy after refactoring and cross-entropy before refactoring) of the file being refactored. When reading the table, we have to be aware of the fact that high cross-entropy stands for low naturalness. Therefore, when the cross-entropy change is above zero, the naturalness of the code actually drops. Similarly, the naturalness increases when the cross-entropy change is negative.

Table B.2 shows that overall, although the decrease of cross-entropy (increase of naturalness) is more common than the increase of cross-entropy (decrease of naturalness), the difference is not substantial (*i.e.,* 50.8% *vs* 44.5%). When it comes to specific refactoring types, "Inline Method", "Pull Up Method", "Rename Method", and "Move Method" are more likely to reduce the code naturalness. Among these five refactoring types, "Pull Up Method" has the highest possibility (73.3%) to reduce the naturalness. All other refactoring types tend to increase the code naturalness, despite the fact that there is still a large percentage of cases in which the naturalness decreases. Thus, our preliminary analysis of the achieved results does not show any clear relationship between refactoring and code naturalness.

Table B.2. Detected Refactorings and Their Impact on the Code Naturalness. Only "Rename Method" contains refactoring operations with unchanged cross-entropy (68 operations, 14.5% of "Rename Method" refactorings, and 4.7 % of all refactorings). Thus, the column "# cross-entropy" is omitted.

Refactoring type	Total	# cross-entropy increased	# cross-entropy decreased
Extract Method	488	174 (35.7%)	314 (64.3%)
Inline Method	57	37 (64.9%)	20 (35.1%)
Pull Up Method	45	33 (73.3%)	12 (26.7%)
Push Down Method	5	2 (40.0%)	3 (60.0%)
Rename Method	468	220 (47.0%)	180 (38.5%)
Move Method	126	76 (60.3%)	50 (39.7%)
Extract & Move Method	162	60 (37.0%)	102 (63.0%)
Pull Up Field	18	7 (38.9%)	11 (61.1%)
Push Down Field	10	4 (40.0%)	6 (60.0%)
Move Field	69	32 (46.4%)	37 (53.6%)
Sum	**1,448**	645 (44.5%)	735 (50.8%)

Table B.3. Statistical Tests of File Cross-Entropy Before and After Refactoring

Refactoring type	P-Value	Effect size
Extract Method	< 0.001	0.180 (small)
Inline Method	0.202	0.119 (small)
Pull Up Method	< 0.001	0.414 (medium)
Rename Method	0.177	0.044 (negligible)
Move Method	0.029	0.138 (small)
Extract and Move Method	< 0.001	0.213 (small)
Pull Up Field	0.122	0.258 (small)
Move Field	0.727	0.030 (negligible)
Overall	0.453	0.003 (negligible)

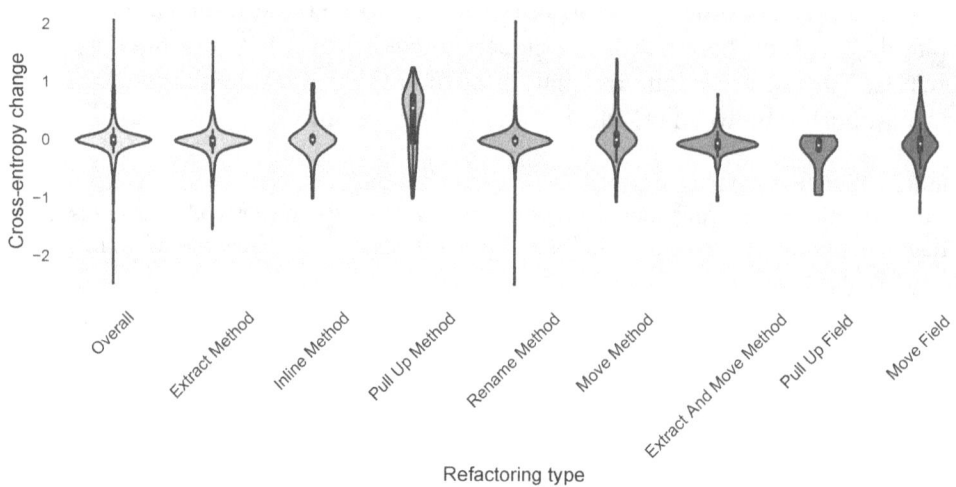

Figure B.1. Cross-entropy change after refactoring

To better understand the impact of refactoring operations on the code naturalness, we applied statistical tests to the cross-entropy values before and after refactoring for all the files being refactored. In Table B.3, we can find that for half of the refactoring types, there is no statistically significant difference (p-value ≥ 0.05) between the cross-entropy before and after refactoring. Meanwhile, the magnitude of the difference is mostly limited (with negligible or small effect size). The only exception here is the "Pull Up Method" refactoring. The comparison of cross-entropy values result in a statistically significant difference (p-value < 0.05), with a medium effect size. The result is in line with our findings from Table B.2.

To further understand how the impact of different types of refactoring on code naturalness differs, we also visualize the cross-entropy difference with violin plots in Fig. B.1. In the violin plots, the thickness of the outer layer represents how likely the cross-entropy change will fall into this value. In the center of each violin plot, the white dot represents the median; the thick black bar represents the interquartile range, and thin black line represents the 95% confidence interval.

Looking at Fig. B.1 we can see that "Extract Method", "Pull Up Field", "Rename Method", and "Extract And Move Method" refactorings are the least likely to impact the code naturalness, as most of the cross-entropy changes are close to zero. "Pull Up Method" can often bring large naturalness change to files, especially by reducing the code naturalness.

B.4.2 Examples of Cross-Entropy Change

To gain a more intuitive impression on how refactoring impacts the code naturalness, we extracted some examples from our dataset.

"Inline Method" refactoring was performed on the class "View" from the project "*Carbon*"[5]. In this refactoring operation, the calls to method "setTint" were replaced with the body of "setTint", consisting in a call to the method "setTintList". The replaced method "setTint" was also deleted in the class. After this refactoring, the cross-entropy of this class file increased from 2.418 to 2.430, thus resulting in a reduction of code naturalness. Intuitively, since the refactored method was used multiple times in the class, one might think that the increase of cross-entropy was caused by the fact that the replaced token "setTint" is much more common (*i.e.,* has a lower cross-entropy) in the source code than "setTintList". We inspected the cross-entropy of each token in the class before and after the refactoring to verify this assumption. However, we found out that the cross-entropy of the tokens "setTint" and "setTintList" are actually similar (whose value varies in different token positions due to the difference of preceding tokens). As a matter of fact, the removed tokens with significantly lower cross-entropy were those composing the method declaration, such as "public" and "void". Indeed, since the idea behind naturalness is based on the repetitiveness of tokens, these reserved keywords often have a much lower cross-entropy. One interesting direction to explore in future is how the cross-entropy of identifiers, which are the tokens carrying semantic information, changes during refactoring.

An "Extract Method" refactoring operation was performed on the "CacheHandler" class from the project "*AutoLoadCache*"[6]. In this refactoring operation, multiple lines of code in the method "proceedDeleteCacheTransactional" were moved to a newly created method "clearCache", and a call to "clearCache" replaced these lines. After refactoring, the cross-entropy of this class file was reduced to 3.776 from 3.813, namely the code naturalness increased. "Extract Method" is the opposite operation of "Inline Method", therefore, it is unsurprising that the naturalness change caused by "Extract Method" displays an opposite trend. Similarly, the major difference between the versions (before and after refactoring) is the extra tokens needed for declaring the new method.

B.4.3   Comparison with the Study by Arima et al.

We compare the results we achieved with the results from the study by Arima *et al.* [AHK18]. Some interesting facts are spotted.

In our study, only 50.8% of the total refactorings increase the code naturalness, which is much lower than what has been observed in [AHK18] (67.9%). The reason behind this different finding could be explained by the different datasets employed in the two studies. First, the dataset used in [AHK18] is composed of only 28 refactorings (as compared to the 1,448 considered in our study), thus possibly indicating peculiarities of the specific refactoring operations considered. Second, the 28 refactorings used in [AHK18] have all been mined from a single, well-known project, namely JUnit 4, while in our study we extracted the studied refactorings from a variegated set

---

[5]https://goo.gl/NBRBah
[6]https://goo.gl/r4FE26

of 619 projects. It is possible that the "quality" of the refactorings applied in JUnit 4 is higher, thus resulting in a naturalness increase that we did not observe in our dataset. Clearly, this is only an assumption, which needs to be carefully verified. However, it also indicates a direction to work with: We might need to better understand the association between code quality and naturalness, which is not fully disclosed in the research community.

In the work of Arima *et al.* [AHK18], 7 out of 9 (77.8%) "Extract Method" refactorings increase the code naturalness, which is in line with our result: 64.3% of the "Extract Method" refactorings result in increased naturalness. Although no significant difference between the cross-entropy before and after refactoring was found during our statistical analysis, there are indications that "Extract Method" refactoring might help in improving the naturalness of code. Similarly, 2 out of 3 "Inline Method" refactorings in their study lead to a naturalness decrease, meanwhile, the same trend applies to 64.9% of our cases. However, since they inspected a smaller number of "Inline Method" refactorings, much more refactorings need to be examined to make a solid comparison.

B.5　Threats to Validity

Threats to construct validity concern the relation between theory and observation. In this work, we use RMINER to detect refactorings. While the precision achieved by this tool is very high [TME+18], we are aware that our results can be affected by the presence of false positives. Also, RMINER can identify a specific set of refactoring operations, while the definition of refactoring is broader.

Threats to internal validity concern external factors we did not consider that could affect the variables and the relations being investigated. In our study, when calculating the entropy for source code, we did not experiment with all possible configurations of the used language model. An adapted 3-gram model with an additional cache is used. We do not expect to observe a significant difference in the overall result trend with different configurations.

Threats to external validity concern the generalizability of our findings. While we investigated a large number of refactoring operations, we are aware that only Java and open source software projects are considered in our study.

B.6　Conclusion and Future Work

We investigated how refactoring impacts the naturalness of source code by inspecting 1,448 refactoring operations from 619 Java projects. We studied the impact of refactoring types on the naturalness of the modified code components. Our results show that refactorings do not necessarily make source code more natural, and that naturalness changes in different ways for different types of refactorings.

Our study serves as the first step toward using naturalness information to support refactoring activities. In the future, we will conduct more thorough empirical studies to understand the correlation between refactoring quality and code naturalness. That is, we would like to examine whether naturalness can be a good indicator for effective refactorings with high quality code. We will also investigate the possibility of use the naturalness of source code combined with other metrics, such as Chidamber and Kemerer metrics [HM96], to support the identification of code components in need of refactoring.

Using of Code Analysis and NLP to Promote a Consistent Usage of Identifiers

Meaningless identifiers as well as inconsistent use of identifiers in the source code might hinder code readability and result in increased software maintenance efforts. Over the past years, effort has been devoted to promoting a consistent usage of identifiers across different parts of a system through approaches exploiting static code analysis and natural language processing (NLP). These techniques have been evaluated in small-scale studies, but it is unclear how they compare to each other and how they complement each other. Furthermore, a full-fledged larger empirical evaluation is still missing.

We aim at bridging this gap. We asked developers of five projects to assess the meaningfulness of the recommendations generated by three techniques, two already existing in the literature (one exploiting static analysis, one using NLP) and a novel one we propose. With a total of 922 rename refactorings evaluated, this is, to the best of our knowledge, the largest empirical study conducted to assess and compare rename refactoring tools promoting a consistent use of identifiers. Our study sheds light on the current state-of-the-art in rename refactoring recommenders, and indicates directions for future work.

This study is based on the following publication [LSM+17]:

Investigating the Use of Code Analysis and NLP to Promote a Consistent Usage of Identifiers

Bin Lin, Simone Scalabrino, Andrea Mocci, Rocco Oliveto, Gabriele Bavota, Michele Lanza. In *Proceedings of the 17th International Working Conference on Source Code Analysis and Manipulation (SCAM 2017) – Research Track*, pp. 81-90, 2017

C.1   Introduction

In programming languages, identifiers are used to name program entities; *e.g.,* in Java, identifiers include names of packages, classes, interfaces, methods, and variables. Identifiers account for ∼30% of the tokens and ∼70% of the characters in the source code [DP06]. Naming identifiers in a careful, meaningful, and consistent manner likely eases program comprehension and supports developers in building consistent and coherent conceptual models [DP06].

Instead, poorly chosen identifiers might create a mismatch between the developers' cognitive model and the intended meaning of the identifiers, thus ultimately increasing the risk of fault proneness. Indeed, several studies have shown that bugs are more likely to reside in code with low quality identifiers [BWYS09, AAT⁺12]. Arnaoudova *et al.* [AEO⁺10] also found that methods containing identifiers with higher physical and conceptual dispersion are more fault-prone. This suggests the important role played by a specific class of identifiers, *i.e.,* local variables and method parameters, in determining the quality of methods.

Naming conventions can help to improve the quality of identifiers. However, they are often too general, and cannot be automatically enforced to ensure consistent and meaningful identifiers. For example, the Java Language Specification[1] indicates rules for naming local variables and parameters: *e.g., "should be short, yet meaningful".* Clearly, these requirements do not guarantee consistent variable naming.

For example, developers might use "`localVar`" and "`varLocal`" in different code locations even if these two names are used in the same context and with the same meaning. Also, synonyms might be used to name the same objects, such as "`car`" and "`auto`". Finally, developers might not completely adhere to the rules defined in project-specific naming conventions.

Researchers have presented tools to support developers in the consistent use of identifiers. Thies and Roth [TR10] analyzed variable assignments to identify pairs of variables likely referring to the same object but named differently. Allamanis *et al.* [ABBS14] pioneered the use of NLP techniques to support identifiers renaming. Their NATURALIZE tool exploits a language model to infer from a code base the naming conventions and to spot *unnatural* identifiers (*i.e.,* unexpected identifiers), that should be renamed to promote consistency.

To obtain a reliable evaluation of approaches supporting automatic identifier renaming, the original authors of the source code should be involved in assessing the meaningfulness of the suggested refactorings. However, running such evaluations is expensive, thus refactoring techniques are often evaluated in "artificial scenarios" (*e.g.,* injecting a meaningless identifier in the code and check whether the tool is able to recommend a rename refactoring for it) and/or by relying on the manual evaluation of a limited number of recommended rename refactorings. For example, Thies and Roth [TR10] manually assessed the meaningfulness of 32 recommendations generated by their tool. Instead, Allamanis *et al.* [ABBS14] firstly analyzed 33 rename

---

[1]https://docs.oracle.com/javase/specs/jls/se7/html/jls-6.html

recommendations generated by NATURALIZE, and then opened pull requests in open source projects to evaluatethe meaningfulness of 18 renaming recommended by NATURALIZE (for a total of 51 data points).

We aim at assessing the meaningfulness of the rename refactorings recommended by state-of-the-art approaches on a larger scale (922 evaluations in total) and by only relying on developers having a first-hand experience on the object systems of our study. We evaluated two existing approaches, *i.e.,* the one by Thies and Roth [TR10] exploiting static code analysis, and the NATURALIZE tool [ABBS14] using NLP techniques to support identifier renaming. In addition, we propose a variation of NATURALIZE, named LExicAl Renaming (LEAR), exploiting a different concept of language model more focused on the lexical information present in the code. We conducted extensive empirical comparison of these three tools. Our results support the potential practical use of the identifier renaming approaches and indicates directions for improvement.

Structure of the Chapter

In Section C.2 we discuss the related work, while Section C.3 presents LEAR. In Section C.4 we report the evaluation study and the comparison with the baseline approach. Section C.5 discusses the threats to validity. Finally, Section C.6 outlines the conclusions.

C.2   Related Work

We discuss the literature related to the study of identifiers' quality and to techniques supporting the automatic identifier renaming. We describe in detail two of the techniques that are part of our empirical study, and in particular the approach by Thies and Roth [TR10] and the NATURALIZE tool by Allamanis *et al.* [ABBS14]. The third approach involved in our evaluation, named LEAR, is described in Section C.3.

Lawrie *et al.* [LMFB06] report the results of an experiment in which over 100 developers were asked to describe 12 different functions. The functions used three different types of identifiers, *i.e.,* single letters, abbreviations, and full words. The results showed that developers tend to comprehend identifiers composed of full words better than single letters/abbreviations. Lawrie *et al.* [LFB07b] also investigated the identifier quality based on almost 50 million lines of code, covering different programming languages. They found that modern software projects have better quality of identifier names than old projects.

Butler *et al.* [BWYS09] used eleven identifier naming guidelines for Java to evaluate the quality of identifiers. They found statistically significant associations between the identifier names violating at least one guideline and code quality issues reported by a static analysis tool. Based on this finding, Butler *et al.* [BWYS10] conclude that some of these naming guidelines can be used as a light-weight diagnostic to identify areas of potentially problematic code. Murphy-Hill *et al.* [MPB12] investigated the adoption of refactoring tools in the IDE, reporting that *rename refactoring* is among the most frequently performed operations.

Much effort has been devoted to improving the quality of identifier names, for example via identifier splitting [GPAG13, CMM12, EHPV09] and expansion [HFB+08, LB11]. However, these approaches cannot address the problem caused by non-adherence to naming conventions or by the inconsistent use of identifiers.

Reiss [Rei07] proposed a tool that learns code style from existing source code, such as identifier conventions and indentation, and applies it automatically on a new code artifact, thus making it consistent with the rest of the system. A similar tool is SmartFormatter [CGP07] that also learns the lexical form of terms used in identifiers.

Caprile and Tonella [CT00] proposed an approach to restructure identifiers with the goal of enhancing their meaningfulness. The approach builds a standard lexicon dictionary and a synonyms dictionary by analyzing a set of programs. Then, when analyzing a new program, the devised approach decomposes each identifier into the terms composing it and checks whether each term is "standard" according to the built dictionary. Non-standard terms are suggested to be replaced by their standard forms (*e.g.*, expand upd into update). While their approach was foundational for the field of identifier restructuring, we do not consider it in our empirical study since we focus on techniques aimed at promoting a consistent use of identifiers across a system. The approach by Caprile and Tonella [CT00] is focused on improving the meaningfulness of identifiers, without considering their consistent use.

Høst and Østvold [HØ09a] presented an approach to identify *naming bugs, i.e.,* a method name not representative of its implementation. The approach mines method naming rules from a corpus of Java applications, and suggests renamings for methods not following the learned rules. In our study we did not consider the approach by Høst and Østvold since we focus on techniques recommending identifier renames for methods' variables and parameters. Feldthaus and Møller [FM13] proposed a technique to support rename refactorings in JavaScript. When a developer decides to rename a variable v, a static analysis technique is applied to identify v's occurrences that need to be consistently renamed. The list of identified occurrences is provided to the developer for inspection. Jablonski and Hou [JH07] proposed Consistent ReNaming (CReN), a tool to track copy-and-paste clones and support identifier renaming in the IDE. A set of rules based on relationships between identifiers is used to infer developers' intentions (*e.g.*, two identifiers that are frequently renamed together). Also these two approaches have not been considered in our study since we focus on techniques suggesting renaming operations to promote a consistent use of identifiers.

C.2.1 Thies and Roth [TR10] - Static code analysis

Thies and Roth [TR10] present a tool to support identifier renaming based on information extracted via static code analysis. They exploit information of variable assignments to identify the inconsistent identifier use to name variables referring to the same object. The authors consider two types of assignments: 1) a variable is assigned to another variable (*e.g.*, paper = bestPaper); 2) a variable is assigned to a method invocation (*e.g.*, `paper = getBestPaper()`). For the latter, the assignment can be seen as the assignment to the returned variable. In our example, assume that the method `getBestPaper()` returns a variable named "`bestPaper`", the assignment is treated as `paper = bestPaper`. Once the information about variable assignments is extracted for all variables, an assignment graph is constructed where each node represents a variable and an edge connecting two variables represents an assignment. If an edge connects two nodes named with different identifiers but representing two variables of the same type, the tool generates a rename recommendation.

To evaluate their approach, Thies and Roth [TR10] applied their tool to four open source projects, and manually inspected renaming suggestions generated for variables with non-primitive types. As a result, 21 out of 32 suggestions appear to be beneficial. Among the 21 useful suggestions, 4 of them are related to synonyms and 17 to inaccurate choice of the identifiers.

In our study, we re-implemented the approach proposed by Thies and Roth since their tool is not publicly available and we refer to this approach as CA-RENAMING, to stress the fact that it only relies on static code analysis. We selected this approach because it is one of the very few existing approaches aiming to reduce the inconsistent use of identifiers, while most approaches focus on increasing the meaningfulness of identifiers without considering naming consistency.

C.2.2 Allamanis *et al.* [ABBS14] - NLP

Allamanis *et al.* [ABBS14] present a framework, named NATURALIZE, to recommend natural identifier names and formatting conventions by applying NLP to source code. One of the goals of NATURALIZE is to promote identifier consistency. NATURALIZE exploits a *n*-gram language model to estimate the probability that a specific identifier should be used in a given context to name a variable. Language models are widely employed in many domains such as speech recognition and code completion. The *n*-gram model is one of the most commonly used language models and it determines the probability of having a word w_i given the previous *n*-1 words. This probability is denoted by $p(w_i|w_{i-1}, w_{i-2}, \ldots, w_{i-n+1})$, where $w_{i-n+1}, \ldots, w_{i-1}, w_i$ are *n* continuous words. The probability that w_i follows $w_{i-n+1}, \ldots, w_{i-2},$ w_{i-1} is estimated by training the language model on a training set, composed of textual documents. When applying the language model to software-related tasks, like code completion, the training set is composed of code documents.

NATURALIZE follows a two-step approach to recommend a rename refactoring for a variable *v*:

1. **Generating candidate names.** NATURALIZE uses the abstract syntax tree (AST) of the program under analysis to find the set of locations, *L*, in which *v* appears. Then, it builds a snippet *S* representing the *context* in which *v* is used by taking the lowest common ancestor in AST of nodes in *L* [ABBS14]. *S* is then linearly scanned by using a moving window of length *n*, where *n* is the number of tokens. A token could be an identifier, a syntactic symbol of the programming

language, like ";", a reserved keyword of the language and so on. All n-grams containing v are extracted and the collection of these n-grams becomes the context set of v. If another variable v_i other than v occurs in at least one similar context (*i.e.,* in at least one similar n-gram), a new snippet S_i is created, *i.e.,* S with all v replaced by v_i, and it is added to the list of alternative candidates.

2. **Ranking candidates**. A score function leveraging a language model is defined to rank the candidates generated in the previous step. While any probability model can be used in the score function, the authors apply the n-gram language model we previously describe to assess the probability of a given candidate. In other words, given the context (*i.e.,* the set of n-grams) where an identifier v is used, the probability of renaming v into v_i is higher if v_i is used in the training set in which the language model has been built in a similar context.

To evaluate NATURALIZE, the authors assessed the meaningfulness of the refactorings recommended for 30 methods (for a total of 33 variable renamings). Half of the suggestions were identified as meaningful. Also, they submitted 18 patches to five GitHub projects, among which 14 were accepted.

The goal of NATURALIZE (*i.e.,* promoting consistency), its peculiarity of relying on NLP techniques, and its availability[2], made it an obvious choice for our study.

We started from the core idea behind NATURALIZE (*i.e.,* using a language model to promote a consistent identifier use) to define an alternative rename refactoring approach, named LEAR , that is presented in the next section and tries to overcome some limitations of the NATURALIZE approach. For example, NATURALIZE uses all textual tokens in the n-gram language model (including, *e.g.,* punctuation) to characterize the context in which an identifier is used; we believe that all the *syntactic sugar* in the programming language could mostly represent noise for the language model, thus reducing the quality of the rename recommendations. Also, NATURALIZE does not verify whether the recommended rename refactorings are valid or not (*e.g.,* it is not possible to rename an identifier id used in id_s in a method m, if id_s is already used in m to name any other variable/parameter. We present LEAR in the next section, by paying particular attention to stressing its main differences with respect to NATURALIZE.

C.3   LExicAl Renaming

Our LEAR recommends renaming operations related to (i) variables declared in methods and (ii) method parameters. The renaming of methods/classes as well as of instance/class variables is not currently supported, since, as it will be clearer later, LEAR works at method level. The support of other types of identifiers is part of our future work agenda. In the following we describe in detail the main steps of LEAR.

Identifying methods and extracting the vocabulary. LEAR parses the source code of the input system by relying on the SRCML infrastructure [CDM13]. The goal

---

[2]http://groups.inf.ed.ac.uk/naturalize/

of the parsing is to extract (i) the complete list of methods, and (ii) the identifiers' vocabulary, defined as the list of all the identifiers used to name parameters and variables (declared at both method and class level) in the whole project. From now on we refer to the identifiers' vocabulary simply as the *vocabulary*. Once the vocabulary and the list of methods have been extracted, the following steps are performed for each method m in the system. We use the method in Listing C.1 as a running example.

N-gram Extraction from m. We extract all textual tokens from the method m under analysis, by removing (i) comments and string literals, (ii) all non-textual content, *i.e.*, punctuation and (iii) non-interesting words, such as Java keywords and the name of method m itself. Basically, we only keep tokens referring to identifiers, excluding the name of m, and non-primitive types, which are Java keywords. This is one of the main differences with respect to NATURALIZE.

Indeed, while NATURALIZE uses all textual tokens in the n-gram language model (including, *e.g.*, Java keywords), we only focus on tokens containing *lexical* information. We expect sequences of only lexical tokens to better capture and characterize the context in which a given identifier is used.

Listing C.1. Example of method analyzed

```
public void printUser(int uid) {
    String q = "SELECT  WHERE user_id = " + uid;
    User user = runQuery(q);
    System.out.println(user);
}
```

The list of identifiers extracted from `printUser` includes: uid, String, q, uid, User, user, runQuery, q, System, out, println, user. Again, our conjecture is that such a list of tokens captures the *context*—referred to method `printUser`—where an identifier (*e.g.*, q) is used. After obtaining the identifier list, we extract n-grams from it such that the language model can use them to estimate the probability that a specific identifier should be used in a given context.

Lin *et al.* [LPM$^+$17] found that the n-gram language model achieves the best accuracy in supporting code completion tasks when setting $n = 3$. The same value was used in the original work by Hindle *et al.* [HBS$^+$12] proposing the usage of the language model for code completion. Therefore, we build 3-grams from the extracted list of tokens. In our running example, ten 3-grams will be extracted, including: ⟨uid, String, q⟩, ⟨String, q, uid⟩, ⟨q, uid, User⟩, ⟨uid, User, user⟩, etc.

Generating candidate rename refactoring. For each variable/parameter identifier in m (in the case of `printUser`: uid, q, and user), LEAR looks for its possible renaming by exploiting the *vocabulary* built in the first step. Given an identifier under analysis id, LEAR extracts from the *vocabulary* all the identifiers id_s which meet the following constraints:

- C_1: id_s is used to name a variable/parameter of the same type as the one referred by id. For example, if id is a parameter of type int, id_s must be used at least once as an int variable/parameter;

- C_2: id_s is not used in m to name any other variables/parameters. Indeed, in such a circumstance, it would not be possible to rename id in id_s in any case;

- C_3: id_s is not used to name any attribute of the class C_k implementing m nor in any class C_k extends, for the same reason explained in C_2.

The constraint checking not considered in NATURALIZE represents another difference between LEAR and NATURALIZE.

We refer to the list of valid identifiers fulfilling the above criteria as VI_{id}. Then, LEAR uses a customized version of the 3-gram language model to compute the probability that each identifier id_s in VI_{id} appears, instead of id, in all the 3-grams of m including id.

Let TP_{id} be the set of *3-gram patterns* containing at least once id, and $tp_{id \to id_s}$ be a 3-gram obtained from a pattern $tp_{id} \in TP_{id}$ where the variable id is replaced with a valid identifier $id_s \in VI_{id}$. We define the probability of a given substitution to a variable as:

$$P(tp_{id \to id_s}) = \frac{count(tp_{id \to id_s})}{\sum_{y \in VI_{id}} count(tp_{id \to y})} \tag{C.1}$$

When the pattern is in the form of $\langle id_1, id_2, id \rangle$, the probability of a substitution corresponds to the classic probability as computed by a 3-gram language model, that is:

$$P(\langle id_1, id_2, id \rangle_{id \to id_s}) = P(id_s | id_1, id_2) = \frac{count(\langle id_1, id_2, id_s \rangle)}{count(\langle id_1, id_2 \rangle)} \tag{C.2}$$

To better understand this core step of LEAR, let us discuss what happens in our running example when LEAR looks for possible renaming of the `uid` parameter identifier. The 3-grams of `printUser` containing uid are: $\langle$uid, String, q$\rangle$, $\langle$String, q, uid$\rangle$, $\langle$q, uid, User$\rangle$, and $\langle$uid, User, user$\rangle$.

Assume that the list of identifiers VI_{id} (*i.e.*, the list of valid alternative identifiers for uid) includes `userId` and `localCount`. LEAR uses the language model to compute the probability that `userId` occurs in each of the 3-grams of `printUser` containing uid. For example, the probability of observing `userId` in the 3-gram $\langle$q, uid, User$\rangle$ is:

$$p(q, userId, User) = \frac{count(q, userId, User)}{count(q, y, User)} \tag{C.3}$$

where $count(q, userId, User)$ is the number of occurrences of the 3-gram $\langle$q, userId, User$\rangle$ in the system, and $count(q, y, User)$ is the number of occurrences of the corresponding 3-gram, where y represents any possible identifier (including userId itself). Note that the *count* function only considers n-grams where id_s has the same type as id. Also, it does not take into account n-grams extracted from the method under analysis. This is done to avoid favoring the probability of the current identifier name used in the method under analysis as compared to the probability of other identifiers.

How the probability for a given identifier to appear in a n-gram is computed also differentiates LEAR from NATURALIZE. In the example reported above, NATURALIZE in fact computes the probability of observing User following $\langle$q, userId$\rangle$:

$$p(\text{User}|\text{q}, \text{userId}) = \frac{count(\text{q}, \text{userId}, \text{User})}{count(\text{q}, \text{userId})} \tag{C.4}$$

The two probabilities (*i.e.*, the one computed by LEAR and by NATURALIZE), while based on similar intuitions, could clearly differ. Our probability function is adapted from the standard language model (*i.e.*, the one used by NATURALIZE) in an attempt to better capture the context in which an identifier is used. This can be noticed in the way our denominator is defined: it keeps intact that identifiers' context in which we are considering injecting userId instead of uid.

The average probability across all these 3-grams is considered as the probability of id_s being used instead of id in m.

This process results in a ranked list of VI_{id} identifiers having on top the identifier with the highest average probability of appearing in all the 3-grams of m as a replacement (*i.e.*, rename) of id. We refer to this top-ranked identifier as T_{id}.

Finally, LEAR uses the same procedure to compute the average probability that the identifier id itself appears in the 3-grams where it currently is. If the T_{id} has the higher probability of appearing in the 3-grams is than id, a candidate rename refactoring has been found (*i.e.*, rename id in T_{id}). Otherwise, no rename refactoring is needed.

Assessing the confidence and the reliability of the candidate recommendations. LEAR uses two indicators acting as proxies for the *confidence* and the *reliability* of the recommended refactoring. Given a rename refactoring recommendation $id \rightarrow T_{id}$ in the method m, the confidence indicator is the average probability of T_{id} to occur instead of id in the 3-grams of m where id appears.

We refer to this indicator as C_p, and it is defined in the $[0, 1]$ interval. The higher C_p, the higher the confidence of the recommendation. We study how C_p influences the quality of the recommendations generated by LEAR in the following.

The "reliability" indicator, named C_c, is the number of distinct 3-grams used by the language model in the computation of C_p for a given recommendation $id \rightarrow T_{id}$ in the method m. Given $\langle id_1, id_2, id \rangle$ a 3-gram where id appears in m, we count the number of 3-grams in the system in the form $\langle id_1, id_2, x \rangle$, where x can be any possible identifier. This is done for all the 3-grams of m including id, and the sum of all computed values is represented by C_c. The conjecture is that the higher C_c, the higher is the reliability of the C_p computation. Indeed, the higher C_c, the higher the number of 3-grams from which the language model learned that T_{id} is a good substitution for id. C_c is unbounded on top. We study what is the minimum value of C_c allowing reliable recommendations in the following.

Note that while NATURALIZE does also provide a scoring function based on the probability derived by the n-gram language model to indicate the confidence of the recommendation (*i.e.*, the equivalent of our C_p indicator), it does not implement a "reliability" indicator corresponding to C_c.

Tuning of the C_c and C_p indicators. To assess the influence of the C_p (confidence) and C_c (reliability) indicators on the quality of the rename refactorings generated by LEAR, we conducted a study on one system, named SMOS. We asked one of the SMOS developers (having nowadays six years of industrial experience) to assess the meaningfulness of the LEAR recommendations. SMOS is a Java web application developed by a team of Master students, and composed by 121 classes for a total of ~23 thousand lines of code (KLOC). We used the SMOS system only for the tuning of the indicators C_p and C_c, i.e., to identify minimum values needed to receive meaningful recommendations for both of them. SMOS is not used in the actual evaluation of our approach, presented in Section C.4.

We ran LEAR on the whole system and asked the participant to analyze the 146 rename refactoring generated by LEAR and to answer, for each of them, the question *Would you apply the proposed refactoring?*, assigning a score on a three-point Likert scale: 1 (yes), 2 (maybe), and 3 (no). We clarified with the participant the meaning of the three possible answers:

1 (yes) must be interpreted as *"the recommended renaming is meaningful and should be applied"*, i.e., the recommended identifier name is better than the current one;

2 (maybe) must be interpreted as *"the recommended renaming is meaningful, but should not be applied"*, i.e., the recommended identifier is a valid alternative to the one currently used, but is not a better choice;

3 (no) must be interpreted as *"the recommended rename refactoring is not meaningful"*.

The participant answered *yes* to 18 (12%) of the recommended refactoring, *maybe* to 15, and *no* to 113. This negative trend is expected, considering the fact that we asked the participant to assess the quality of the recommended refactoring independently from the values of the C_p and the C_c indicators. That is, given the goal of this study, also recommendations having very low values for both indicators (e.g., $C_p = 0.1$ and $C_c = 1$) were inspected, despite we do not expect them to be meaningful. Table C.1 reports five representative examples of rename refactoring tagged with a *yes* by the developer.

Table C.1. Five rename refactoring tagged with a *yes*

Original name	Rename	C_p	C_c
mg	managerUser	1.00	146
e	invalidValueException	0.90	356
buf	searchBuffer	0.89	5
result	classroom	0.87	15
managercourseOfStudy	managerCourseOfStudy	0.67	12

By inspecting the assessment performed by the participant, the first thing we noticed is that recommendations having $C_c < 5$ (i.e., less than five distinct 3-grams have been used by the language model to learn the recommended rename refactoring) are generally unreliable, and should not be considered. Indeed, out of the 28 rename refactoring having $C_c < 5$, one (3%) was accepted (answer "yes") by the developer and three (10%) were classified as *maybe*, despite the fact that 22 of them had $C_p = 1.0$ (i.e., the highest possible confidence for the generated recommendation). Thus, when $C_c < 5$ even recommendations having a very high confidence are simply not reliable. When $C_c \geq 5$, we noticed that its influence on the quality of the recommended renames is limited, i.e., no other clear trend in the quality of the recommended refactoring can be observed for different values of C_c. Thus, we excluded the 28 refactoring recommendations having $C_c < 5$ and studied the role played by C_p in the remaining 118 recommendations (17 *yes*, 12 *maybe*, and 89 *no*).

Fig. C.1 reports the recall and precision levels of our approach when excluding the recommendations having $C_p < t$, with t varying between 1.0 and 0.1 at steps of 0.1. Note that in the computation of the recall and precision we considered the 29 recommendations accepted with a *yes* (17) or assessed as meaningful with a *maybe* (12) as correct (i.e., the *maybe* answers are equated to the *yes* answers, and considered correct). This choice was dictated by the fact that we see the meaningful recommendations tagged with *maybe* as valuable for the developer, since she can then decide whether the alternative identifier name provided by our approach is valid or not. For a given value of t, the recall is computed as the number of correct recommendations having $C_p \geq t$ divided by 29 (the number of correct recommendations). This is an "approximation" of the *real recall* since we do not know the actual number of correct renamings that are needed in SMOS. In other words, if a correct rename refactoring was not recommended by LEAR, it was not evaluated by the participant and thus is not considered in the computation of the recall.

The precision is computed as the number of correct recommendations having $C_p \geq t$ divided by the number of recommendations having $C_p \geq t$. For example, when considering recommendations having $C_p = 1.0$, we only have three recommended renames, two of which have been accepted by the developer. This results in a recall of 0.07 (2/29) and a precision of 0.67 (2/3)—see Fig. C.1.

Looking at Fig. C.1, we can see that both recall and precision increase moving from $C_p = 1.0$ to $C_p = 0.8$, reaching recall=0.42 (12/29) and precision=0.92 (12/13). This means that only one among the top-13 recommendations ranked by C_p has been considered as not meaningful by the developer. Moving toward lower values of C_p, the recall increases thanks to the additional recommendations considered, while the precision decreases, indicating that the quality of the generated recommendations tend to decrease with lower C_p values (i.e., there are higher chances of receiving a meaningless recommendation for low values of C_p). It is quite clear in Fig. C.1 that the likelihood of receiving good rename recommendations when $C_p < 0.5$ is very low.

Based on the results of the performed tuning, we modified our tool in order to generate refactoring recommendations only when $C_c \geq 5$ *and* $C_p \geq 0.5$. This parameter

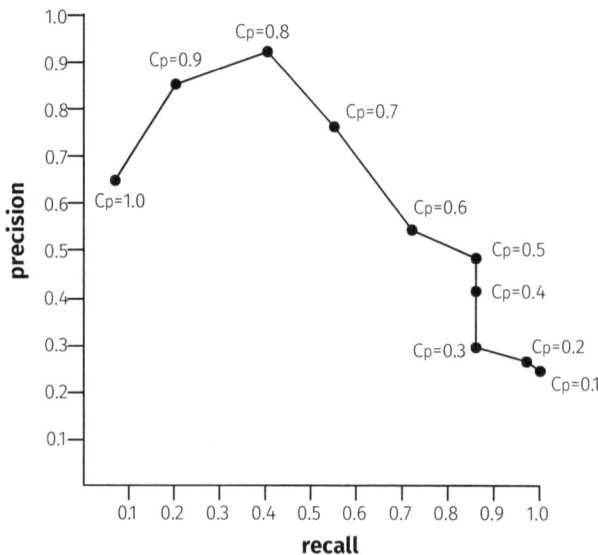

Figure C.1. Precision and recall of the LEAR recommendations when varying C_p

setting will be used for all the projects subject of our evaluation, *i.e.,* no project-specific tuning will be performed. In the evaluation reported in Section C.4 we will further study the meaningfulness of the generated recommendations of rename refactorings for different values of C_p in the significant range, *i.e.,* varying between 0.5 and 1.0.

C.4 Evaluation

This section presents the design and the results of the empirical study we carried out to compare the three previously introduced approaches for rename refactoring.

C.4.1 Study Design

The *goal* of the study is to assess the meaningfulness of the rename refactorings recommended by CA-RENAMING, NATURALIZE, and LEAR.

The *perspective* of the study is of researchers who want to investigate the applicability of approaches based on static code analysis (*i.e.,* CA-RENAMING) and on the *n*-gram language model (*i.e.,* NATURALIZE and LEAR) to recommend rename refactorings. The *context* is represented by *objects, i.e.,* five software projects on which we ran the three experimented tools to generate recommendations for rename refactorings, and *subjects, i.e.,* seven developers of the *objects* assessing the meaningfulness of the recommended rename refactorings.

To limit the number of refactoring recommendations to be evaluated by the developers, we applied the following "filtering policy" to the experimented techniques:

Table C.2. Context of the study (systems and participants)

(a) Context of the study – systems

System	Type	# of classes	LOCs	Developers
THERIO	Web App	79	13K	2
LIFEMIPP	Web App	72	7K	2
MYUNIMOLANDROID	Android App	96	27K	4
MYUNIMOLSERVICES	Web Services	100	8K	7
OCELOT	Desktop App	182	22K	2

(b) Context of the study – participants

System	Participants	Experience (mean)	Occupation
THERIO	1	7+ years	PhD Student
LIFEMIPP	2	7+ years	Professional; PhD Student
MYUNIMOLANDROID	1	5+ years	Professional
MYUNIMOLSERVICES	2	3+ years	Bachelor students
OCELOT	1	7+ years	PhD student

- LEAR: Given the results of the tuning of the C_p and the C_c indicators, we only consider the recommendations having $C_c \geq 5$ and $C_p \geq 0.50$.

- NATURALIZE: We used the original implementation made available by the authors with the recommended $n = 5$ in the n-gram language model. To limit the number of recommendations, and to apply a similar filter with respect to the one used in LEAR, we excluded all recommendations having a probability lower than 0.5. Moreover, since NATURALIZE is also able to recommend renamings for identifiers used for method names (as opposed to the other two competitive approaches), we removed these recommendations, in order to have a fair comparison.

- CA-RENAMING: No filtering of the recommendations was applied (*i.e.,* all of them were considered). This is due to the fact that, as it will be shown, CA-RENAMING generates a much lower number of recommendations as compared to the other two techniques.

Despite these filters, our study involves a total of 922 manual evaluations of recommendations for rename refactoring. Note also that no comparison will be performed in terms of running time (*i.e.,* the time needed by the techniques to generate the recommendations), since none of them requires more than a few minutes (<5) per system.

Research Questions and Context

Our study is steered by the following research question:

- **RQ$_1$** *Are the rename refactoring recommendations generated by approaches exploiting static analysis and NLP meaningful from a developer's point of view?*

The *object* systems taken into account are five Java systems developed and actively maintained at the University of Molise in the context of research projects or as part of its IT infrastructure. As *subjects*, we involved seven of the developers maintaining these systems. Table C.2 shows size attributes (number of classes and lines of code (LOC)) of the five systems, the number of developers actively working on them (column "Developers"), the number of developers we were able to involve in our study (column "Participants"), the average experience of the involved participants, and their occupation[3].

As it can be seen we involved a mix of professional developers and Computer Science students at different levels (Bachelor, Master, and PhD). All the participants have at least three years of experience in Java and they are directly involved in the development and maintenance of the object systems.

THERIO is a Web application developed and maintained by Master and PhD students. It is currently used for research purposes to collect data from researchers from all around the world. LIFEMIPP is a Web application developed and maintained by a professional developer and a PhD student. LIFEMIPP has been developed in the context of a European project and it is currently used by a wide user base. MYUNIMOLANDROID is an Android application developed and maintained by students and professional developers. It is available on the Google PlayStore, and has been downloaded over 1,000 times, and it is mostly used by students and faculties. MYUNIMOLSERVICES is an open-source software developed and maintained by students and professional developers. Such a system is the back-end of the MYUNIMOLANDROID app. Finally, OCELOT is a Java desktop application developed and maintained by PhD students. At the moment, it is used by researchers in an academic context.

Data Collection and Analysis

We run the three experimented approaches (*i.e.,* CA-RENAMING, NATURALIZE, and LEAR) on each of the five systems to recommend rename refactoring operations. Given R the set of refactoring recommended by a given technique on system P, we asked P's developers involved in our study to assess the meaningfulness of each of the recommended refactorings. We did not disclose which tool generated the recommendations to the developers. We adopted the same question/answers template previously presented for the tuning of the LEAR's C_c and C_p indicators. In particular, we asked the developers the question: *Would you apply the proposed refactoring?* with possible answers on a three-point Likert scale: 1 (yes), 2 (maybe), and 3 (no). Again, we clarified the meaning of these three possible answers.

---

[3]Here "Professional" indicates a developer working in industry.

Overall, participants assessed the meaningfulness of 725 rename refactorings, 66 recommended by CA-RENAMING, 357 by NATURALIZE, and 302 by LEAR across the five systems. Considering the number of participants involved (*e.g.,* two participants evaluated independently the recommendations generated for LIFEMIPP), this accounts for a total of 922 refactoring evaluations, making our study the largest empirical evaluation of rename refactoring tools performed with developers having first-hand experience on the object systems.

To answer our research question we report, for the three experimented techniques, the number of rename refactoring recommendations tagged with *yes*, *maybe* and *no*. We also report the precision of each technique computed in two different variants. In particular, given *R* the set of refactorings recommended by an experimented technique, we compute:

- $Prec_{yes}$, computed as the number of recommendations in *R* tagged with a *yes* divided by the total number of recommendations in *R*. This version of the precision considers as meaningful only the recommendations that the developers would actually implement.

- $Prec_{yes \cup maybe}$, computed as the number of recommendations in *R* tagged with a *yes* or with a *maybe* divided by the total number of recommendations in *R*. This version of the precision considers as meaningful also the recommendations indicated by the developers as a valid alternative to the original variable name but not calling for a refactoring operation.

Due to lack of space, we discuss the results aggregated by technique (*i.e.,* by looking at the overall performance across all systems and as assessed by all participants). The tools and raw data are available in our replication package [LSM⁺].

Finally, we analyze the complementarity of the three techniques by computing, for each pair of techniques (T_i, T_j), the following overlap metrics:

$$correct_{T_i \cap T_j} = \frac{|correct_{T_i} \cap correct_{T_j}|}{|correct_{T_i} \cup correct_{T_j}|} \tag{C.5}$$

$$correct_{T_i \setminus T_j} = \frac{|correct_{T_i} \setminus correct_{T_j}|}{|correct_{T_i} \cup correct_{T_j}|} \tag{C.6}$$

$$correct_{T_j \setminus T_i} = \frac{|correct_{T_j} \setminus correct_{T_i}|}{|correct_{T_i} \cup correct_{T_j}|} \tag{C.7}$$

The formulas above use the following metrics:

- $correct_{T_i}$ represents the set of meaningful refactoring operations recommended by technique T_i;

- $correct_{T_i \cap T_j}$ measures the overlap between the set of meaningful refactorings recommended by T_i and T_j;

- $correct_{T_i \setminus T_j}$ measures the meaningful refactoring operations recommended by T_i only and missed by T_j.

The latter metric provides an indication on how a rename refactoring tool contributes to enrich the set of meaningful refactorings identified by another tool. Such an analysis is particularly interesting for techniques relying on totally different strategies (*e.g.,* static code analysis *vs* NLP) to identify different rename refactoring opportunities. Due to space limitation, we only report the three overlap metrics when considering both the recommendations tagged with *yes* and *maybe* as correct. The overlap metrics obtained when only considering the "*yes* recommendations" as meaningful are available in [LSM+].

C.4.2   Results

Table C.3 reports the answers provided by the developers to the question "*Would you apply the proposed rename refactoring?*". Results are presented by approach, starting with the technique based on static code analysis (*i.e.,* CA-RENAMING [TR10]) followed by four different variations of NATURALIZE and of LEAR using different thresholds for the confidence of the generated recommendations. Table C.3 does also report the $Prec_{yes}$ and $Prec_{yes \cup maybe}$ computed as described in Section C.4.1.

General Trends. Before discussing in detail the performance of the experimented techniques, it is worthwhile to comment on some general trend reported in Table C.3. First of all, *the approaches based on NLP generate more recommendations than* CA-RENAMING. This holds as well when considering the highest confidence threshold we experimented with (*i.e.,* 0.8). Indeed, in this case LEAR generates a total of 130 rename refactorings (on average 18.57 per system) and NATURALIZE 88 (12.57 on average), as compared to the 80 recommended by CA-RENAMING (11.43 on average).

Another consideration is that LEAR *recommends a higher number of refactorings that are accepted by the developers with respect to* NATURALIZE *and to* CA-RENAMING. Overall, 111 rename refactorings recommended by LEAR have been fully accepted with a *yes*, as compared to the 76 by NATURALIZE and 21 by CA-RENAMING.

Also, the higher number of accepted refactorings does not result in a lower precision. Indeed, LEAR does also achieve a higher $Prec_{yes}$ with respect to CA-RENAMING (29.21% *vs* 26.25%) and to NATURALIZE (16.56%). The precision of NATURALIZE is negatively influenced by the extremely high number of recommendations it generates when considering all those having confidence ≥ 0.5 (*i.e.,* 459 recommendations). Finally, LEAR's *and* NATURALIZE's *precision is strongly influenced by the chosen confidence threshold*. The values on Table C.3 show an evident impact of the confidence threshold on $Prec_{yes}$ and $Prec_{yes \cup maybe}$ for both the approaches. Indeed, going to the least to the most conservative configuration for the confidence level, $Prec_{yes \cup maybe}$ increases by ~14% (from 66.05% to 80.77%) for LEAR and by ~38% for NATURALIZE (from 38.13% to 76.14%), while $Prec_{yes}$ increases by ~13% for LEAR (from 29.21% to 42.31%) and by ~6% for NATURALIZE (from 16.56% to 22.73%).

Table C.3. Participants' answers to the question *Would you apply the proposed rename refactoring?*

(a) Statistics of "yes", "maybe", "no" answers

Approach	Conf.	# yes		# maybe		# no	
		overall	mean	overall	mean	overall	mean
CA-RENAMING	N/A	21	3.00	30	4.29	29	4.14
NATURALIZE	>=0.5	76	10.86	99	14.14	284	40.57
NATURALIZE	>=0.6	59	8.43	67	9.57	193	27.57
NATURALIZE	>=0.7	35	5.00	43	6.14	107	15.29
NATURALIZE	>=0.8	20	2.86	21	3.00	47	6.71
LEAR	>=0.5	111	15.86	140	20.00	129	18.43
LEAR	>=0.6	99	14.14	112	16.00	85	12.14
LEAR	>=0.7	67	9.57	69	9.86	50	7.14
LEAR	>=0.8	55	7.86	50	7.14	25	3.57

(b) Precision of the compared techniques

Approach	Conf.	# recomm.		$Prec_{yes \cup maybe}$	$Prec_{yes}$
		overall	mean		
CA-RENAMING	N/A	80	11.43	63.75%	26.25%
NATURALIZE	>=0.5	459	65.57	38.13%	16.56%
NATURALIZE	>=0.6	319	45.57	39.50%	18.50%
NATURALIZE	>=0.7	185	26.43	42.16%	18.92%
NATURALIZE	>=0.8	88	12.57	46.59%	22.73%
LEAR	>=0.5	380	54.29	66.05%	29.21%
LEAR	>=0.6	296	42.29	71.28%	33.45%
LEAR	>=0.7	186	26.57	73.12%	36.02%
LEAR	>=0.8	130	18.57	80.77%	42.31%

These results indicate one possibility offered by these two approaches based on a similar underlying model: Depending on the time budget developers have, they can decide whether to have a higher or a lower number of recommendations, being informed of the fact that the most restrictive threshold is likely to generate very few false positives, but also to potentially miss some good suggestions.

Per-project analysis. Table C.4 reports examples of recommendations generated by the three approaches and tagged with *yes*, *maybe*, and *no*. Moving to the assessment performed by participants on each project (data available in our replication package [LSM+]), we found that the accuracy of the recommendations generated by the three tools substantially varies across the subject systems. For example, on the

Table C.4. Refactorings tagged with *yes*, *maybe*, and *no*

	System	Original name	Rename	*Conf.*	Tag
CA-RENAMING	LIFEMIPP	i	insect	N/A	*yes*
	THERIO	pk	idCollection	N/A	*yes*
	MYUNIMOLANDROID	data	result	N/A	*maybe*
	OCELOT	hash	md5final	N/A	*maybe*
	OCELOT	navigator	this	N/A	*no*
	MYUNIMOLANDROID	fullname	fullnameOk	N/A	*no*
NATURALIZE	OCELOT	callString	macro	0.92	*yes*
	MYUNIMOLANDROID	factory	inflater	0.75	*yes*
	OCELOT	declaration	currentDeclaration	0.79	*maybe*
	MYUNIMOLSERVICES	moduleName	name	0.69	*maybe*
	LIFEMIPP	species	t	0.64	*no*
	MYUNIMOLSERVICES	username	token	0.91	*no*
LEAR	LIFEMIPP	image	photo	1.00	*yes*
	MYUNIMOLSERVICES	careerId	pCareerId	0.63	*yes*
	OCELOT	type	realType	0.91	*maybe*
	LIFEMIPP	file	fileFullName	0.67	*maybe*
	THERIO	pUsername	pName	0.59	*no*
	MYUNIMOLANDROID	info	o	1.00	*no*

LIFEMIPP project, CA-RENAMING is able to achieve very high values of precision, substantially better than the ones achieved by the approaches based on NLP. The refactoring recommendations for the LIFEMIPP project have been independently evaluated by two developers. Both of them agreed on the meaningfulness of all eight recommendations generated by CA-RENAMING. Indeed, the first developer would accept all of them, while the second tagged five recommendations with *yes* and three with *maybe*. NATURALIZE and LEAR, instead, while able to recommend a higher number of *yes* and *maybe* recommendations as opposed to CA-RENAMING (on average 19 for NATURALIZE and 22 for LEAR *vs* the 8 for CA-RENAMING), present a high price to pay in terms of false positives to discard (0 false positives for CA-RENAMING as compared to 49 for NATURALIZE and 19 for LEAR). Such a cost is strongly mitigated when increasing the confidence threshold. Indeed, when only considering recommendations having confidence ≥ 0.8, the number of false positives drops to 1 (first developer) or 0 (second developer) for LEAR and to 8 or 6 for NATURALIZE. However, LEAR and NATURALIZE still keep an advantage in terms of number of *yes* and *maybe* generated recommendations (13 and 14—depending on the developer—for LEAR, and 12, for both developers, for NATURALIZE). A similar trend has also been observed for MYUNIMOLSERVICES.

When run on MYUNIMOLANDROID, CA-RENAMING only recommends three rename refactorings, two tagged with a *maybe* and one discarded (*no*). NATURALIZE generates 65 recommendations, with nine *yes*, 14 *maybe*, and 42 *no*. Finally, LEAR generates 35 suggestions, with six *yes*, 12 *maybe*, and 17 *no*.

This is the only system in which we did not observe a clear trend between the quality of the refactoring recommended by LEAR and the value used for the C_p threshold. Indeed, the precision of our approach is not increasing with the increase of the C_p value. This is due to the fact that the developer involved in the evaluation of the refactoring for the MYUNIMOLANDROID rejected with a *no* seven recommendations having $C_p \geq 0.8$.

We asked the developer for further comments to check what went "wrong" for this specific system, and in particular we asked to comment on each of these seven cases. Some of the explanations seemed to indicate more a *maybe* recommendation rather than the assigned *no*. For example, our approach recommended with $C_p = 0.9$ and $C_c = 54$ the renaming *activity* → *navigationDrawer*. The developer explained that the *activity* identifier refers to an object of `FragmentActivity` that is casted as a `NavigationDrawer` and, for this reason, he prefers to keep the *activity* name rather than the recommended one. Another false positive indicated by the developer was renaming *info* → *o*, where *info* is a method parameter of type `Object`. LEAR learned from the MYUNIMOLANDROID's trigrams that the developers tend to name a parameter of type `Object` with *o*. This is especially true in the implementation of `equals` methods. Thus, while the renaming would have been consistent with what is present in the system, the developer preferred to keep the original name as being "*more descriptive*", rejecting the recommendation. MYUNIMOLANDROID is also the only system in which NATURALIZE achieves a higher precision than LEAR when considering the most restrictive confidence (*i.e.,* ≥ 0.8).

Finally, on the THERIO and on the OCELOT projects, LEAR substantially outperforms the two competitive approaches. On THERIO, The CA-RENAMING approach achieves $Prec_{yes} = 0.33$ and $Prec_{yes \cup maybe} = 0.47$, as compared to the $Prec_{yes} = 0.37$ and $Prec_{yes \cup maybe} = 0.74$ achieved by LEAR when considering only recommendations having $C_p \geq 0.6$. LEAR also generates a much higher number of *yes* (35 *vs* 5) and *maybe* (13 *vs* 2) recommendations. Examples of recommendations generated by LEAR and accepted by the developers include *pk* → *idTaxon* and *o* → *occurrences*, while an example of rejected recommendation is *pUsername* → *pName*. NATURALIZE also achieves its best performance on THERIO when considering all the recommendations having confidence ≥ 0.6 ($Prec_{yes} = 0.35$ and $Prec_{yes \cup maybe} = 0.74$), but with a lower number of *yes* (23) and *maybe* (8) recommendations with respect to LEAR. A similar trend can also be observed on OCELOT, where LEAR is able to recommend 89 renamings with a $Prec_{yes \cup maybe} = 0.93$.

Table C.5. Overlap metrics

T_i	T_j	$correct_{T_i \cap T_j}$	$correct_{T_i \setminus T_j}$	$correct_{T_j \setminus T_i}$
CA-RENAMING	LEAR	1.00%	16.05%	82.94%
CA-RENAMING	NATURALIZE	0.00%	22.57%	77.43%
LEAR	NATURALIZE	4.16%	57.21%	38.63%

Overlap Metrics Analysis. Table C.5 reports the three overlap metrics between the experimented techniques.

The overlap in terms of meaningful recommendations provided by the different tools is extremely low; 1% between CA-RENAMING and LEAR, 0% between CA-RENAMING and NATURALIZE, and 4% between LEAR and NATURALIZE. While the low overlap between the techniques using static code analysis and NLP is somehow expected, the 4% overlap observed between LEAR and NATURALIZE is surprising considering the fact that LEAR is inspired by the core idea behind NATURALIZE. This means that the differences between the two techniques described in Section C.3 (*e.g.,* only considering the lexical tokens in the language model as opposed to using all tokens) have a strong impact on the generated recommendations. While this was already clear by the different performance provided by the two approaches (see Table C.3), it is even more evident from Table C.5.

LEAR is able to recommend 82.94% of meaningful renamings that are not identified by CA-RENAMING, and 57.21% that are not recommended by NATURALIZE. However, there is also a high percentage of meaningful rename refactorings recommended by CA-RENAMING (16.05%) and NATURALIZE (38.63%) but not identified by LEAR. This confirms the very high complementarity of the different techniques, paving the way to novel rename refactoring approaches based on their combination, which will be investigated in our future work.

C.5   Threats to Validity

Threats to *construct validity* are mainly related to how we assessed the developers' perception of the refactoring meaningfulness. We asked developers to express on a three-point Likert scale the meaningfulness of each recommended refactoring making sure to carefully explain the meaning of each possible answer from a practical point of view.

Threats to *internal validity* are represented, first of all, by the calibration of the LEAR confidence C_p and C_c indicators. We performed the calibration of these indicators on one project (SMOS) not used in the LEAR's evaluation, by computing the recall *vs* precision curve for different possible values of the C_p indicator. This was not really needed for the C_c indicator, for which we just observed the unreliability of the recommendations having $C_c < 5$. Concerning the other approaches, for the NATURALIZE's n-gram model parameter we adopted the one used by its authors (*i.e.,* $n = 5$) and we relied on their implementation of the approach. To limit the number of refactoring recommendations, we excluded the ones having a probability lower than 0.5. This choice certainly does not penalize NATURALIZE, since we are only considering the best recommendations it generates. As for CA-RENAMING, we used our own implementation (available in [LSM$^+$]).

Threats to *external validity* are related to the set of chosen objects and to the pool of participants. Concerning the objects, we are aware that our study is based on refactorings recommended on five Java systems only and that the considered systems, while not trivial, are generally of small-medium size (between 7 and 27 KLOC). Also, we were only able to involve in our study seven developers. Still, as previously said, (i) we preferred to limit our study to developers having a first-hand experience with the object systems, rather than inviting also external developers to take part in our study, and (ii) despite the limited number of systems and developers, our results are still based on a total of 922 manual inspections performed to assess the quality of the refactorings.

C.6 Conclusion

We assessed the meaningfulness of recommendations generated by three approaches—two existing in the literature (*i.e.,* CA-RENAMING [TR10] and NATURALIZE [ABBS14]) and one presented in this chapter (*i.e.,* LEAR)—promoting a consistent use of identifiers in code. The results of our study highlight that:

1. Overall, LEAR achieves a higher precision, and it is able to recommend a higher number of meaningful refactoring operations with respect to the competitive techniques.

2. While being the best performing approach, LEAR still generates a high number of false positives, especially when just considering as meaningful the recommendations tagged with a *yes* by the developers (*i.e.,* the ones they would actually implement). This means that there is large room for improvement in state-of-the-art tools for rename refactoring.

3. The experimented approaches have unstable performance across the different systems. Indeed, even if LEAR is, overall, the approach providing the most accurate recommendations, it is not the clear winner on all the object systems. This indicates that there are peculiarities of the software systems that can influence the performance of the three techniques.

The above observations will drive our research agenda, including: (i) revising our approach to exploit more information (*e.g.,* data flow graph) to increase its performance, and (ii) studying the characteristics of the software systems that influence the accuracy of the rename refactoring tools.

On The Quality of Identifiers in Test Code

Meaningful, expressive identifiers in source code can enhance the readability and reduce comprehension efforts. Over the past years, researchers have devoted considerable effort to understanding and improving the naming quality of identifiers in source code. However, little attention has been given to test code, an important resource during program comprehension activities.

To better grasp identifier quality in test code, we conducted a survey involving manually written and automatically generated test cases from ten open source software projects. The survey results indicate that test cases contain low quality identifiers, including the manually written ones, and that the quality of identifiers is lower in test code than in production code. We also investigated the use of three state-of-the-art rename refactoring recommenders for improving test code identifiers. The analysis highlights their limitations when applied to test code and supports mapping out a research agenda for future work in the area.

This study is based on the following publication [LNB$^+$19]:

On The Quality of Identifiers in Test Code

Bin Lin, Csaba Nagy, Gabriele Bavota, Andrian Marcus, Michele Lanza. In *Proceedings of the 19th International Working Conference on Source Code Analysis and Manipulation (SCAM 2019) – Research Track*, pp. 204–215, 2019

D.1   Introduction

Identifiers represent a major part of the source code [DP06] and program comprehension becomes significantly harder when they are not meaningful [LMFB06, LFB07b]. Indeed, while comprehending code, programmers rely on the meaning encoded in names [HØ09b], since those are supposed to record knowledge and communicate key concepts in the source code [DP06, But09]. Poor identifier names can hinder code comprehension and negatively affect code quality [BWYS09]. Moreover, studies have found that the low quality of identifiers may also threaten the performance of identifier based SE tools [PVH+11, GMPV13].

Consequently, many naming conventions, guidelines, and best practices have been distilled to help developers to choose appropriate names for their identifiers. For example, the Java Language Specification[1] indicates rules for naming local variables and parameters: *e.g., "should be short, yet meaningful"; "one-character identifiers should be avoided, except for temporary and looping variables, or where a variable holds an undistinguished value of a type"*. Researchers have also extensively studied what makes an identifier good or bad [LMFB06, LFB07b, HØ09a, HØ09b, BDL+13], and how it is possible to automatically improve existing ones using natural language processing (NLP) [BHL11], thesauruses [CT00], or statistical language models [ABBS15, LSM+17].

Existing empirical studies and rename refactoring techniques target the source code as a whole when studying/improving identifier names, often ignoring the test code, despite its important peculiarities. For instance, many studies found that developers take less care of the quality of test code as compared to production code, thus leading to possible quality issues in the tests [BGP+19, BGPZ15, ZRvDD11, ANVZ14, CDL+16, SPZ+18], including specific types of smells [DMBK01, BQO+15, TPB+16] accompanied by refactorings aimed at removing them [DMBK01].

The quality problem of test code is further exacerbated when using automated test suite generators [PPZ+16, GSGO18]. These tools [FA11] represent a useful aid to identify defects through a systematic, automatic approach and to improve the coverage of a test bed. Another possible use case is to generate an initial test suite and then manually improve/evolve it. In any case, the generated code, and especially the assertions of tests, need to be manually validated. Hence, the quality of the generated code matters, including the meaningfulness of the used identifiers.

We first present an empirical investigation of the quality of identifiers in test code and compare it to the quality of production code. Given the result that the quality of identifiers is often unsatisfactory, especially for the test code, we investigate whether the identifier quality can be improved by three state-of-the-art renaming recommenders: CA-RENAMING [TR10], NATURALIZE [ABBS14], and LEAR [LSM+17]. More specifically, in this chapter we address the following research questions:

RQ$_1$: What is the quality of identifiers in the test code of open source projects? We conducted a survey asking 19 participants to inspect the quality of identifiers in both, human-written manually and automatically generated, test code. As target

---

[1]https://docs.oracle.com/javase/specs/jls/se7/html/jls-6.html

systems, we select ten open source Java projects maintained by companies/organizations or by small teams of developers, ensuring high popularity and diversity of the target projects. The participants were asked to judge the identifiers and to list for the characteristics of high- and low-quality identifiers. To ease the interpretation of the achieved results and to have a baseline for comparison, we also asked four of the 19 participants to evaluate the quality of identifiers in the production code of two of the subject systems.

RQ_2: *What is the accuracy of rename refactoring approaches when applied on test code identifiers?* We evaluate three state-of-the-art rename refactoring approaches, namely CA-RENAMING, NATURALIZE, and LEAR. We use the same ten projects used to answer RQ_1 and 429 additional projects from GitHub. We assess the rename refactorings with two different datasets as oracle: 1) the high-quality identifiers obtained as an output of RQ_1, 2) identifiers from the test code of open source projects that underwent code reviews. We also used the two systems for which we collected evaluations related to the quality of identifiers in production code to compare the performance of the renaming tools on the test and on the production code.

Our results show that low-quality identifiers are spread both in manually written and in automatically generated tests, and this problem is more relevant in test than in production code (RQ_1). State-of-the-art rename refactoring tools are of little help in improving the identifier quality of test code while their performance is more promising for production code (RQ_2). Major advances are needed in this field. Given our findings, we outline a research agenda for future work in the area.

Structure of the Chapter

Section D.2 provides an overview of the related literature. Section D.3 presents the design and results of our survey investigating the quality of identifiers in test code, while Section D.4 examines whether state-of-the-art rename refactoring techniques can improve the identifier quality in test code. In Section D.5 we discuss the threats that could affect the validity of our studies. Finally, Section D.6 concludes the chapter.

D.2   Related Work

D.2.1   Quality of Identifiers

Strong connections have been discovered between bad identifier names and code quality issues [BWYS09]. Researchers have put a considerable amount of effort into investigating which characteristics of identifier names can influence program comprehension, positively or negatively.

Deissenboeck and Pizka [DP06] introduced two important concepts for good identifier naming: consistency and conciseness. They also proposed a model based on bijective mappings between concepts and names. The model requires that each concept should have a unique name and this name should represent the concept correctly.

Lawrie *et al.* [LMFB06, LFB07b] studied the impact of identifier length on program comprehension and found out that developers can easily comprehend source code with full word identifiers or well-formed abbreviations. However, excessively long identifiers might hinder program comprehension as they overload short-term memory. A recent study with 72 professional C# developers conducted by Hofmeister *et al.* [HSH17] provides evidence that using full words in identifiers helps developers in code comprehension, compared to letters and abbreviations.

Lawrie *et al.* [LFB07b, LFB07a] also analyzed identifier usage in 186 programs written in four different programming languages. Their findings disclose that better programming practices are producing higher quality identifiers.

Binkley *et al.* [BDL+13] conducted an experiment with 150 participants to understand the impact of identifier styles on program comprehension. As a result, they discovered that camel casing can help novices detect identifiers more accurately, at a cost of more time needed.

Researchers have also investigated practical issues (*e.g.,* bad smells, inconsistencies) originating from identifier naming. Kim *et al.* [KK16] performed interviews with developers, finding that developers often deal with inconsistent identifiers and the inconsistency is more common in larger projects. Butler *et al.* [BWY15] analyzed 3.5 million Java reference name declarations in 60 well-known Java projects, and manually tagged around 46,000 names. Their study shows that the use of unknown abbreviations and words is not rare in the source code and might potentially hinder program comprehension.

Abebe *et al.* [AHTM09] introduced the notion of "lexicon bad smell" to indicate potential problems in identifier names. With the tool they built, they were able to identify 15,633 bad smells in *Alice*, an open-source software system containing around 1.5 million lines of code, demonstrating the wide spread of imperfect identifiers.

Arnaoudova *et al.* [APA16] presented a catalogue of 17 linguistic antipatterns (LAs) capturing inconsistencies among the naming, documentation, and implementation of attributes and methods, showing that LAs are negatively perceived by developers who highlighted their negative impact on code comprehension.

Fakhoury *et al.* investigated how poor lexica of source code negatively affects the readability of source code, thus hindering comprehension processes [FMAA18].

To the best of our knowledge, our study is the first focusing on the quality of identifiers used in **test code**.

D.2.2 Rename Refactoring

Identifiers are often composed of abbreviations, and researchers have proposed techniques like identifier splitting [HBL+14, GPAG13, CMM12, EHPV09] and expansion [HFB+08, LB11] to ease their comprehension. However, in practice, lots of identifiers do not follow naming conventions and can be composed of meaningless tokens. Researchers have also investigated rename refactoring approaches, which rename the identifier with a more meaningful and/or consistent name.

Corbo *et al.* [CGP07] and Reiss [Rei07] proposed renaming approaches able to learn code identifier conventions from existing code. The rename refactoring approaches proposed by Feldthaus and Møller [FM13] and by Jablonski and Hou [JH07], instead, focus on the relations between variables, inferring whether one variable should be changed together with others.

Caprile and Tonella [CT00] proposed an approach to enhance the meaningfulness of identifiers with a standard lexicon dictionary and a thesaurus collected by analyzing a set of programs, replacing non-standard terms used in identifiers with a standard one from the dictionaries.

Thies and Roth [TR10] proposed a static analysis based approach to support identifier renaming: if a variable v_1 is assigned to an invocation of method m (*e.g.*, name = getFullName), and the type of v_1 is identical to the type of the variable v_2 returned by m, then rename v_1 to v_2. This was effective when experimented on open source projects.

Allamanis *et al.* [ABBS14] proposed NATURALIZE, a n-gram language model based approach which suggests new names to identifiers. The n-gram model predicts the probability of the next token given the previous n-1 tokens. NATURALIZE learns coding conventions from the codebase, promoting the consistent use of identifiers. The approach trains a language model on the rest of the project code, and then predicts the identifier names for the target files. Building on top of NATURALIZE, Lin *et al.* [LSM+17] proposed LEAR, combining code analysis and n-gram language models. The differences between LEAR and NATURALIZE are 1) while NATURALIZE considers all the tokens in the source code, LEAR only focuses on tokens containing lexical information; 2) LEAR also considers the type information of variables.

The approach proposed by Daka *et al.* [DRF17] is explicitly designed to rename identifier in test code and, in particular, in automatically generated unit tests. It generates descriptive method names for automatically generated unit tests by summarizing API-level coverage goals. A relevant work by Høst and Østvold [HØ09a] identifies the "bugs" in method names, meaning names that do not reflect the responsibilities implemented in the method. This approach recommends new method names by learning naming rules from a corpus of Java applications. Since these tools [HØ09a, DRF17] only recommend method names, they cannot be used in our study to suggest names for variables.

We assess the accuracy of three identifier renaming techniques [TR10, ABBS14, LSM+17] when applied on test code, including a comparison of their performance on production code.

D.3   Study I: Quality of Identifiers in Test Code

Our *goal* is to better understand the characteristics of good/bad identifiers used by local variables in test methods.

D.3.1   Research Question

Studies [LMFB06, HØ09a, HØ09b] have investigated the quality of identifiers in production code, yet little attention has been given to test code. We aims to answer the
Research Question (RQ):

RQ$_1$: *What is the quality of identifiers in the test code of open source projects?*

The quality of the identifiers was judged by 19 participants, who were also required to justify their quality assessment by explicitly reporting what makes an identifier good or bad. Given the advances in automatic test case generation [FA11], we
also asked participants to judge the quality of identifiers in automatically generated
test cases for the same set of projects. Instructions were distributed to participants,
stressing that high-quality identifiers make the code easier to read and understand.

The set of identifiers deemed as "good" in this study will be used as a ground truth
in our second study (Section D.4).This allows to have a manually validated ground
truth, overcoming one of the limitations of experimentations performed to evaluate
the performance of naming approaches, in which researchers often use the identifiers
defined by developers in open source projects as oracle [ABBS15].

D.3.2   Study Context and Data Collection

Table D.1. Subject projects for Study I: Identifier quality.

Project	Repository	# Java files	ELOC
Community projects			
COMMONS LANG	https://goo.gl/wdZMf9	323	75,958
GSON	https://goo.gl/JkG9CV	176	22,272
JACKSON CORE	https://goo.gl/WTeh3N	238	42,150
PLEXUS-UTILS	https://goo.gl/j3ckGk	128	24,710
REST ASSURED	https://goo.gl/ivx7jK	171	9,175
Team projects			
JESQUE	https://goo.gl/GJxAuv	121	10,339
JONGO	https://goo.gl/M2nDdK	155	8,190
LA4J	https://goo.gl/fPKYDX	117	13,480
NATTY	https://goo.gl/RBznPG	27	3,854
ORMLITE CORE	https://goo.gl/TXaRiR	280	34,970

The *study context* consists of the 10 open source Java projects from GitHub (Table D.1). We selected well-known projects maintained by companies/organizations
(from now on *community projects*), as well as projects maintained by small teams
(from now on *team projects*). We selected five projects for each of these two categories, by adopting the following selection criteria:

- **Popularity.** For *community projects*, we selected popular libraries hosted on Maven (`https://mvnrepository.com/`) and used by at least 500 client projects. For the *team projects*, we select projects having more than 300 stars on GitHub, to filter out "toy projects".

- **Diversity.** The projects are of different size and type and run by different entities, preventing the bias of internal coding conventions and programming practices.

To answer RQ_1, we conducted a survey asking 19 participants to manually inspect the quality of identifiers in both, human-written and automatically generated, test code.

Manually written test code. For each of the 10 projects, we randomly selected eight test methods from different classes to guarantee the generalizability and parsed them with JavaParser (`https://javaparser.org/`). In total, we extracted 237 manually written identifiers from these 80 test methods.

Automatically generated test code. We used EvoSuite [FA11] to generate test code for the selected projects, randomly selecting two test methods from each project. We collected 46 automatically generated identifiers.

Summarizing, we extracted 283 identifiers, 237 manually written and 46 automatically generated. We preferred to have more manually written than automatically generated identifiers since we expect automatically generated identifiers to follow a limited number of naming patterns and, thus, a smaller number of instances is necessary to observe a trend in the data.

We also asked four participants to judge the quality of identifiers in the production code of JACKSON CORE and ORMLITE CORE (*i.e.*, one community and one team project). This was done to (i) have a term of comparison when discussing the results achieved in terms of quality of the identifiers in test code, and (ii) verify whether there is a difference in the quality of identifiers used in test and production code. In this case, we extracted 47 identifiers from 20 methods (10 per system) contained in 20 different classes of the two systems. Note that the study on the production code identifiers was only conducted on two systems since we preferred to polarize the participants' effort toward the evaluation of test identifiers, being this the main goal of our study. Table D.2 summarizes the identifiers judged for each project.

Judgment of identifiers quality

Through convenience sampling, we invited 19 participants, including 4 professional developers, 11 computer science students (BSc, MSc, PhD), 2 academic staff to evaluate the quality of the identifiers collected, based on how well the identifiers support code comprehension. Participants had an average of 6.6 years experience of Java development (median=7.0, min=1, max=15), 1.5 years industrial experience (median=1, min=0, max=5), and 2.8 years experience of software testing (median=1, min=0, max=12). None of the participants was involved in the development of the subject projects.

Table D.2. Number of identifiers inspected for each project

Project	# human written test identifiers	# auto. gener. test identifiers	# human written prod. identifiers	Total
COMMONS LANG	17	7	-	24
GSON	20	4	-	24
JACKSON CORE	38	8	26	46
PLEXUS-UTILS	16	2	-	18
REST ASSURED	12	3	-	15
JESQUE	25	7	-	32
JONGO	15	3	-	18
LA4J	26	6	-	32
NATTY	28	3	-	31
ORMLITE CORE	40	3	21	43
Sum	237	46	47	330

Participants judged the identifiers from one test (or production) method at a time using a Web app we developed[2]. The app showed one test case/method at a time together with links to the methods in the production code that it tests. Participants are not explicitly informed whether the displayed method is manually written or automatically generated. The quality of an identifier was judged on a 3-point scale: "*good*", "*acceptable*", "*poor*". Participants could also select a "*not sure*" option.

Participants were asked to motivate their judgment by explaining the positive and negative characteristics of identifiers. An identifier judged as having a good (poor) quality could have both positive and negative characteristics. We provided two lists of predefined categories based on a literature review we performed (one for positive and one for negative characteristics, the detailed lists can be found in Section D.3.4), and participants could also add their own quality attributes. Moreover, they had the option to suggest a new name for the identifiers.

On average, each participant assessed the quality of 33.3 identifiers (median=23, min=16, max=118). Each identifier was evaluated by two participants, totaling 566 manual evaluations for test code and 94 for production code identifiers.

D.3.3 Data Analysis

To answer RQ_1, we plot the distribution of quality scores for the identifiers used in the subject test code. We discuss the characteristics of good and poor identifiers as reported by participants and compare the assessments provided for community projects and team projects, and the differences between human written and automatically generated identifiers. We also compare the quality of manually written identifiers in test and production code for JACKSON CORE and ORMLITE CORE.

---

[2]The screenshots can be found at `https://identifierquality.bitbucket.io/webapp/`

D.3.4   Results

Table D.3 reports the evaluations given by the participants to the quality of the identifiers subject of our study. Since each identifier has been judged by two evaluators, we
report the frequency of each possible pair of evaluations and their ratio to the total
number of evaluation pairs.

Table D.3. Evaluation of identifier quality given by evaluators

Evaluation of identifiers	Manually written		Automatically generated	
both good	59	(24.9%)	0	(0.0%)
both acceptable	13	(5.5%)	4	(8.7%)
both poor	36	(15.2%)	9	(19.6%)
both unsure	0	(0.0%)	0	(0.0%)
good & acceptable	43	(18.1%)	8	(17.4%)
good & poor	36	(15.2%)	6	(13.0%)
good & unsure	2	(0.8%)	0	(0.0%)
acceptable & poor	46	(19.4%)	19	(41.3%)
acceptable & unsure	1	(0.4%)	0	(0.0%)
poor & unsure	1	(0.4%)	0	(0.0%)
Sum	237	(100.0%)	46	(100.0%)

Agreement Analysis

Assessing the quality of an identifier is subjective and depends on the experience and
coding habits of developers. We first look at the level of agreement reached by the
study participants. For manually written variables, 45.6% of evaluations for the same
identifier reached an agreement: both evaluators rate the same identifier as "*good*"
(24.9%), "*acceptable*" (5.5%) or "*poor*" (15.2%). Since each identifier was judged on
a 3-point scale, we also computed the cases of "weak agreement", meaning a 1-point
difference on the quality assessment scale (*i.e.,* "*good vs acceptable*" and "*acceptable
vs poor*"). In this case, the ratio of agreement reaches 83.1%. 15.2% quality assessments gave totally different quality scores (*i.e.,* "*good vs poor*"), which confirms that
developers can have very different views on *what* a good identifier actually is.

   For automatically generated variables, evaluators agreed in 28.3% of cases (as
opposed to the 45.6% of the manually written code) and weakly agreed in 87.0% of
cases. 13.0% obtained an inconsistent assessment (*i.e.,* "*good vs poor*"). The obtained
agreement level confirmed the high subjectiveness of this task. It also highlighted
a good level of agreement in discriminating between *good* and *poor* identifiers, with
only ~15% of identifiers falling in this strong disagreement scenario. We also manually inspected these ~15% of identifiers, and illustrate them with some examples.
One interesting controversial identifier is "notDao". In that test case, "dao" was created to represent an object of type LocalBigDecimalNumeric. The developer used

"notDao" to represent another object of a different numeric class. While one evaluator believes this identifier is informative enough, the other considers "notDao" misleading as readers might think it is a Boolean value. Another example is the identifier "value", assigned to a string "easter '06". "value" is intended to be parsed by a date parser. While one evaluator thinks this identifier is meaningful and concise, the other believes "value" is too general.

Quality of Identifiers

Table D.4 reports the quality scores assigned by participants to test code identifiers.

Table D.4. Frequency of scores given to identifier quality

Evaluation	Manually written		Automatically generated		Sum	
good	199	(42.0%)	14	(15.2%)	213	(37.6%)
acceptable	116	(24.5%)	35	(38.0%)	151	(26.7%)
poor	155	(32.7%)	43	(46.7%)	198	(35.0%)
unsure	4	(0.8%)	0	(0.0%)	4	(0.7%)
Sum	474	(100.0%)	92	(100.0%)	566	(100.0%)

Manually written *vs* automatically generated. For manually written identifiers, 42% of the ratings indicate a *good* quality and an additional 24.5% an *acceptable* quality. ~33% of evaluations pointed to *poor*-quality identifiers. This indicates that poor identifiers are frequent in manually written test code.

For automatically generated variables we obtained only 15.2% *good* evaluations (as compared to the 42% of manually written ones), with an additional 38% of *acceptable* ratings, *i.e.,* evaluators were not satisfied with the quality of identifiers in automatically generated test cases in almost half of the cases.

If we compare the results for manually written and automatically generated variables, the quality of manually written identifiers is better overall, especially considering that the automatic test case generation approach rarely generates "good" identifiers according to the study participants. It is worth highlighting that in ~53% of the cases the evaluators considered the automatically generated identifiers at least as *acceptable*, indicating the use of good naming heuristics in EvoSuite.

We further analyze the obtained results in Section D.3.4 to better understand the reasons behind these quantitative findings.

Community projects *vs* team projects. Table D.5 reports the quality scores assigned to manually written variables in *community projects* and *team projects*.

A quality score is assigned by a single participant to one identifier (*i.e.,* a single evaluation). This means that each identifier results in two quality scores assigned by the two participants evaluating it, thus 237 manually written identifiers lead to 474 scores. As explained before, the same identifier could have both a *good* and a *poor* evaluation.

Table D.5. Evaluation of manually written variables

Evaluation	Community projects manual variables		Team projects manual variables	
good	65	(31.6%)	134	(50.0%)
acceptable	62	(30.1%)	54	(20.1%)
poor	77	(37.4%)	78	(29.1%)
unsure	2	(1.0%)	2	(0.7%)
sum	206	(100%)	268	(100%)

Table D.6. Identifier quality in test & production code for JACKSON CORE and ORMLITE CORE

Evaluation	Test code manual variables		Production code manual variables	
good	55	(35.3%)	49	(52.1%)
acceptable	41	(26.3%)	38	(40.4%)
poor	58	(37.2%)	7	(7.5%)
unsure	2	(0.2%)	0	(0.0%)
sum	156	(100%)	94	(100%)

We can see from the table that for *community projects*, the ratios of "good", "acceptable", and "poor" quality evaluations are quite similar (~30%), while for *team projects* around half of the evaluations pointed to a good identifier quality. This seems to indicate that the presence of organizations behind *community projects* does not guarantee better code quality assurance, at least not for identifiers quality in test code.

Test Code *vs* Production Code. Finally, we conclude our quantitative analysis by comparing the quality of manually written identifiers in test and production code as judged by four participants for two subject systems (*i.e.,* JACKSON CORE and ORMLITE CORE). Table D.6 shows the achieved results: For production code, 92.5% of identifiers are judged as having a good or an acceptable quality, as compared to the 61.6% of the test code identifiers from the same systems. While a full comparison of the quality of identifiers in test and production code is out of the scope of this chapter , the results obtained on these two systems seem to indicate that the quality problem is more evident in test code rather than in production code. Additional data is present in our online appendix [LNB+].

Qualitative Analysis

Fig. D.1 summarizes the reasons provided by participants when classifying a test code identifier as having a good quality (a), an acceptable quality (b), or a poor quality (c). These reasons are the characteristics that make an identifier perceived as good, acceptable, or poor. We did not report characteristics listed in less than 1% of cases.

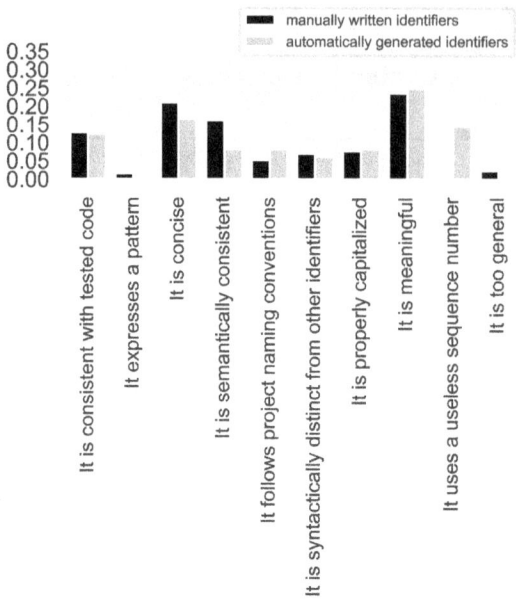

(a) Characteristics of "good" identifiers

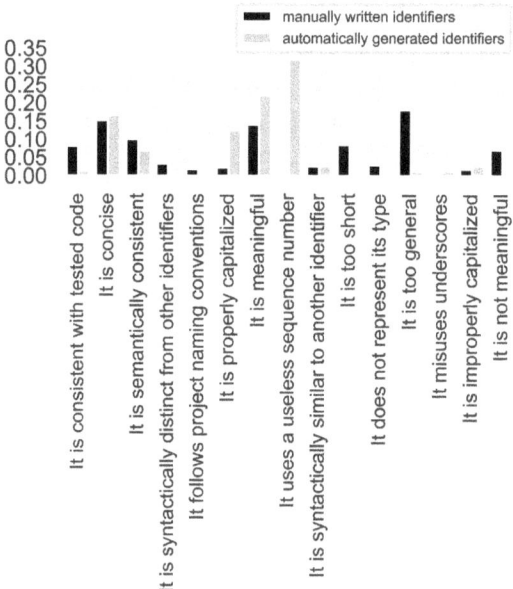

(b) Characteristics of "acceptable" identifiers

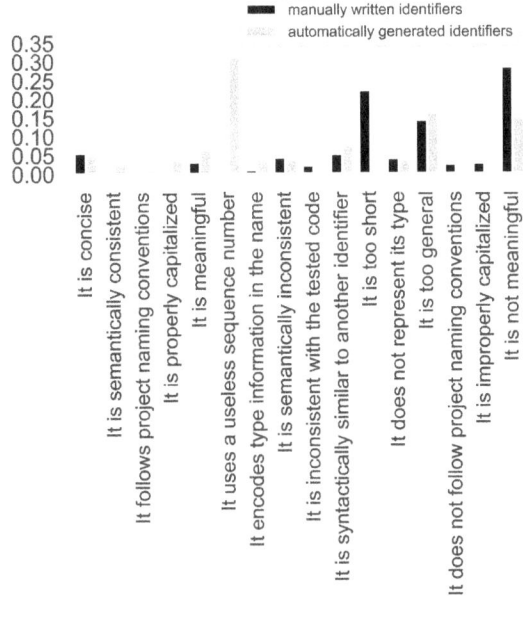

(c) Characteristics of "bad" identifiers

Figure D.1. Characteristics of identifiers having different quality levels, as perceived by the study participants

Concerning "good" identifiers, "*it expresses a pattern*", "*it is too general*", and "*it uses a useless sequence number*" are the characteristics provided by the evaluators, while all others were predefined by us, based on the related literature. Among the listed characteristics, the most selected ones are "*it is meaningful*" and "*it is concise*": Participants appreciated short identifiers having, however, a clear meaning (*e.g.,* config is considered good as it refers to an object of type HeaderConfig).

Two factors considered by evaluators as contributing to high quality identifiers are semantic consistency (*i.e.,* no different identifiers are used for the same concept), and consistency with the tested code (*i.e.,* it uses the same terms used in the tested code to represent a specific concept). For example, the methods setIndexName and getIndexName appear in multiple test cases, all the identifiers they interact with are consistently named as indexName, without any use of other names such as index and name. Moreover, indexName is also consistently used in the methods tested by these test cases.

Good-quality identifiers also had some negative characteristics highlighted by the participants, and in particular "*it is too general*" (*e.g.,* when an object is named with the name of the class it instantiates) and "*it uses a useless sequence number*" which is one of the main issues with the automatically generated identifiers. Moving to the poor-quality identifiers, besides the predefined characteristics, one additional characteristic has been contributed by the evaluators: "*it does not represent its type*". Fig. D.1-(c) shows that different problems exist in the low-quality *manually written* and *automatically generated* variables. For *manually written variables*, the major issues include: 1) "*the identifiers are not meaningful*" (*e.g.,* a for a matrix); 2) "*the identifiers are too general*" (*e.g.,* type for the type of a token); and 3) "*the identifiers are too short*" (*e.g.,* g for a JsonGenerator object). Two other attributes which account for around 5% of occurrences each are "*syntactically similar to another identifier*" (*i.e.,* similar identifiers are used for other concepts, such as applicationConfigurator and applicationConfiguration) and "*not representing its type*" (*e.g.,* strings is used to name a DateMap object).

For *automatically generated variables*, the dominant issue is that identifiers include "*useless sequence numbers*". Indeed, EvoSuite assigns the object type as variable names followed by a progressive number (*e.g.,* a new instance of a JsonReader object is called jsonReader0). This heuristic, while very simple, helps EvoSuite obtain some meaningful identifiers, especially in the case where a single variable of a specific type is used (*e.g.,* a single JsonReader is instantiated). In this case, the progressive number is not disturbing and there is no reason for a more specific name (since only one variable of that type exists in the test method), explaining why the identifiers are assessed as *good* by the participants, despite the presence of a "*useless sequence number*" (see Fig. D.1-(a)).

More specific names and advanced heuristics are needed when the role played in the test method by two variables of the same type must be *disambiguated* through their identifiers.

Being "*not meaningful*" and "*too general*" are two evident problems for automatically generated identifiers, accounting for 12% and 14% of the negative characteristics mentioned by the evaluators for the automatically generated tests. In very few cases, evaluators report the *misuse of underscore or of capitalization* as negative characteristics of identifiers in both *manually written* and *automatically generated* variables. These are issues that could be easily fixed with existing tools.

Finally, the *acceptable* identifiers (see Fig. D.1-(b)) represent a mix of good and bad practices, justifying their rating in between good and poor identifiers.

Participants' recommendations to improve poor identifiers

As previously said, participants could suggest a new name for an identifier, when it was judged as not good enough. The recommendations can be found in our replication package. By inspecting the identifiers rated as *good* and the 205 identifiers suggested by participants, we observed three patterns:

(1) Participants prefer full name identifiers to abbreviations. For example, both evaluations judging the quality of the qb identifier recommended to rename it into queryBuilder, thus confirming the importance of techniques supporting the automatic expansion of identifiers (*e.g.,* [HFB+08, LB11]).

(2) Plural format of an object type is recommended for the list of a certain type of objects. For example, dataGroups is suggested to replace dataGroup, which is a list of DataGroup objects.

③ Identifiers assigned to `get` methods and identifiers used as parameters of `set` methods are suggested to be consistent with the method names. For example, `foreignCollection` is considered a good name for a local variable assigned to the `getForeignCollection()` method.

We plan to conduct larger surveys in the future to distill a list of additional good naming practices and integrate them in rename refactoring and code generation tools.

D.4 Study II: Identifier Renaming in Test Code

The *goal* of this study is to assess whether state-of-the-art rename refactoring techniques can improve the identifier quality, especially for the test code.

D.4.1 Research Question

Given the fact that the quality of identifiers in test code is indeed a problem, one might wonder whether we can automatically improve it. While rename refactoring techniques have been proven useful on the production code by several studies [TR10, ABBS14, LSM+17], their effectiveness on test code remains unknown.

We aim at answering the following research questions:

RQ₂: *What is the accuracy of rename refactoring approaches when applied on test code identifiers?*

This RQ aims at exploring the possibility of using state-of-the-art rename refactoring techniques [TR10, ABBS14, LSM+17] to improve identifier quality of test code.

D.4.2 Study Context

The *study context* consists of the same ten projects used in our first study and 429 additional projects mined from GitHub and used for the training/test of the refactoring techniques.

To select the tools, we first investigated which rename refactoring techniques can be applied to rename *variable* identifiers. This led to the identification of three state-of-the-art approaches, namely CA-RENAMING[3] [TR10], NATURALIZE [ABBS14], and LEAR [LSM+17]. These techniques are described in Section D.2. We used the original implementations provided by the authors of NATURALIZE and LEAR, and reimplemented CA-RENAMING.

We consider two types of ground truths to assess the accuracy of the experimented techniques. One is the set of 201 high-quality identifiers obtained as output of Study I, including the identifiers that were assessed by both evaluators as at least *acceptable* (*i.e.,* good-good, good-acceptable, acceptable-acceptable) as well as the identifiers

---

[3]Note that CA-RENAMING is not the original name proposed by Thies and Roth, the researchers presenting this approach (that has no specific name), but the name assigned in [LSM+17], in which LEAR was compared to CA-RENAMING.

suggested by participants as a good alternative to the poor identifiers. From now on, we refer to this ground truth as the *manual-oracle*. The second set includes reviewed test code identifiers used in the 429 additional projects we mined for this study (from now on, *mined-oracle*). Similarly to what has been done in the literature, the idea for the *mined-oracle* is to assess the ability of the experimented techniques in recommending identifiers for a given variable in a test method. The assumption is that these identifiers are meaningful and, as seen in RQ_1, such a strong assumption does not always hold, since low-quality identifiers are still prevalent in manually written code. We mitigate this issue in two ways. First, we also compute the accuracy of the rename refactoring techniques on the *manual-oracle* including manually checked identifiers assessed to be meaningful. Second, we only consider in *mined-oracle* identifiers from the test methods of the 429 projects that have been submitted in pull requests on GitHub and underwent a code review process. This should increase the confidence in the high quality of the identifiers in *mined-oracle*.

To understand how the performance of rename refactoring approaches differ for production code, we also constructed the *manual-oracle* for production code identifiers in the same way with the data collected in our first study, which consists of 42 identifiers from JACKSON CORE and ORMLITE CORE.

To build the *mined-oracle*, we first mined Java projects from GitHub on Sept. 1, 2018, using the following selection criteria:

- **Activity level.** To exclude inactive projects, the projects must have at least one commit in the three months preceding the data collection.

- **Popularity.** Projects must have at least 100 forks and 100 stars, in order to exclude "toy-projects".

This process resulted in the selection of 2,583 Java projects. Then, we excluded the projects for which the test methods that underwent a review process in the latest version have less than 50 identifiers usable in our dataset, to ensure a good representativeness for each of the included projects. This led to the final 429 projects part of our dataset, including 24,355 reviewed test files. The test files were identified when their name started with "Test" or when they were located under a folder named "src/test" or "tests". Table D.7 summarizes the dataset used in this study.

Table D.7. Dataset Statistics

	Overall	Per project		
		Mean	Median	St. deviation
Java files	166,558	388.2	256.0	385.6
# total test files	46,260	107.8	62.0	138.7
# test files for study	24,355	56.8	24.0	99.7
# variables for study	397,936	927.6	396.0	1533.6

D.4.3 Data Collection and Analysis

The three considered rename refactoring techniques rely on a training phase to learn naming patterns: LEAR [LSM$^+$17] and NATURALIZE [ABBS14] need to build a language model based on n-grams extracted from the training code, while CA-RENAMING [TR10] needs to extract static type information and returned identifiers from declared methods in the training code. We experimented with different training scenarios to understand whether projects themselves or other projects are more helpful for training recommenders to rename identifiers in test code:

- **Training on production code.** Given the test code of a system A on which we apply a given renaming technique T, we train T on A's production code. Thus T learns naming conventions that are specific to project A.

- **Training on test code.** We train T on the large corpus of test code, extracted from reviewed and merged pull requests of 429 open source projects. Thus T learns naming conventions specific for test code, across several projects. The idea behind this scenario is that software is in general very repetitive and natural [HBS$^+$12]. Due to the high computational cost of this procedure, this second training scenario has only been performed by using the 429 projects for training and the 10 projects used in Study I as testing (*i.e.,* the ones part of the *manual-oracle*).

We ran the three techniques on the *manual-oracle* (both scenarios) and on the *mined-oracle* (only in the "training on production code" scenario). For production code identifiers, we only performed training on other production code in the project. We also only ran the three techniques on the *manual-oracle*.

We used two different matching approaches to determine whether the techniques provide correct renaming recommendations: 1) exact match (the recommended identifier is identical to the one in the oracle); 2) fuzzy match, meaning that at least 50% of the tokens (words identified through CamelCase splitting) composing the identifier in the oracle appear among the tokens used in the recommended identifier.

For test code identifiers, we compare via box plots the precision of the techniques in the different training scenarios and on the two oracles. The comparisons are also performed via the Mann-Whitney test [Con99], with results intended as statistically significant at $\alpha = 0.05$. To control the impact of multiple pairwise comparisons (*e.g.,* the precision of CA-RENAMING is compared with both NATURALIZE and LEAR), we adjust p-values with the Holm's correction [Hol79]. We estimate the magnitude of the differences by using the Cliff's Delta (d), a non-parametric effect size measure [GK05]. We follow well-established guidelines to interpret the effect size: negligible for $|d| < 0.10$, small for $0.10 \leq |d| < 0.33$, medium for $0.33 \leq |d| < 0.474$, and large for $|d| \geq 0.474$ [GK05].

For identifiers in production code, we list in a table the precision of the techniques for the two projects, and we also display the performance of the same projects when applying these techniques in their test code.

D.4.4 Results

Training on production code

We analyze the performance of rename refactoring techniques from two aspects: 1) the ability to generate recommendations for rename refactoring, 2) the correctness of the generated recommendations.

Ability to generate recommendations. Understanding how many recommendations can be generated can help us assess the applicability of rename refactoring tools in practice. Therefore, as the first step of our analysis, we inspect the percentage of identifiers involved in our study for which the three techniques can recommend an identifier name. Note that with "recommending an identifier name" we do not refer to the scenario in which a **new** name is recommended for a variable, but to the scenario in which a name (any name) is recommended, even the original one. Indeed, for a given variable, the three techniques might not be able to generate a recommendation. In particular, CA-RENAMING does not generate a recommendation in the case in which: 1) the variable to rename is not assigned to a method invocation (*e.g.*, for `String name = "Max"`, CA-RENAMING cannot be applied — see Section D.2 for a description of the CA-RENAMING technique) or if the invoked method returns a variable of a different type (*e.g.*, `String age = (String) getAge()` with `getAge()` returning an integer). The other two techniques (NATURALIZE and LEAR) are both based on *n*-gram language models, and do not trigger any recommendation when a minimum confidence threshold set by the original authors is not met for a generated identifier.

Tables D.8 and D.9 report descriptive statistics (*e.g.*, mean across projects) of the ratio of variables with renaming recommendations for test code generated by CA-RENAMING, NATURALIZE and LEAR on the *manual-oracle* and the *mined-oracle*, respectively. CA-RENAMING is omitted in Table D.8 as it is unable to generate any renaming recommendation.

The achieved results show the limited percentage of cases in which these approaches are actually able to generate a recommendation. Indeed, even by considering the approach generating the highest number of recommendation (*i.e.*, LEAR), it can only be applied on ∼20% of the test code identifiers of a given project. Not surprisingly, CA-RENAMING has the lowest applicability, given its strong constraint making it applicable only to variables assigned to a method invocation returning the same type. NATURALIZE can generate refactoring recommendations for around 10% of the variables in the *manual-oracle*, while for *mined-oracle* this percentage significantly drops. This difference might be the consequence of test method sampling when building the *manual-oracle* dataset.

Table D.8. Ratio of variables for which a rename refactoring is generated (*manual-oracle*)

Approach	Mean	Median	St. deviation
NATURALIZE	12.2%	9.9%	0.133
LEAR	22.1%	17.9%	0.199

Table D.9. Ratio of variables for which a rename refactoring is generated (*mined-oracle*)

Approach	Mean	Median	St. deviation
CA-RENAMING	0.9%	0.1%	0.023
NATURALIZE	3.6%	0.0%	0.075
LEAR	26.1%	24.0%	0.251

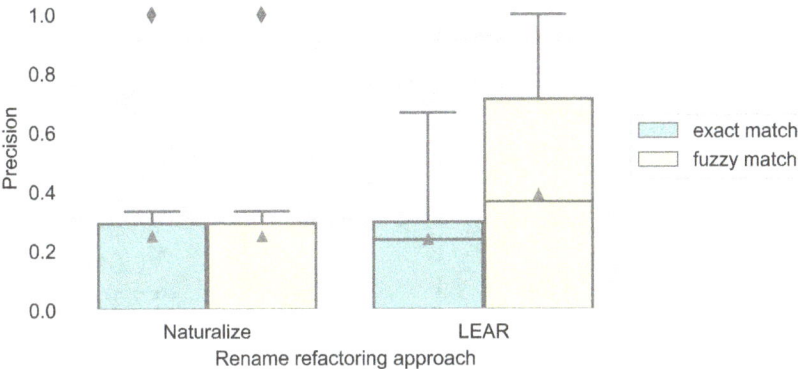

(a) Precision of rename refactoring techniques on *manual-oracle*

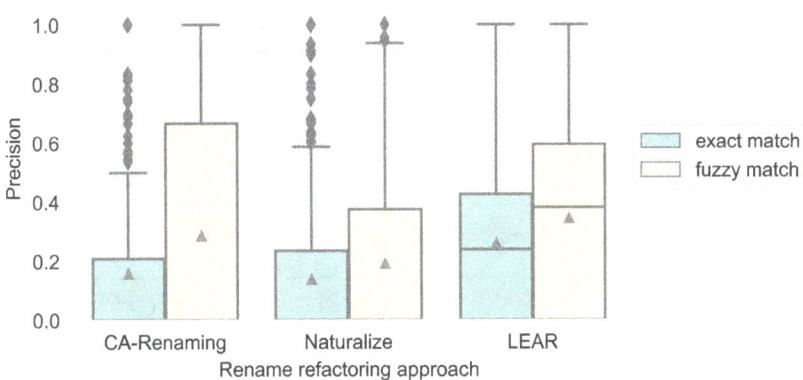

(b) Precision of rename refactoring techniques on *mined-oracle*

Figure D.2. Precision of rename refactoring techniques on test code

Correctness of the generated recommendations. Fig. D.2 compares the precision of rename refactoring techniques when applied on the *manual-oracle* and the *mined-oracle*. Since CA-RENAMING does not generate any recommendation for the *manual-oracle*, it is not plotted on Fig. D.2a. The main message of Fig. D.2 is that the precision is in general quite low in terms of recommending good identifiers for test code. Moreover, although LEAR significantly outperforms the other two approaches

Table D.10. Performance comparison of rename refactoring techniques for identifiers in production code and test code

(a) Results of NATURALIZE

Project	# var.	# Recomm.	NATURALIZE Prec. (exact)	Prec. (fuzzy)
JACKSON CORE (Prod. code)	24	5	40.0%	40.0%
JACKSON CORE (Test code)	35	4	0.0%	0.0%
ORMLITE CORE (Prod. code)	18	8	37.5%	62.5%
ORMLITE CORE (Test code)	37	0	0.0%	0.0%

(b) Results of LEAR

Project	# var.	# Recomm.	LEAR Prec. (exact)	Prec. (fuzzy)
JACKSON CORE (Prod. code)	20	55.0%	60.0%	
JACKSON CORE (Test code)	3	0.0%	0.0%	
ORMLITE CORE (Prod. code)	7	42.9%	57.1%	
ORMLITE CORE (Test code)	0	0.0%	0.0%	

Table D.11. Statistical tests of precisions of rename refactoring techniques for *mined-oracle*

(a) Results of *P-value*

Comparison	P-Value (exact match)	P-Value (fuzzy match)
CA-RENAMING *vs* NATURALIZE	0.74	0.0037
CA-RENAMING *vs* LEAR	<0.0001	0.0003
NATURALIZE *vs* LEAR	<0.0001	<0.0001

(b) Results of *effect size*

Comparison	Effect size (exact match)	Effect size (fuzzy match)
CA-RENAMING *vs* NATURALIZE	0.01 (Negligible)	0.10 (Negligible)
CA-RENAMING *vs* LEAR	0.29 (Small)	0.14 (Negligible)
NATURALIZE *vs* LEAR	0.31 (Small)	0.29 (Small)

(see Table D.11), the average and median precision is still lower than 50% even when only fuzzy match is required. However, it is worth noting that the low precision does not necessarily mean the generated identifiers are wrong, due to the matching rules we adopted to define "correctness". As we know, in practice, often many variants of identifiers can well fit in the code context. Therefore, the precision people perceive with these tools could be higher than the values presented here.

To better compare these rename refactoring approaches, we applied statistical analysis to the precisions of the renaming recommendations. For the *manual-oracle*, we compared NATURALIZE against LEAR. The p-value of 0.35 (exact match)/0.44 (fuzzy match) indicates that the precision difference between NATURALIZE and LEAR is not statistically significant. However, the situation changes on the *mined-oracle*. In the Table D.11, we can find that there is no statistically significant difference (adjusted p-value ≥ 0.05) between CA-RENAMING and NATURALIZE when exact match is required. However, the advantage of LEAR is visible in any case. All of the statistical comparisons with CA-RENAMING and NATURALIZE result in a statistically significant difference, with small or negligible effect sizes.

Test Code vs Production Code. Table D.10 compares the performance of rename refactoring techniques when they are applied to production code and test code (*manual-oracle*). CA-RENAMING is also omitted as no recommendation was generated for both production and test code. We can notice that rename refactoring approaches can generate more recommendations for production code, and the precision is much higher. This result indicates that rename refactoring techniques are less effective when used to improve the quality of test code identifiers as compared to production code identifiers.

Training on test code

Table D.12 reports the performance of NATURALIZE and LEAR on the *manual-oracle* of test code identifiers, when training on test code from other projects. In this case, CA-RENAMING was unable to generate any recommendation, as it heavily relies on program analysis. Since no production code was used for training, CA-RENAMING could not retrieve the declarations of methods used in test cases. Therefore, CA-RENAMING is excluded in this study.

Both NATURALIZE and LEAR perform poorly in this task. The unsatisfactory performance comes from two aspects: the amount and the precision of generated refactoring recommendations. More specifically, NATURALIZE failed to generate recommendations for six projects, while LEAR could not recommend any identifier for five projects. As a side note, LEAR can generate at maximum five refactoring recommendations when applied on the *manual-oracle* and trained with *test code*. When it comes to the precision of exactly matched recommendations, the performance is extremely poor for LEAR. That is, none of the generated recommendations is correct, which is not the case for NATURALIZE.

We can also spot some major differences between these results and the previous ones. Although the performance of both techniques drop significantly, in this study NATURALIZE performs better than LEAR in terms of the number of exactly matched generated recommendations. The reason could be the nature of the training materials. Unlike the previous study, in which the training of the techniques was performed on the production code of the same system for which the test code identifiers were recommended, training on the test code from other projects likely results in the learning of linguistic patterns that are not representative of the "test project" (*i.e.,* the one

Table D.12. Results of rename refactoring techniques for *manual-oracle* when trained on test code

(a) Results of NATURALIZE

Project	# variables	NATURALIZE		
		# recomm.	Precision (exact)	Precision (fuzzy)
NATTY	22	12	50.0%	50.0%
JONGO	12	0	0.0%	0.0%
COMMONS LANG	14	10	0.0%	0.0%
JACKSON CORE	35	0	0.0%	0.0%
PLEXUS-UTILS	14	0	0.0%	0.0%
JESQUE	21	10	10.0%	10.0%
GSON	18	14	28.6%	43.0%
REST ASSURED	12	0	0.0%	0.0%
LA4J	16	0	0.0%	0.0%
ORMLITE CORE	37	0	0.0%	0.0%

(b) Results of LEAR

Project	# variables	LEAR		
		# recomm.	Precision (exact)	Precision (fuzzy)
NATTY	22	1	0.0%	0.0%
JONGO	12	0	0.0%	0.0%
COMMONS LANG	14	1	0.0%	0.0%
JACKSON CORE	35	3	0.0%	66.7%
PLEXUS-UTILS	14	5	0.0%	40.0%
JESQUE	21	0	0.0%	0.0%
GSON	18	0	0.0%	0.0%
REST ASSURED	12	0	0.0%	0.0%
LA4J	16	0	0.0%	0.0%
ORMLITE CORE	37	2	0.0%	50.0%

for which identifiers must be recommended). This might be due to a vocabulary mismatch between the code used for training and the one used for test. LEAR seems to be more sensitive to this change since it only considers tokens carrying out semantic information during the training (*i.e.,* the identifiers used in method names, parameters, and variables), while NATURALIZE, also learns from syntax-related tokens (*e.g.,* Java keywords), thus being able to better deal with the vocabulary mismatch.

Although researchers have proved that source code is repetitive [GS10, HBS⁺12, LPM⁺17], our study discloses that to recommend renaming operations for test code, it might be more effective to train these approaches on the related production code rather than from a massive dataset containing thousands of projects.

D.5   Threats to Validity

Construct validity. In Study I, instead of using proxy measures, we preferred to let participants evaluate the quality of identifiers used in test code. While how to perceive the identifier quality may vary among different participants, the subjectiveness of such an evaluation was mitigated by involving two evaluators for each identifier. Also, although a four or five-level Likert scale [Opp92] could have provided a more accurate evaluation of the identifiers' quality, we preferred a simpler three-level scale to facilitate the task to the respondents.

In Study II, we assessed the performance of the experimented techniques by adopting two different ground truths that complement each other. Indeed, the *manual-oracle* is small in size, but includes identifiers manually classified as meaningful. The *mined-oracle*, instead, includes 397,936 identifiers, thus ensuring a good generalizability at the risk, however, of including some poor-quality identifiers in the ground truth. This threat was mitigated by only considering in the *mined-oracle* identifiers from test code that underwent code review.

Internal validity. The experience of the participants involved in Study I could have played a role in the identifier quality assessment. We only involved participants with at least one year of Java experience but, due to the limited participants, we did not analyze the influence of their experience on the quality assessments they provided.

External validity. The validity of Study I is limited by the 19 participants and the selected projects. This, as a consequence, partially impacted the generalizability of Study II concerning the results achieved on the *manual-oracle*. Also, when running our studies on production code, we only considered identifiers from two systems (and their respective evaluations provided by four participants in Study I). This is a clear limitation to the generalizability of the findings related to the comparison between test and production code performed in both studies. However, our focus is on test code identifiers, and production code identifiers were only considered to have a baseline for comparison, easing the interpretation of the achieved results. Details about the results achieved on production code identifiers are available in our appendix [LZB+a].

D.6   Conclusion and Future Work

We studied the the quality of identifiers in test code and compared it with identifiers in production code. We also analyzed the attributes that are deemed important in determining the quality of identifiers and assessed the performance of three state-of-the-art rename refactoring techniques in suggesting good identifiers. The results of our study provide us with a number of lessons learned.

The quality of identifiers in test code is a notable problem. Even in well-known projects run by open source organizations, one out of three quality assessments performed by developers would result in the identification of a poor-quality identifier. This highlights the need for techniques and tools able to help developers in identifying and fixing these problematic identifiers, and leads us to our next point.

The performance of state-of-the-art rename refactoring techniques is far from promising for improving the unsatisfactory identifier quality of test code. In the best case scenario, these techniques achieve a limited precision, lower than 50% on average. We observed that training language models on the production code of the same system for which test code identifiers should be recommended as a more promising training approach as compared to the usage of a large set of test cases extracted from other systems. Techniques specifically tailored for test code and, for example, exploiting its relationship with the tested production code, might be required to substantially increase the automated support provided to developers for the renaming of test code identifiers.

Automatically generated test code suffers even more from identifiers' quality issues. This result, while expected, highlights the need for integrating more sophisticated naming heuristics in tools for the automatic generation of test cases. Our findings in Study I disclose that some simple heuristics (*e.g.,* the use of plural for naming variables representing collections of objects) could be implemented with very little effort, and would generate identifiers appreciated by software developers.

These findings dictate our future research agenda.

Reproducibility. The data used in our studies as well as the experimented renaming approaches are available for replication[4]. This includes the *manual-oracle* output of Study I that could represent a valuable resource for testing rename refactoring approaches tailored for test code.

---

[4]https://identifierquality.bitbucket.io/

Knowledge Transfer in Modern Code Review

Knowledge transfer is one of the main goals of modern code review, as shown by several studies that surveyed and interviewed developers. While knowledge transfer is a clear expectation of the code review process, there are no analytical studies using data mined from software repositories to assess the effectiveness of code review in "training" developers and improve their skills over time. We present a mining-based study investigating how and whether the code review process helps developers to improve their contributions to open source projects over time. We analyze 32,062 peer-reviewed pull requests (PRs) made across 4,981 GitHub repositories by 728 developers who created their GitHub account in 2015. We assume that PRs performed in the past by a developer D that have been subject to a code review process have "transferred knowledge" to D. Then, we verify if over time (*i.e.,* when more and more reviewed PRs are made by D), the *quality* of the contributions made by D to open source projects increases (as assessed by proxies we defined, such as the acceptance of PRs, or the polarity of the sentiment in the review comments left for the submitted PRs). With the above measures, we were unable to capture the positive impact played by the code review process on the quality of developers' contributions. This might be due to several factors, including the choices we made in our experimental design. Additional investigations are needed to confirm or contradict such a *negative result*.

This study is based on the following publication [CLB+20]:

Knowledge Transfer in Modern Code Review

Maria Caulo, Bin Lin, Gabriele Bavota, Giuseppe Scanniello, Michele Lanza. In *Proceedings of the 28th International Conference on Program Comprehension (ICPC 2020) – Research Track*, accepted

E.1   Introduction

Code review is the process by which peer developers inspect the code written by a teammate to assess its quality, to recommend changes and, finally, to approve it for merging [BLNS16]. Previous works have investigated code review from several perspectives. Some authors studied the factors influencing the likelihood of getting a patch accepted as the results of the code review process [WND08, BKHG13], while others studied the reviewing habits of developers in specific contexts [RS11]. Several works focused on the benefits, motivations, and expectations of the review process. Most of these studies are qualitative in nature [RGS08, BB13, BBZJ14], and were conducted by surveying/interviewing developers or by inspecting their conversations in mailing lists or issue trackers of open source projects. Only a few researchers analyzed data from a quantitative perspective, mostly to assess the impact of code review on code quality (*e.g.,* the relationship between code review and post-release defects) [KP09, MKAH14, MMK15, BR15].

The work conducted at Microsoft by Bacchelli and Bird [BB13] provided qualitative evidence of the central role played by code review in knowledge transfer among developers. However, no quantitative, mining-based study has tried to investigate this phenomenon, and in particular to answer the following high-level research question (RQ): *Does code review enable knowledge transfer among developers?*. Answering this RQ, by mining software repositories, is far from trivial since: *(i)* quantitatively measuring knowledge transfer is challenging and an open research problem by itself and *(ii)* many confounding factors come into play when collecting developer-related data from online repositories. We quantitatively answer the above research question by making the following assumptions:

- *The number of **reviewed** pull requests (PRs) a developer made in the past across all repositories she contributed to is a proxy of the transferred knowledge she benefited of.* Given a developer D, we assume that the higher the number of closed PRs (*i.e.,* accepted and rejected ones) that were subject to review (*i.e.,* received comments from peer developers) D performed, the higher the knowledge transfer D benefited of.

- *We can measure the actual benefits of the knowledge transfer experienced through the code review process by a developer, by observing if, with the increase of the received knowledge transfer, the quality of her contributions to open source projects increases as well.* Given the various types of projects involved, it is necessary to adopt contribution quality measures which are independent from project languages and domains. We assume that how code reviewers respond to developers' PRs can reflect the quality of the submitted contribution.We use as proxies for the quality of the contributions provided by D: *(i)* the percentage of D's PRs that are accepted (expected to increase over time); *(ii)* the time required to review the changes D contributes (expected to decrease); *(iii)* the amount of recommendations provided by the reviewers to improve the code D contributes in PRs (expected to decrease); and *(iv)* through sentiment analysis, the polarity of the sentiment in the discussion of the PRs D submits (expected to be more positive).

Based on these assumptions, we analyzed the contribution history of 728 developers across 4,981 repositories hosted on GitHub. We studied whether the number of reviewed PRs opened in the past by a developer impacts the quality of her contributions over time.

We grouped developers into different sets based on the amount of knowledge transfer they benefited of (low, medium-low, medium-high, high), as assessed by the number of reviewed PRs they performed in the past. Any result achieved with such an experimental design may be due to a simple increase of the developer's experience over time rather than to the knowledge transfer that took place over the reviewed PRs. To control for this, we replicated our analysis by grouping the developers based on the number of commits rather than the number of reviewed PRs they performed in the past (into the four groups listed above). Using our experimental design with the measures mentioned above, we were not able to capture the positive impact played by the code review process on the quality of developers' contributions. Such a negative result might be due to several factors, including the choices we made in our experimental design (see Section E.3). For this reason, additional studies are needed to corroborate or contradict our findings.

Structure of the Chapter

In Section E.2, we discuss related work, while the design of our mining-based study is presented in Section E.3. The results and the threats that could affect their validity are discussed in Section E.4 and Section E.5, respectively. We conclude the chapter in Section E.6.

E.2   Related Work

Recent works [RR14, TDH14, SdLJMP15a, SdLJMP15b, SVT16, PM18, KRB$^+$18, CSM19] have focused on the motivations of acceptance or rejection of changes proposed in the form of PRs after the code review process, identifying various influencing factors, such as:

- **Programming Language**: proposed changes in Java are the least easily accepted, whereas for C, Typescript, Scala and Go the opposite happens [RR14], [SdLJMP15a];

- **Size and Complexity of the PR**: the greater the size and complexity of the PR to be reviewed (*e.g.,* the number of the commits, or the committed files) the lower the likelihood of acceptance [TDH14], [SdLJMP15b], [SVT16], [PM18], [KRB$^+$18];

- **Addition and Change of files**: PRs which propose to add files have a 8% lower chance of acceptance [SdLJMP15a]; the same applies for PRs which contain many changed files [PM18];

- **Excessive forking**: PR acceptance reduces when many forks are present [RR14];

- **Tests**: contributions including test code have higher chances to be merged [TDH14], [CSM19];

- **Developer's type**: if the PR was made by a member of the core team, it has more chances to be accepted as compared to a PR made by an external. The existence of a social connection between the requester, the project and the reviewer, positively influences merge decisions [SdLJMP15a], [TDH14], [KRB+18];

- **Experience in making PRs**: the higher the percentage of previously merged PRs by a developer, the higher the chances of acceptance [CSM19]. Developers with 20 to 50 months of experience are the most productive in submitting and being accepted their PRs [RR14]. When a PR is the first made by a developer, the chance of a merge considerably decreases [TDH14], [SdLJMP15b], [SdLJMP15a], [KRB+18];

- **Number of comments**: the more comments have been made in the PR discussion, the lower the chance of acceptance [TDH14], [SVT16].

Bosu *et al.* [BGB15] investigated which factors lead to qualitatively high code reviews. To discern if a code review feedback is useful or not, the authors built and verified a classification model, and executed it on 1.5 million review comments from 5 Microsoft projects, finding several factors that affect the usefulness of reviews feedback: *(i)* the working period of the reviewer in the company: in the first year she tends to provide more useful comments than afterward; *(ii)* reviewers from different teams gave slightly more useful comments than reviewers from the same team; *(iii)* the density of useful comments increases over time; *(iv)* source code files had the highest density of useful comments than other types of files; and *(v)* the higher the size of the change (*i.e.*, the number of files involved) that the author would bring to a project, the lower the usefulness of the review comments to such an author, confirming in some sense the results by Weißgerber *et al.* [WND08]. Weißgerber *et al.* studied the email archives of two open source projects to find which factors affect the acceptance of patches. They found that small patches (at most 4 lines changed) have higher chances to get accepted, but the size of a patch does not significantly influence acceptance time.

Baysal *et al.* [BKHG13] investigated which factors affect the likelihood of a code change to be accepted after code review. They extracted both "ordinary" factors (code quality-related) and non-technical ones, such as organizational (company-related) and personal (developers-related) features, finding that nontechnical factors significantly impact the code review outcome.

Company and developers-related factors of code reviews practices in open-source projects have been qualitatively studied also by Rigby *et al.* [RGS08, RS11], who compared, by means of emails archives and version control repositories, the two techniques used by developers of Apache server project: review-then-commit and commit-then-review [RGS08]. Apache reviews resulted to be early and frequent, related to small and completed patches (in line with Weißgerber *et al.* [WND08]), and conducted by a small number of developers. Rigby *et al.* [RS11] also investigated *(i)* the mechanisms and behaviors that developers use to find (or ignore) code changes they are competent to review and *(ii)* how developers interact with one another during the review process.

Research has also been conducted to study how software quality is impacted by code reviews, and how they allow to identify defects. Kemerer and Paulk [KP09] studied the review rate to adopt to have effective reviews when removing defects or influencing the software quality. The authors studied two datasets from a personal software process (PSP) approach with regression and mixed models. The PSP review rate turned out to be significant for the bug-fixing effectiveness. Mäntylä *et al.* [ML09] classified the issues found by both students and professional developers during code review. They found that 75% of issues concerned "evolvability" (*e.g.,* limited readability/maintainability of code). Beller *et al.* [BBZJ14] confirmed this finding by classifying changes brought by the reviewed code of two open-source software projects. They found a 3:1 ratio between maintainability-related and functional defects. They also found that bug-fixing tasks need fewer changes than others, and the person who conducts the review does not impact the number of required changes. Czerwonka *et al.* [CGT15] observed that code reviews often do not identify functionality problems. The authors found that code reviews performed by unskilled developers are not effective, highlighting the importance of social aspects in code review.

McIntosh *et al.* quantitatively studied the relationship between software quality and *(i)* the amount of changes that have been code reviewed, and, *(ii)* code review participation, *i.e.,* the degree of reviewer involvement in the code review process [MKAH14]. The authors studied three projects and found that both aspects are linked to software quality: poorly reviewed code leads to components with up to two post-release defects; low participation up to five. Bavota and Russo [BR15] studied the impact of code review on the quality of the committed code. They found that unreviewed commits have twice more chances of introducing bugs as compared to reviewed commits. Also, code committed after a review is more readable than unreviewed code.

Morales *et al.* [MMK15] studied the effect of code review practices on software design quality. They considered the occurrences of 7 design and implementation anti-patterns and found that lower review coverage leads to higher likelihood to observe those anti-patterns in code. Bernart *et al.* [BMG10, BG13] highlighted that continuous code review practices in agile development produce high benefits to a project, such as *(i)* the reduction of the effort in SE practices, *(ii)* the support of collective ownership; and *(iii)* the improvements in the general understandability of the code.

Recent research work also focused on the content of conversations deriving from the code review activity, the topic of the discussions, and how developers emotionally felt [LYY+17, DOB+18, OMT19]. Li *et al.* [LYY+17] classified review comments according to a custom taxonomy of topics, finding that *(i)* PRs submitted by inexperienced contributors are likely to have potential problems even if they passed the tests; and *(ii)* external contributors tend to not follow project conventions in their early contributions. Destefanis *et al.* [DOB+18] analyzed GitHub issues commenters (*i.e.,* those users who only post comments without posting any issues nor proposing changes to repositories) from the effectiveness perspective. The authors found that commenters are less polite and positive, and express a lower level of emotions in their comments than other types of users. Ortu *et al.* [OMT19] found that GitHub issues with a high level of Anger, Sadness, Arousal and Dominance are less likely to be merged, while high values of Valence and Joy tend to make issues merged.

Bacchelli and Bird [BB13] studied the tool-based code review practices adopted at Microsoft, reporting that even if finding defects remains the main motivation for reviews, they provide additional benefits, such as knowledge transfer, increased team awareness, and creation of alternative solutions to problems.

E.2.1 Taking Stock

The relevance of code reviews has been investigated from different perspectives. The effect of code reviews on knowledge transfer has been only marginally studied, let alone from a quantitative perspective, which is the goal of this chapter: We used the number of past reviewed PRs submitted by a developer as a proxy for the amount of knowledge transfer she has been subject to. Then, we assess whether with the increase in received knowledge transfer, the quality of submitted code contributions improves over time. From this perspective, the most similar work is the recent one by Chen *et al.* [CSM19], in which the authors found that the highest the percentage of previously merged PRs by a developer, the higher the chances of acceptance of new PRs.

Differently from Chen *et al.* [CSM19], we consider past submitted PRs (both accepted and rejected) that have been actually reviewed (*i.e.,* received at least one comment from peer developers), to get a "reliable" proxy of the amount of knowledge transfer of a developer in the past. Also, besides analyzing the impact of the received knowledge transfer on the likelihood of acceptance for future submitted PRs, we consider many other proxies to assess the quality of the contributions submitted by a developer.

E.3 Study Design

E.3.1 Hypothesis

Software development is a knowledge-intensive activity [BD08]. Qualitative research provided evidence that code review plays a pivotal role in knowledge transfer among developers [BB13]. However, no quantitative evidence exists in support of this claim. In this study, we mine software repositories to quantitatively assess the knowledge transfer happening thanks to code review.

There is no well-established metric to assess the "quantity of knowledge" involved in a given process. Knowledge can be classified as either *explicit* (which *"can be spoken and codified in words, figures or symbols"*) or *tacit* (which *"is embedded in individuals' minds and is hard to express and communicate to others"*) [EH04]. We focus on the tacit knowledge acquired by developers over time, which cannot be easily seen and quantified. More specifically, we investigate whether the experience gained by receiving feedback during code review improves the quality of developers' future contributions to open source projects. Intuitively, one might expect that developers gradually gain knowledge by receiving feedback from their peers, thus improving their skills over time. Therefore, we formulated and studied the following hypothesis:

> **H.** *The quality of developers' contributions to software projects will increase with the experience gained from their past reviewed PRs.*

E.3.2 Study Context

The *study context* consists of 728 developers, 4,981 software repositories they contributed to, and 77,456 closed PRs (among which 32,062 PRs are peer-reviewed).

Developers selection

To run our study, we collected information about GitHub users (from here onward referred to also as developers), who created their account in 2015. This was done to collect at least four years of contribution history for each developer. Since data was collected in September 2019, we can observe ~4 years of contributions even for users who created their GitHub account in December 2015. A four-year time window is long enough to observe enough PRs submitted by developers and, consequently, to study the knowledge transfer over time.

We used the *GitHub Search API*[1] to retrieve the developers who joined GitHub on the first day of each month in 2015. Since the *GitHub Search API* only provides up to 1,000 results for search, we collected a total of 12,000 developers who created their account in 2015 (*i.e.,* 1,000 per month). As the next step, we collected all the PRs submitted by these 12,000 developers across all GitHub repositories they contributed to.

---

[1]https://developer.github.com/v3/search/

Since the *GitHub Search API* cannot return over 1,000 PRs for a single developer, to ensure the data completeness, we excluded nine developers who submitted over 1,000 PRs in the studied time window. This reduced the number of developers to 11,991.

We removed from our dataset developers who submitted too few PRs. This was needed since we want to analyze how the quality of developers' contributions to open source projects changes over time. Having only one or two PRs submitted by a developer would not allow to perform such an analysis. For this reason, we excluded from our study all developers who submitted less than 30 PRs in the considered time period (*i.e.,* 2014-2019). This further filter removed 11,173 developers, leaving 818 developers in total.

Pull requests collection and filtering

We collected all the *"closed"* PRs submitted by the 818 subject developers from the day they joined GitHub until the end of September 2019, when we collected the data. This led to a total of 77,456 PRs spanning 9,845 repositories. We only focused on closed PRs to be sure that the PRs underwent a code review process and, thus, were either accepted or rejected instead of still pending. For each PR, we collected the following information:

1. *Creation date:* the date in which the PR was submitted.

2. *Acceptance:* whether the closed PR was accepted.

3. *Closing date:* the date in which the PR was closed.

4. *Source code comments:* the comments left by the reviewers that are explicitly linked to parts of the code submitted for review. Comments left by the PR author are excluded.

5. *General comments:* all the comments left in the PR discussion by all the developers other than the PR author, excluding *source code comments*. These comments are generally used to ask for clarifications or to explain why a PR should be accepted/rejected. Source code comments, instead, reports explicit action items for the PR author to improve the submitted code. We separate the *source code comments* and the *general comments*, as there might be different levels of technical details in these two categories.

6. *Author:* the author of the PR.

7. *Contributors:* all the developers who have been involved in the discussion and handling of the PR.

Since we plan to use the comments related to each PR as one of the variables for our study, *i.e.,* to assess the amount of feedback received by developers as well as to check whether a PR was actually subject to code review (meaning, it received at least one comment), we removed general comments posted by bots (this problem does not occur for source code comments). We discriminated whether a comment was left by a bot following the steps below:

1. We calculated how many general comments each commenter (*i.e.*, entity who posted at least one comment in the considered PRs) left in the PRs and sorted them in descending order. As a result, around 60% of the comments were left by the top-500 commenters, with a long tail of commenters only posting a handful of comments in their history.

2. For these top-500 commenters, we manually checked their usernames and profile images. If the username contained "bot," or the profile image represented a robot, we then further inspected whether their comments followed a predefined structure, *e.g.*, "Automated fastforward with [GitMate.io] (https://gitmate.io) was successful!", by *gitmate-bot*. If this was the case, we considered the commenter as a bot.

3. For the rest of the commenters, we manually checked the GitHub profiles of those whose username contained "bot".

This process led to the disclosure of 147 bot commenters. The manual identification of the bots was done by a collaborator of this study, and the final output (*i.e.*, the 147 removed bots) is available in our replication package [CLB$^+$].

After this cleaning process, we further excluded 90 developers from our study since they authored less than 30 closed PRs (including those which did not receive comments). This led to the final number of 728 developers considered in our study, who authored a total of 77,456 PRs (among which 32,062 PRs received comments).

Project collection

We cloned all the projects[2] in which the selected developers submitted at least one PR, for a total of 4,981 repositories. To provide a better overview of the collected projects, our replication package[CLB$^+$] also includes basic information (*e.g.*, programming languages, project size) of these repositories.

E.3.3 Measures

To verify our hypothesis, we use proxies to measure the knowledge transfer experienced by developers through their past reviewed PRs and to assess the quality of developers' contribution over time.

---

[2]This was done since we also used in our analysis the number of commits performed by the studied developers over time. While this information can be collected through the GitHub APIs as well, cloning the repositories simplified data collection.

Knowledge measures

We use the number of **reviewed** PRs a developer contributed (authored) in the past (*i.e.,* before the current PR) as a proxy of the amount of knowledge transferred to her thanks to the code review process. That is, we assume that the more closed and peer-reviewed PRs a developer has, the more knowledge the developer gained. In our study, we consider that peer-reviewed PRs are those which received at least one comment by non-bot users. The rationale behind this choice is that if no comments are given by other developers, we assume that the PR was not subject of a formal review process and, thus, it is not interesting for our goals, since no transfer knowledge can happen in that PR. We compute this number for each developer before each of their peer-reviewed PR. We use this variable to split developers into different groups based on the knowledge transfer they experienced (*i.e.,* low, medium-low, medium-high, and high), and compare the quality of the submitted contributions (as assessed by the proxies described in the following section) among the different groups. This means that the same developer can belong, in different time periods, to different groups (*i.e.,* she starts in the low transfer knowledge group, she then moves to medium-low, etc.). The exact process used for data analysis is detailed later on.

To verify whether the quality of the submitted contributions is actually influenced by the knowledge transfer during code review or if it is just a result of the increasing developer's experience over time, we also collected the number of commits performed in the past by each developer before submitting each PR. The commits are extracted from all repositories in which the developers submitted at least one PR. As done for the past PRs, we use past commits to split developers into groups and contrast the quality of their contributions over time.

This allows us to see whether potential differences in contribution quality among the groups can be attributed to the code review process put into place in PR (*i.e.,* these differences are visible when splitting developers based on past reviewed PRs, but not when splitting them based on past commits) or if they are mainly due to changes in the experience over time (*i.e.,* the differences can be observed both when splitting by past reviewed PRs as well as by past commits). When retrieving past commits for developers, there are two issues worth noting: 1) The developer's username on GitHub (as extracted using the GitHub API) might be different from the author name in the Git commit history (as extracted from the Git logs); 2) One developer might use several different identities to author commits. Therefore, we employed the following process to map GitHub accounts to their corresponding identities. For each of the 728 developers included in our study, we first tried to match their GitHub account to the author names in the commits of the repositories they contributed to through PRs. As a result, 360 GitHub usernames could be matched to the commit author names, while no link could be established for the remaining 368 accounts. For this latter, we manually checked their GitHub profile and tried to match their displayed name and email to the author names and emails in Git logs. If no match was found, we manually inspected the "contributors" page of their corresponding repositories on GitHub to check if the developer has made any commits. If the developer did not appear in the list of contributors, we assume no commit was made by the developer. Otherwise, we manually browsed developers' commits to those repositories (which is not possible to retrieve with the GitHub API), and obtained the commit hash. Then, in the local repository, we checked the commit information linked to the commit hash, such that we could obtain the author names they used for commits. As developers might use multiple author names in the commits, we also recorded the other author names associated with the same email addresses they used, and iterated this process with the newly found author names until no new author name emerged. Through this manual process, we managed to collect the identities of 715 developers, while for the rest 13 we assume they did not make any commit.

Contribution quality measures

We assume that with the knowledge transfer one of the major benefits developers receive is the improvement of the quality of their contributions (*i.e.,* PRs) over time. While there are a few existing metrics to evaluate code quality (see *e.g.,* Chidamber and Kemerer (CK) metrics [SK03] and bug count [MCP+09]), some limitations hinder their applications in our study context: 1) The software repositories involved can be written in different programming languages, making it impossible to set universal thresholds for CK metrics, let alone not all programming languages are object-oriented. 2) Metrics like bug count rely on the assumption that bugs can be identified thanks to the consistent usage of issue tracking systems, which is not always the case.We do not pick repositories of specific languages or programming domains as we believe knowledge gained from different types of projects can still be beneficial. In our study we adopt quality contribution measures which are independent from the programming language and application domain. Thanks to the code review process, the contribution quality can be manually evaluated by peers, and the corresponding feedback can be mined. For each submitted PR, we use the following contribution quality measures as dependent variables:

General comments received. The number of general comments received from all the developers other than the PR author. We expect that with the increase of past reviewed PRs (*i.e.,* with more knowledge transfer the developer benefited of), fewer discussions will be triggered by the PR, thus leading to a reduction of general comments.

Source code comments received. The number of source code comments received from all the developers other than the PR author. Similarly to general comments received, we would expect that the *source code comments received* will decrease over time as well.

Acceptance Rate. The rate of the past PRs acceptance. We expect that the percentage of accepted PRs over time will increase.

Accepted PR closing time. The time (in minutes) between the creation and the closing of the accepted PRs. We expect that the time needed to accept PRs will decrease over time.

Sentiment of source code comments. The sentiment polarity of all source code comments in the PRs. We expect that with the increase of contribution quality more appreciation will be received in the code review. Thus, the sentiment of the developer embedded in the comments should be increasingly positive over time.

Sentiment of general comments. The sentiment polarity of all the general comments in the PRs. Similarly to source code comments, we expect general comments will also be more positive over time.

Sentiment analysis. To calculate the sentiment polarity of the comments in the PRs, we adopted SENTISTRENGTH-SE [IZ18b] and SENTI4SD [CLMN18]. Both tools are designed to work on software-related datasets. For each PR, we aggregate all comments and feed them into these two sentiment analysis tools. Comments are not considered if 1) they are empty, which is possible in general comments when the reviewer just assigns a status to the PR (*e.g.,* "Approved"); or 2) the text contains special characters other than English letters, numbers, punctuation, or emoticons.

SENTISTRENGTH-SE returns a negative sentiment score (from -1 to -5) and a sentiment score (from +1 to +5). We summed up the two scores and standardized the result in the following way, as suggested by the original authors:

1. a new score "-1" is assigned if the sum is lower than -1;

2. a new score "0" is assigned if the sum is in [-1; 1];

3. a new score "1" is assigned if the sum is higher than 1.

SENTI4SD returns three sentiment polarity categories (*i.e.,* "positive", "negative" or "neutral"), and we standardized these values to "-1", "0", and "1", respectively.

E.3.4 Data Analysis

Our hypothesis suggests that developers, who benefited of higher knowledge transfer thanks to the past reviewed PRs they submitted, are also the ones contributing higher quality PRs in the project. We verify this hypothesis thanks to the data previously extracted: Each peer-reviewed PR_i submitted by any of the studied developers represents a row in our dataset, reporting *(i)* the *knowledge transfer measures*, meaning the number of past reviewed PRs performed by the developer before PR_i as well as our control variable, represented by the number of commits she performed in the past (*i.e.,* before PR_i); and *(ii)* the *contribution quality measures* (*i.e.,* acceptance of PRs, number of general comments, etc.). However, the *contribution quality measures* cannot be only computed for the current PR. Indeed, this would make our analysis heavily biased by outliers. For example, a developer having a certain level of *knowledge transfer measures* may have submitted nine PRs before PR_i, having all of them accepted but PR_i. Indicating a 90% acceptance rate as a proxy for the quality of her recent contributions would be more representative of the actual facts rather than reporting a 0% since only considering PR_i. Therefore, we rely on a *fixed sliding window with a length of five PRs* to compute the *contribution quality measures* for each row in our dataset. Instead of reporting the *contribution quality measures* only for PR_i, we compute these measures on the most recent five PRs (including PR_i) submitted by PR_i's author. There are two exceptions to this process. First, for the measure *accepted PR closing time* we consider the most recent five *accepted* PRs. Second, for the sentiment polarity, we only considered the comments in PR_i, since there is a guarantee that PR_i contains at least one comment. We ignore the history of each developer before she performed at least five PRs. This ensures that there are always five PRs falling into the *fixed sliding window*.

Following the above-described process, we created two different datasets, named *cross-project scenario* and *single-project scenario*. In the first, we consider all PRs and all commits performed across all repositories to which a developer contributed, assuming that knowledge acquired thanks to the code review process performed on project P_x, can help developers in submitting better contributions not only to project P_x, but also to project P_y. While both datasets contain one row for each PR performed by the developer in any repository, they differ in the way we compute the *knowledge transfer measures* and the *contribution quality measures*. Given a row in the dataset representing the PR_i, in the *single-project scenario* only PRs and commits performed in the past by the developer in the same project PR_i belongs to are considered. This means, for example, that a developer who made 50 PRs in the past, only 12 of which belong to the same project as PR_i, will get 12 as the number of past reviewed PRs she submitted in the row corresponding to PR_i. Differently, in the *cross-project scenario*, these measures are computed by considering all PRs and commits submitted in any project by PR_i's developer (50 in the example).

Once the datasets were created, we split their rows (*i.e.*, contributions representing PRs) based on the *knowledge transfer measures* of the developer who submitted them. In particular, we extract the first (Q1), second (Q2), and third (Q3) quartile of the distributions for the *number of past reviewed PRs submitted* and the *number of past commits* performed by developers. Then, we split the rows into four groups based on the *number of past reviewed PRs submitted*: *low* ($\leq$ Q1), *medium-low* ($>$ Q1 & $\leq$ Q2), *medium-high* ($>$ Q2 & $\leq$ Q3), and *high* ($>$ Q3). Note that, while a contribution (*i.e.*, a row in our dataset) can only appear in one of these groups, the PRs submitted by a developer can appear in more than one group, since her *number of past reviewed PRs submitted* increases over time. We perform the same grouping also for the *number of past commits*. Table E.1 lists the value ranges of each "knowledge" measure (the value denoted by n) for each group in both *cross-project* and *single-project* scenarios. For example, when we are considering the single project scenario and the knowledge measure # past reviewed PRs, all the PRs whose author made up to eleven PRs in the past fall into the *low experience group*.

Statistical methods

For both *cross-project* and *single-project* scenarios and each of the experience measures (*i.e.*, # past reviewed PRs, # past commits), we compare via box plots the contribution quality measures in different knowledge groups. The comparisons are

Table E.1. Groups for each "knowledge" measure

Knowledge measure	Knowledge group	Study scenario	
		Single project	Cross project
# past reviewed PRs	low	n≤11	n≤19
	median-low	11<n≤26	19<n≤46
	median-high	26<n≤64	46<n≤110
	high	n>64	n>110
# past commits	low	n≤20	n≤52
	median-low	20<n≤67	52<n≤171
	median-high	67<n≤215	171<n≤446
	high	n>215	n>446

also performed via the Mann-Whitney test [Con99], with results intended as statistically significant at $\alpha = 0.05$. Mann-Whitney test is a robust non-parametric test when we did not know *a priori* (and we could not assume) what kind of distribution of data we had [Mot10]. To control the impact of multiple pairwise comparisons (*e.g.,* the *"low knowledge group"* is compared with all the other three groups), we adjust *p*-values with Holm's correction [Hol79]. We estimate the magnitude of the differences by using the Cliff's Delta (d), a non-parametric effect size measure. We follow well-established guidelines to interpret the effect size: negligible for $|d| < 0.148$, small for $0.148 \leq |d| < 0.33$, medium for $0.33 \leq |d| < 0.474$, and large for $|d| \geq 0.474$ [GK05].

Note that, before running these analyses, we first remove outliers from the compared data distributions. Given Q1 and Q3 the first and third quartile of a given distribution, and IQR the interquartile range computed as Q3-Q1, we remove all values lower than Q1-(1.5×IQR) or higher than Q3+(1.5×IQR)[Tuk77]. This was done for the analyses carried out for *(i)* the number of *general comments received, (ii)* the number of *source code comments received*, and *(iii)* the *accepted PR closing time*. This was instead not needed for the percentage of accepted PRs (as it is always between 0 and 1), and for the comment sentiment scores (always between -1 and 1).

E.4   Results

The box plots in Figures E.1, E.2, E.3, and E.4 show the trends of the dependent variables (*i.e., the contribution quality measures*), for both the cross- (left) and single-(right) project scenarios, with respect to the two independent variables (*i.e., the knowledge measures*).

In particular, the top part of each figure reports the results obtained when splitting developers into "knowledge groups" based on the past reviewed PRs they submitted, while the bottom part shows the same results when grouping developers based on the number of past commits they performed. The red dot represents the mean value in each box plot.

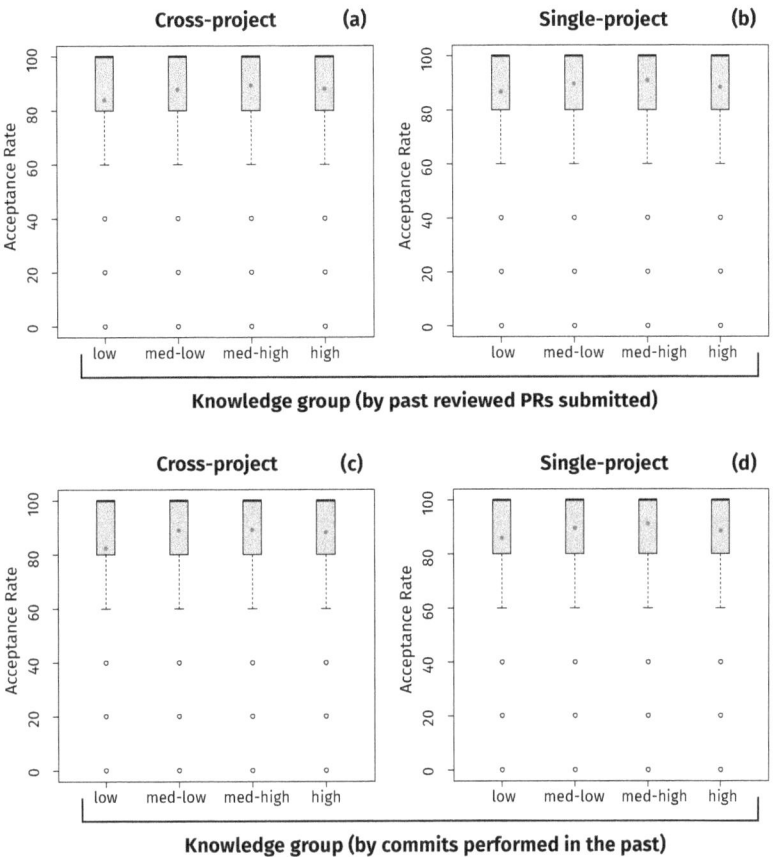

Figure E.1. Acceptance rate for PRs submitted by developers.

In Table E.2, we report the results of the Mann-Whitney test and Cliff's Delta for past reviewed PRs in the cross-project scenario. The same analyses are reported in Tables E.3 (cross-project) and E.4 (single-project) for past commits. Due to lack of space, the tables only report results of comparisons that are *(i)* statistically significant (*i.e.,* adjusted p-value lower than 0.05), and *(ii)* have at least a small effect size (*i.e.,* Cliff's $|d| \geq 0.148$). For the same reason, the table reporting the results achieved in the single-project scenario when using past reviewed PRs as independent variable is not reported, since all comparisons where either not significant or with a negligible effect size. Tables reporting the complete results of the statistical analyses are available in our replication package [CLB+].

In the following, we discuss the achieved results grouping them by dependent variable, commenting the results obtained when using both the past PRs and the past number of commits as criteria to split developers into "knowledge groups".

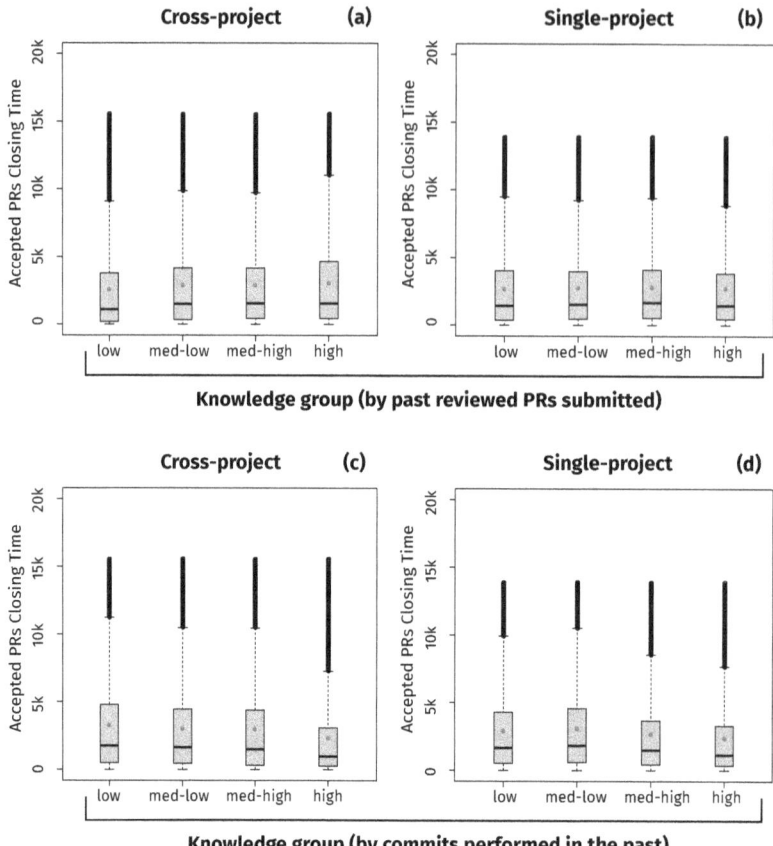

Figure E.2. Closing time (in minutes) for PRs submitted by developers.

E.4.1 PRs Acceptance Rate

From Fig. E.1 (a) and (b), we can observe an almost flat trend of the *Acceptance Rate* (expressed in percentage) of PRs when the past reviewed PRs submitted by a developer serve as a proxy for her knowledge. That is, at least by looking at Fig. E.1 (top part), we did not observe any effect of the knowledge transfer on the likelihood of future PRs to be accepted. Looking at the results of the statistical tests, we can also observe that none of the performed comparisons have at least a small effect size (see Table E.2). Concerning our "control variable," meaning the number of commits, we achieved a slight different result: significant differences (with at least a small effect size) can be observed between the knowledge groups (see Table E.3). However, this only holds: 1) in the cross-project scenario (no such differences are observed in the single-project setting), and 2) when comparing the *low* group with the top two groups (*i.e., medium-high* and *high*), as well as comparing *medium-low* and *high*. Actually, the effect of the experience acquired through commits over time seems to have an imperceptibly higher impact on the acceptance rate of future PRs as compared to the experience gained through past PRs (compare top and bottom part of Fig. E.1).

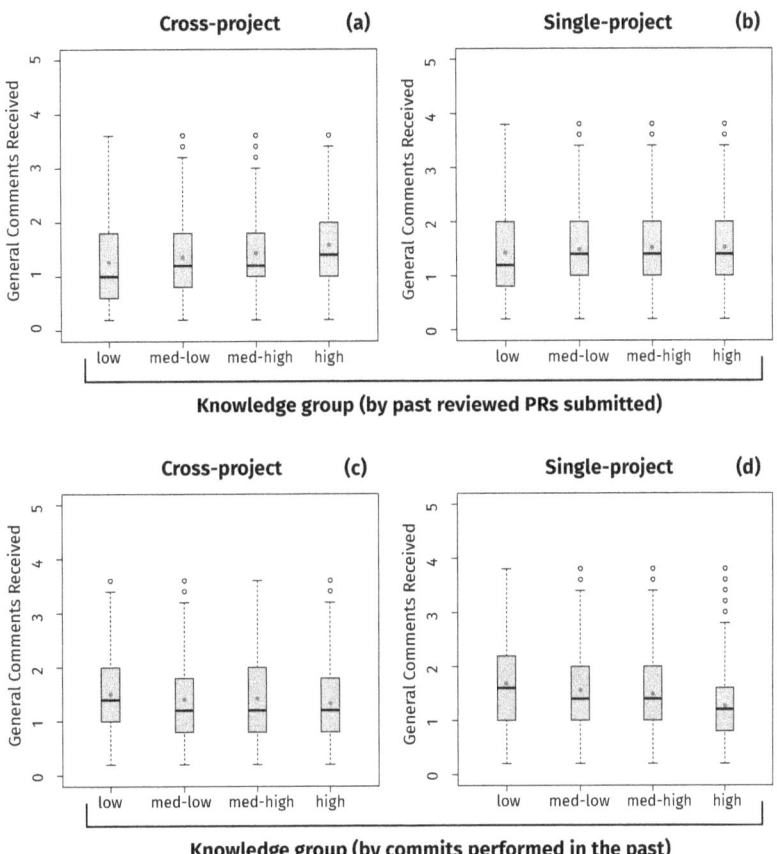

Figure E.3. Number of general comments for PRs submitted by developers.

To summarize, we do not observe any apparent positive impact of the past reviewed PRs submitted by a developer on the likelihood that her future PRs will be accepted (contradicting some previous findings in the literature, *e.g.,* [CSM19, RR14, SdLJMP15a, TDH14]). Note, however, that we adopted a completely different experimental design, and we only considered past reviewed PRs as independent variable.

Instead, developers are more likely to improve their PR acceptance along with the increase of their committing experience (as observed through the commits-based analysis).

E.4.2 Accepted PRs Closing Time

As for the *accepted PR closing time*, the top part of Fig. E.2 is also quite flat, for both cross- and single-project scenarios. This finding is also supported by the results of the statistical analysis, reporting *negligible* effect sizes for all performed comparisons.

Such a result was quite surprising for us, since we expected that the higher the knowledge acquired by developers through PRs, the lower the closing time of their accepted PRs. While we do not have any empirical evidence to explain the lack of such a trend, one possibility is that more experienced developers are responsible for

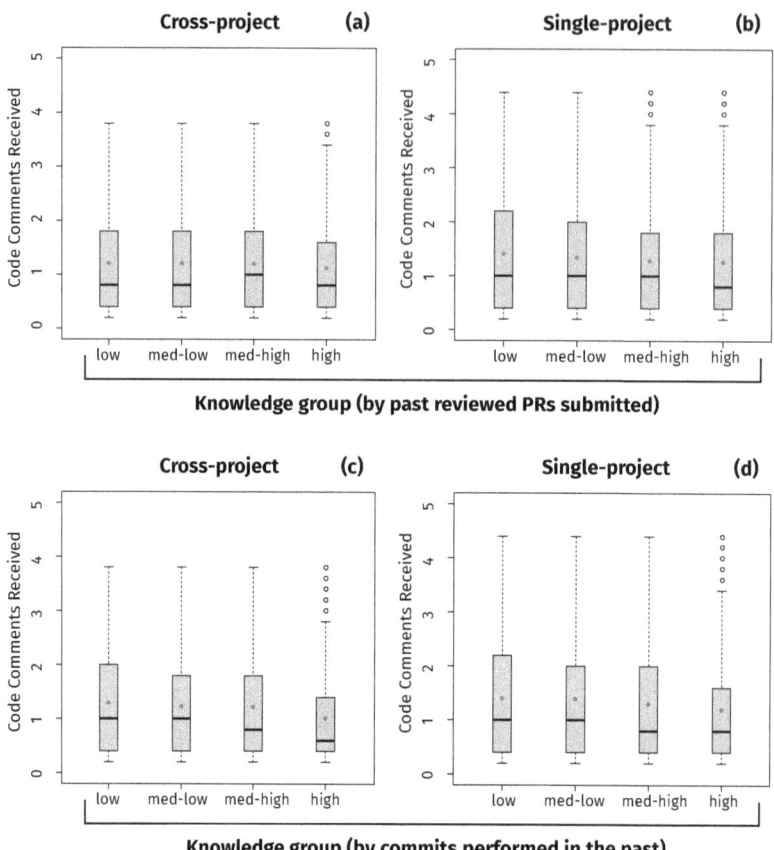

Figure E.4. Number of source code comments for PRs submitted by developers.

more complex PRs, that require longer reviewing time thus "nullifying" the advantage brought by the acquired knowledge. Such a finding would be in line with what discussed by Zeller in his book *Why Programs Fail* [Zel09], in which the author reports that Erich Gamma, the master developer of Eclipse, was the second most defect-prone Eclipse developer. The explanation for such a finding was indeed that more experienced developers tend to perform more complex and critical tasks [Zel09].

When performing the same analysis for the *past commits* independent variable (bottom part of Fig. E.2), we observe a slight decrease of reviewing time when moving from the *low* toward the *high* group in the cross-project scenario, with the statistical tests reporting a significant difference with a non-negligible effect size only when comparing the *low* and the *high* groups (see Table E.3).

E.4.3   Comments Posted in PRs

We discuss together our findings for both the number of *general comments* (Fig. E.3) and *source code comments* (Fig. E.4) posted in the PRs submitted by different groups of developers. We first focus on the top part of both figures (*i.e.,* results related to the past reviewed PRs).

Table E.2. Cross-project scenario - Knowledge groups created by past PRs: Results of the Mann-Whitney test (adj. p-value) and Cliff's Delta (d). We only report results of comparisons that are: *(i)* statistically significant and *(ii)* have at least a *small* effect size.

Test	Adj. p-value	d
Acceptance Rate		
No significant differences with at least small d		
Accepted PR Closing Time		
No significant differences with at least small d		
General Comments Received		
low *vs* medium-high	**<0.01**	-0.15 (Small)
low *vs* high	**<0.01**	-0.27 (Small)
medium-low *vs* high	**<0.01**	-0.19 (Small)
Source Code Comments Received		
No significant differences with at least small d		
Sentiment Analysis on General Comments: SENTISTRENGTH-SE		
No significant differences with at least small d		
Sentiment Analysis on General Comments: SENTI4SD		
No significant differences with at least small d		
Sentiment Analysis on Code Comments: SENTISTRENGTH-SE		
No significant differences with at least small d		
Sentiment Analysis on Code Comments: SENTI4SD		
No significant differences with at least small d		

These two figures together tell an interesting story. While developers who acquired more knowledge over time receive more general comments (possibly indicating the higher complexity of the changes they implement), the number of *source code comments*, meaning specific recommendations on how to improve the code, does not increase with the increase of the knowledge. This means that, despite the PRs submitted by developers who performed a higher number of reviewed PRs in the past are discussed more, they do not receive a higher number of comments for source code. This is also confirmed by the statistical tests for the cross-project scenario (see Table E.2), with: 1) significant differences observed for the number of general comments received in the *low* and *medium-low* groups when compared with the *high* group, as well as in the *low* group when compared with the *medium-low* group, and 2) no differences found for what concerns the number of received code comments among the different groups. When looking at the commits-based analysis (bottom part of Figures E.3 and E.4), significant differences with a small effect size can be observed regarding the number of general comments received when comparing the *high*

Table E.3. Cross-project scenario - Knowledge groups created by past commits: Results of Mann-Whitney test (adj. *p*-value) and Cliff's Delta (*d*). We only report results of comparisons that are *(i)* statistically significant, and *(ii)* have at least a *small* effect size.

Test	Adj. *p*-value	*d*
Acceptance Rate		
low *vs* medium-low	**<0.01**	-0.16 (Small)
low *vs* medium-high	**<0.01**	-0.16 (Small)
low *vs* high	**<0.01**	-0.21 (Small)
Accepted PR Closing Time		
low *vs* high	**<0.01**	0.17 (Small)
General Comments Received		
No significant differences with at least small *d*		
Source Code Comments Received		
low *vs* high	**<0.01**	0.16 (Small)
Sentiment Analysis on General Comments: SENTISTRENGTH-SE		
low *vs* high SSE	**<0.01**	0.16 (Small)
Sentiment Analysis on General Comments: SENTI4SD		
low *vs* high 4SD	**<0.01**	0.17 (Small)
Sentiment Analysis on Code Comments: SENTISTRENGTH-SE		
No significant differences with at least small *d*		
Sentiment Analysis on Code Comments: SENTI4SD		
No significant differences with at least small *d*		

group to all other groups (see Table E.4) in single-project scenario. Meanwhile, similar differences can also be found when comparing the source code comments received between the *low* group and the *high* group in cross-project scenario.

Overall, the comments posted during the PRs reviewing process seem to be the only dependent variable in our study for which we observed some possible positive influence of the knowledge acquired in the code review process. Indeed, while PRs submitted by more experienced developers (in terms of reviewed PRs they submitted in the past) are more discussed, they do not receive more requests for code changes. Such an effect is also visible when using the past commits as independent variable in single-project setting.

E.4.4 Sentiment Polarity of Comments

As far as the Sentiment Polarity is concerned, we do not show any box plot for space reason (they are available in our replication package [CLB+]). However, the results of the statistical tests are reported in the Tables E.2 (cross-project, past PRs), E.3 (cross-

Table E.4. Single-project scenario - Knowledge groups created by past commits: Results of Mann-Whitney test (adj. p-value) and Cliff's Delta (d). We only report results of comparisons that are *(i)* statistical significant, and *(ii)* have at least a *small* effect size.

Test	Adj. p-value	d
Acceptance Rate		
No significant differences with at least *small d*		
Accepted PR Closing Time		
No significant differences with at least *small d*		
General Comments Received		
low *vs* high	**<0.01**	0.31 (Small)
medium-low *vs* high	**<0.01**	0.21 (Small)
medium-high *vs* high	**<0.01**	0.16 (Small)
Source Code Comments Received		
No significant differences with at least *small d*		
Sentiment Analysis on General Comments: SENTISTRENGTH-SE		
No significant differences with at least *small d*		
Sentiment Analysis on General Comments: SENTI4SD		
No significant differences with at least *small d*		
Sentiment Analysis on Code Comments: SENTISTRENGTH-SE		
No significant differences with at least *small d*		
Sentiment Analysis on Code Comments: SENTI4SD		
No significant differences with at least *small d*		

project, past commits), and E.4 (local-project, past commits). As previously said, no results are reported for the local-project scenario when using past PRs due to the non-significant p-values and/or negligible d effect size achieved in all comparisons.

We found that neither positive nor negative polarities in the source code discussions prevail in both the cross and single-project studies. Such an outcome is plausible due to the fact that code review discussions mostly concern topics like *(i)* defect detecting, *(ii)* reviewer assigning, *(iii)* contribution encouraging, and so on [LYY+17]. Second, only the comparison of sentiment polarity in general comments between the *low* group and the *high* group provides a significant result (*i.e.,* the two extremes, with "newcomers" and very experienced developers). In this case, we found that the sentiment polarity is generally higher in discussions related to PRs opened by developers in the *low* group in the cross-project scenario. This may be due to the fact that reviewers tend to be more positive with newcomers to not discourage them in contributing again in the future. Note that the findings related to the sentiment polarity of comments are confirmed by both sentiment analysis tools used in our study.

E.4.5 Answering our Research Question

Our study led to what we can define a negative result. For most of the analyzed dependent variables we did not find any strong impact of the knowledge transfer in the code review process on the quality of the contributions submitted by developers in open source projects. In particular, for the *PRs acceptance rate*, we did not observe positive effects in the cross-project scenario when using past PRs as a proxy for knowledge transfer. Instead, an increase of experience over time might be more important for the improvement of the *PRs acceptance rate*, as demonstrated by the obtained results when using past commits as independent variable.

For the *closing time of accepted PRs*, most of the times we found no impact of the knowledge acquired in past PRs. As said, this may be due to the fact that more experienced developers tend to submit more complex PRs that, in some way, nullify the shorter reviewing time they would benefit of otherwise. Additional investigations are needed to understand the reasons behind such a result.

The *comments posted in PRs* are the only dependent variables for which we observed some influence of the knowledge acquired in past reviewed PRs. Indeed, while the PRs submitted by developers in the *high* group are generally more discussed, they receive a similar amount of recommendations for improving the contributed code, indicating a higher quality of the submitted PR. Also, such a phenomenon was not observable when using commits as independent variable in the cross-project scenario. Finally, no major differences were observed in the polarity of sentiments for comments posted in PRs submitted by developers having different levels of knowledge as assessed by both past PRs and past commits.

Overall, our findings failed to provide some quantitative evidence about the benefits brought by a code review process in improving developers' skills over time. The reasons behind such a result certainly deserve additional investigation, since knowledge transfer is one of the main motivations for modern code review. We believe that different experiments, using different experimental designs (*e.g.*, different dependent and independent variables) are needed to corroborate or contradict our findings.

E.5 Threats to Validity

To comprehend the strengths and limitations of our study, the threats that could affect the results and their generalization are presented and discussed here. Despite our efforts to mitigate as many threats to validity as possible, some are still unavoidable.

Threats to *construct validity* concern the relation between the theory and the observation, and in this work are mainly due to the measurements we performed:

The way in which we measured knowledge transfer in code review. There are no accepted metrics to quantitatively assess the notion of knowledge transfer, especially in a context, such as that of mining software repositories, in which there is no direct access to the studied developers. We assumed that the number of past reviewed PRs, that have been submitted by a developer, represent a good proxy of the knowledge transfer that developer has benefited of. To at least mitigate the threat represented by such an assumption, we only considered past PRs that actually received at least one comment by a peer developer. This should at least ensure that a review process was actually carried out for the considered PRs. These measures may not precisely capture the knowledge transfer process given its complex nature. Based on our study (design and outcomes), additional investigations are needed to understand which quantitative proxies can best quantify the knowledge gained during code review process.

The measures used to assess the quality of contributions over time. We adopt a number of indicators that should reasonably be related to the quality of the contributions submitted by a developer via PRs. For example, we assumed that a higher acceptance rate of the submitted PRs is related to higher quality contributions. While such assumption might look reasonable, there might be corner cases in which they do not hold, *e.g.,* PRs accepted despite the fact that they provide a sub-optimal solution, maybe due to the need for fixing, at least partially, a blocking bug. Also, one of our measures (*i.e.,* closing time of accepted PRs) is based on time-related aspects that, when mined from software repositories, can bring noise to the performed measurements. Indeed, there is no guarantee that a review process started right after the PR submission. Thus, longer/shorter reviewing times might be due to factors completely unrelated to the quality/complexity of the submitted contribution.

The approach for mapping GitHub user names to commit author names. There is still a possibility that some developers might use identities we did not discover, or intentionally hide their identities when authoring commits. However, by iterative linking process and manual inspection, we believe the impact has been limited to the possible minimum.

The sentiment polarity assessment provided by sentiment analysis tools. Previous studies showed that state-of-the-art sentiment analysis tools provide poor performance when used in context different from the ones they have been designed for [LZB$^+$18]. Both tools we adopted [IZ18b, CLMN18] have been designed to work on software-related data. However, they have been experimented on different datasets as compared to the one used in this chapter and, as a consequence, their performance on the PR comments can be different from the one reported in the original papers.

Threats to *internal validity* concern external factors we did not consider that could affect the variables and the relations being investigated. The differences observed between the groups of developers we created may be due to several confounding factors (*e.g.,* developers performing more PRs acquire more skills over time not due to the code review process, but thanks to the accumulated experience). For this reason, we also replicated our analyses by using the number of past commits to split the developers into "knowledge groups". This helped, for example, to provide a better interpretation of the results achieved for the *PRs acceptance rate* independent variable.

Threats to *conclusion validity* concern the relation between the treatment and the outcome. Wherever necessary, we used suitable statistical inferences to support our conclusions: we used the Mann-Whitney test (with adjusted *p*-values due to multiple comparisons) and Cliff's *d* effect size.

Threats to *external validity* concern the generalizability of our findings. We tried to achieve high generalizability by considering the complete contribution history of 728 developers, for a total of 32,062 PRs spanning 4,981 repositories. Also, we did not apply any filter related to the programming language, since all the steps of our study are language-independent.

E.6 Conclusions

We presented a quantitative study to investigate knowledge transfer in code review. Our results were mostly negative: we were not able to capture the positive role played by code review in knowledge transfer among developers, as was previously suggested in the literature [BB13]. This came to us as a surprise, as we were confident to see at least significant traces of the knowledge transfer, because despite not supporting the findings of Bacchelli and Bird [BB13] given our results, we actually are convinced that their claims are correct. This raises a number of questions that we have addressed in part throughout the latter part of the chapter, where we conjecture possible fallacies in our experiment design and notable threats to validity that are difficult to fully address, especially those regarding the measures we used to quantify the impact of knowledge transfer.

We stress the fact that our findings do not contradict previous qualitative results reported in the literature, but rather call for additional investigations aimed at understanding how (and if) we can actually capture the knowledge transfer in code review in a quantitative way. Therefore, our main direction for future work includes additional studies investigating the same research questions with a different experimental design. Specifically, we will investigate which measures can be used as a precise proxy to represent the knowledge transfer, in both quantitative and qualitative way.

The data used in our study is publicly available [CLB+].

Datasets

During our studies, we have manually created multiple datasets. We present these datasets here, such that researchers can use them to either tune their own approaches, or validate relevant techniques. All the datasets can be found at `https://github.com/bin-lin/datasets`.

F.1 Sentiment Polarity Analysis in Software Engineering Contexts

F.1.1 Dataset of Mobile App Reviews

This dataset contains 341 sentiment-annotated sentences from app reviews. The app reviews were originally collected by Villarroel *et al.* [VBR⁺16]. We manually labeled the sentiment of each review. Three scores are used to represent the sentiment: 1 for positive, 0 for neutral, and -1 for negative. The dataset contains 130 positive, 25 neutral, and 186 negative reviews. The dataset can be found in the "`Sentiment/AppReviews`" folder.

F.1.2 Dataset of Stack Overflow Discussions

This dataset contains 1,500 sentences extracted from Stack Overflow discussions and 20k intermediate nodes composing these sentences. All of them are annotated with sentiment polarities. For the 1,500 sentences, three scores are used to represent the sentiment: 1 for positive, 0 for neutral, and -1 for negative. For the intermediate nodes, we present them in the Penn Tree Bank (PTB) format, which can be directly used by STANFORD CORENLP: 4 represents positive, 3 slightly positive, 2 neutral, 1 slightly negative, and 0 negative. The dataset can be found in the folder named "`Sentiment/StackOverflow`".

F.2 Mining Opinions from Q&A Sites to Support Software Design Decisions

F.2.1 Dataset of API-Related Opinions

This dataset contains 1,662 sentences extracted from Stack Overflow discussions. Each sentence is annotated with the sentiment polarity and its corresponding quality aspects. The dataset can be found in the "POME/API" folder.

F.2.2 Dataset of pome and Opiner

This dataset contains 205 sentences extracted by POME and 208 sentences extracted by OPINER. They are annotated in the same way as the "dataset of API-related opinions". Additionally, this dataset also include the original prediction results of POME and OPINER. The dataset can be found in the folder named "POME/Tools".

F.3 On The Quality of Identifiers in Test Code

This dataset contains 283 identifiers extracted from test code and 47 identifiers extracted from production code. Each identifier is annotated with its location in the project files, good attributes of the naming, bad attributes of the naming, proposals for a new name, and other remarks. The dataset can be found in the "TestID" folder.

Bibliography

[AAP+18] Giuliano Antoniol, Kamel Ayari, Massimiliano Di Penta, Foutse Khomh, and Yann-Gaël Guéhéneuc. Is it a bug or an enhancement?: a text-based approach to classify change requests. In *Proceedings of the 28th Annual International Conference on Computer Science and Software Engineering (CASCON 2018)*, pages 2–16. ACM, 2018.

[AARS20] Md. Ahasanuzzaman, Muhammad Asaduzzaman, Chanchal K. Roy, and Kevin A. Schneider. CAPS: a supervised technique for classifying stack overflow posts concerning API issues. *Empirical Software Engineering*, 25(2):1493–1532, 2020.

[AAT+12] Surafel Lemma Abebe, Venera Arnaoudova, Paolo Tonella, Giuliano Antoniol, and Yann-Gaël Guéhéneuc. Can lexicon bad smells improve fault prediction? In *Proceedings of the 19th Working Conference on Reverse Engineering (WCRE 2012)*, pages 235–244. IEEE Computer Society, 2012.

[ABBS14] Miltiadis Allamanis, Earl T. Barr, Christian Bird, and Charles A. Sutton. Learning natural coding conventions. In *Proceedings of the 22nd ACM SIGSOFT International Symposium on Foundations of Software Engineering (FSE 2014)*, pages 281–293. ACM, 2014.

[ABBS15] Miltiadis Allamanis, Earl T. Barr, Christian Bird, and Charles A. Sutton. Suggesting accurate method and class names. In *Proceedings of the 2015 10th Joint Meeting on Foundations of Software Engineering (ESEC/FSE 2015)*, pages 38–49. ACM, 2015.

[ABIR17] Toufique Ahmed, Amiangshu Bosu, Anindya Iqbal, and Shahram Rahimi. Senticr: a customized sentiment analysis tool for code review interactions. In *Proceedings of the 32nd IEEE/ACM International Conference on Automated Software Engineering (ASE 2017)*, pages 106–111. IEEE Computer Society, 2017.

[AEO+10] Venera Arnaoudova, Laleh Mousavi Eshkevari, Rocco Oliveto, Yann-Gaël Guéhéneuc, and Giuliano Antoniol. Physical and conceptual identifier dispersion: Measures and relation to fault proneness. In *Proceedings of the 26th IEEE International Conference on Software Maintenance (ICSM 2010)*, pages 1–5. IEEE Computer Society, 2010.

[AHK18] Ryo Arima, Yoshiki Higo, and Shinji Kusumoto. Toward refactoring evaluation with code naturalness. In *Proceedings of the 26th Conference on Program Comprehension (ICPC 2018)*, pages 316–319. ACM, 2018.

[AHTM09] Surafel Lemma Abebe, Sonia Haiduc, Paolo Tonella, and Andrian Mar-
          cus. Lexicon bad smells in software. In *Proceedings of the 16th Working
          Conference on Reverse Engineering (WCRE 2009)*, pages 95–99. IEEE
          Computer Society, 2009.

[AKU⁺19] Ikram El Asri, Noureddine Kerzazi, Gias Uddin, Foutse Khomh, and
          Mohammed Amine Janati Idrissi. An empirical study of sentiments in
          code reviews. *Information and Software Technology*, 114:37–54, 2019.

[ANVZ14] Dimitrios Athanasiou, Ariadi Nugroho, Joost Visser, and Andy Zaid-
          man. Test code quality and its relation to issue handling performance.
          IEEE Transactions on Software Engineering, 40(11):1100–1125, 2014.

[APA16]   Venera Arnaoudova, Massimiliano Di Penta, and Giuliano Antoniol.
          Linguistic antipatterns: what they are and how developers perceive
          them. *Empirical Software Engineering*, 21(1):104–158, 2016.

[AS14]   Miltiadis Allamanis and Charles A. Sutton. Mining idioms from source
          code. In *Proceedings of the 22nd ACM SIGSOFT International Sympo-
          sium on Foundations of Software Engineering (FSE 2014)*, pages 472–
          483. ACM, 2014.

[Ato20]   Issa Atoum. A novel framework for measuring software quality-in-
          use based on semantic similarity and sentiment analysis of software
          reviews. *Journal of King Saud University - Computer and Information
          Sciences*, 32(1):113 – 125, 2020.

[Bak95]   Brenda S. Baker. On finding duplication and near-duplication in large
          software systems. In *Proceedings of the 2nd Working Conference on Re-
          verse Engineering (WCRE 1995)*, pages 86–95. IEEE Computer Society,
          1995.

[BB13]   Alberto Bacchelli and Christian Bird. Expectations, outcomes, and
          challenges of modern code review. In *Proceedings of the 35th Inter-
          national Conference on Software Engineering (ICSE 2013)*, pages 712–
          721. IEEE Computer Society, 2013.

[BBD⁺14] Earl T. Barr, Yuriy Brun, Premkumar T. Devanbu, Mark Harman, and
          Federica Sarro. The plastic surgery hypothesis. In *Proceedings of the
          22nd ACM SIGSOFT International Symposium on Foundations of Soft-
          ware Engineering (FSE 2014)*, pages 306–317. ACM, 2014.

[BBZJ14] Moritz Beller, Alberto Bacchelli, Andy Zaidman, and Elmar Jürgens.
          Modern code reviews in open-source projects: which problems do they
          fix? In *Proceedings of the 11th Working Conference on Mining Software
          Repositories (MSR 2014)*, pages 202–211. ACM, 2014.

[BD08] Finn Olav Bjørnson and Torgeir Dingsøyr. Knowledge management in software engineering: A systematic review of studied concepts, findings and research methods used. *Information and Software Technology*, 50(11):1055–1068, 2008.

[BDL⁺13] Dave W. Binkley, Marcia Davis, Dawn J. Lawrie, Jonathan I. Maletic, Christopher Morrell, and Bonita Sharif. The impact of identifier style on effort and comprehension. *Empirical Software Engineering*, 18(2):219–276, 2013.

[BG13] Mario Bernhart and Thomas Grechenig. On the understanding of programs with continuous code reviews. In *Proceedings of the IEEE 21st International Conference on Program Comprehension (ICPC 2013)*, pages 192–198. IEEE Computer Society, 2013.

[BGB15] Amiangshu Bosu, Michaela Greiler, and Christian Bird. Characteristics of useful code reviews: An empirical study at microsoft. In *Proceedings of the 12th IEEE/ACM Working Conference on Mining Software Repositories (MSR 2015)*, pages 146–156. IEEE Computer Society, 2015.

[BGP⁺19] Moritz Beller, Georgios Gousios, Annibale Panichella, Sebastian Proksch, Sven Amann, and Andy Zaidman. Developer testing in the IDE: patterns, beliefs, and behavior. *IEEE Transactions on Software Engineering*, 45(3):261–284, 2019.

[BGPZ15] Moritz Beller, Georgios Gousios, Annibale Panichella, and Andy Zaidman. When, how, and why developers (do not) test in their ides. In *Proceedings of the 10th Joint Meeting of the European Software Engineering Conference and the ACM SIGSOFT Symposium on the Foundations of Software Engineering (ESEC/FSE 2015)*, pages 179–190. ACM, 2015.

[BGV92] Bernhard E. Boser, Isabelle Guyon, and Vladimir Vapnik. A training algorithm for optimal margin classifiers. In David Haussler, editor, *Proceedings of the 5th Annual ACM Conference on Computational Learning Theory (COLT 1992)*, pages 144–152. ACM, 1992.

[BHL11] David W. Binkley, Matthew Hearn, and Dawn J. Lawrie. Improving identifier informativeness using part of speech information. In *Proceedings of the 8th International Working Conference on Mining Software Repositories (MSR 2011)*, pages 203–206. ACM, 2011.

[BKHG13] Olga Baysal, Oleksii Kononenko, Reid Holmes, and Michael W. Godfrey. The influence of non-technical factors on code review. In *Proceedings of the 20th Working Conference on Reverse Engineering (WCRE 2013)*, pages 122–131. IEEE Computer Society, 2013.

[BLNS16] Tobias Baum, Olga Liskin, Kai Niklas, and Kurt Schneider. A faceted classification scheme for change-based industrial code review processes. In *Proceedings of the 2016 IEEE International Conference on Software Quality, Reliability and Security (QRS 2016)*, pages 74–85. IEEE, 2016.

[BMD⁺00] Magdalena Balazinska, Ettore Merlo, Michel Dagenais, Bruno Laguë, and Kostas Kontogiannis. Advanced clone-analysis to support object-oriented system refactoring. In *Proceedings of the Seventh Working Conference on Reverse Engineering (WCRE 2000)*, pages 98–107. IEEE Computer Society, 2000.

[BMG10] Mario Bernhart, Andreas Mauczka, and Thomas Grechenig. Adopting code reviews for agile software development. In *Proceedings of the 2010 Agile Conference (AGILE 2010)*, pages 44–47. IEEE Computer Society, 2010.

[BMM09] Marcel Bruch, Martin Monperrus, and Mira Mezini. Learning from examples to improve code completion systems. In *Proceedings of the 7th joint meeting of the European Software Engineering Conference and the ACM SIGSOFT International Symposium on Foundations of Software Engineering (ESEC/FSE 2009)*, pages 213–222. ACM, 2009.

[BMO13] Linda Barros, Pilar Rodríguez Marín, and Alvaro Ortigosa. Automatic classification of literature pieces by emotion detection: A study on quevedo's poetry. In *Proceedings of the 2013 Humaine Association Conference on Affective Computing and Intelligent Interaction (ACII 2013)*, pages 141–146. IEEE Computer Society, 2013.

[BQO⁺15] Gabriele Bavota, Abdallah Qusef, Rocco Oliveto, Andrea De Lucia, and Dave W. Binkley. Are test smells really harmful? an empirical study. *Empirical Software Engineering*, 20(4):1052–1094, 2015.

[BR15] Gabriele Bavota and Barbara Russo. Four eyes are better than two: On the impact of code reviews on software quality. In *Proceedings of the 2015 IEEE International Conference on Software Maintenance and Evolution (ICSME 2015)*, pages 81–90. IEEE Computer Society, 2015.

[BTZ07] Steven Burrows, Seyed MM Tahaghoghi, and Justin Zobel. Efficient plagiarism detection for large code repositories. *Software-Practice and Experience*, 37(2):151–176, 2007.

[But09] Simon Butler. The effect of identifier naming on source code readability and quality. In *Proceedings of the Joint 12th European Software Engineering Conference and 17th ACM SIGSOFT Symposium on the Foundations of Software Engineering (ESEC/FSE 2009)*, pages 33–34. ACM, 2009.

[BWY15] Simon Butler, Michel Wermelinger, and Yijun Yu. A survey of the forms of java reference names. In *Proceedings of the 2015 IEEE 23rd International Conference on Program Comprehension (ICPC 2015)*, pages 196–206. IEEE Computer Society, 2015.

[BWYS09] Simon Butler, Michel Wermelinger, Yijun Yu, and Helen Sharp. Relating identifier naming flaws and code quality: An empirical study. In *Proceedings of the 16th Working Conference on Reverse Engineering (WCRE 2009)*, pages 31–35. IEEE Computer Society, 2009.

[BWYS10] Simon Butler, Michel Wermelinger, Yijun Yu, and Helen Sharp. Exploring the influence of identifier names on code quality: An empirical study. In *Proceedings of the 14th European Conference on Software Maintenance and Reengineering (CSMR 2010)*, pages 156–165. IEEE Computer Society, 2010.

[CBHK02] Nitesh V. Chawla, Kevin W. Bowyer, Lawrence O. Hall, and W. Philip Kegelmeyer. Smote: synthetic minority over-sampling technique. *Journal of artificial intelligence research*, pages 321–357, 2002.

[CCL+19] Zhenpeng Chen, Yanbin Cao, Xuan Lu, Qiaozhu Mei, and Xuanzhe Liu. Sentimoji: an emoji-powered learning approach for sentiment analysis in software engineering. In *Proceedings of the ACM Joint Meeting on European Software Engineering Conference and Symposium on the Foundations of Software Engineering (ESEC/FSE 2019)*, pages 841–852. ACM, 2019.

[CDL+16] Steve Counsell, Giuseppe Destefanis, Xiaohui Liu, Sigrid Eldh, Andreas Ermedahl, and Kenneth Andersson. Comparing test and production code quality in a large commercial multicore system. In *Proceedings of the 42th Euromicro Conference on Software Engineering and Advanced Applications (SEAA 2016)*, pages 86–91. IEEE Computer Society, 2016.

[CDM13] Michael L. Collard, Michael John Decker, and Jonathan I. Maletic. srcml: An infrastructure for the exploration, analysis, and manipulation of source code: A tool demonstration. In *Proceedings of the 2013 IEEE International Conference on Software Maintenance (ICSM 2013)*, pages 516–519. IEEE Computer Society, 2013.

[CdS19] Jonathan Cheruvelil and Bruno C. da Silva. Developers' sentiment and issue reopening. In *Proceedings of the 4th International Workshop on Emotion Awareness in Software Engineering (SEmotion 2019)*, pages 29–33. IEEE / ACM, 2019.

[CG96] Stanley F. Chen and Joshua Goodman. An empirical study of smoothing techniques for language modeling. In *Proceedings of the 34th*

Annual Meeting of the Association for Computational Linguistics (ACL 1996), pages 310–318. Morgan Kaufmann Publishers / ACL, 1996.

[CGC10] Agustin Casamayor, Daniela Godoy, and Marcelo R. Campo. Identification of non-functional requirements in textual specifications: A semi-supervised learning approach. *Information and Software Technology*, 52(4):436–445, 2010.

[CGP07] Filippo Corbo, Concettina Del Grosso, and Massimiliano Di Penta. Smart formatter: Learning coding style from existing source code. In *Proceedings of the 23rd IEEE International Conference on Software Maintenance (ICSM 2007)*, pages 525–526. IEEE Computer Society, 2007.

[CGT15] Jacek Czerwonka, Michaela Greiler, and Jack Tilford. Code reviews do not find bugs. how the current code review best practice slows us down. In *Proceedings of the 37th IEEE/ACM International Conference on Software Engineering (ICSE 2015)*, pages 27–28. IEEE Computer Society, 2015.

[CHA14] Joshua Charles Campbell, Abram Hindle, and José Nelson Amaral. Syntax errors just aren't natural: improving error reporting with language models. In *Proceedings of the 11th Working Conference on Mining Software Repositories (MSR 2014)*, pages 252–261. ACM, 2014.

[CLB⁺] Maria Caulo, Bin Lin, Gabriele Bavota, Giuseppe Scanniello, and Michele Lanza. Replication package of the study "knowledge transfer in modern code review". https://tinyurl.com/wn9my8f.

[CLB⁺20] Maria Caulo, Bin Lin, Gabriele Bavota, Giuseppe Scanniello, and Michele Lanza. Knowledge transfer in modern code review. In *Proceedings of the 28th International Conference on Program Comprehension (ICPC 2020), accepted*, 2020.

[CLH⁺14] Ning Chen, Jialiu Lin, Steven C. H. Hoi, Xiaokui Xiao, and Boshen Zhang. AR-miner: Mining informative reviews for developers from mobile app marketplace. In *Proceedings of the 36th International Conference on Software Engineering (ICSE 2014)*, pages 767–778, 2014.

[CLMN18] Fabio Calefato, Filippo Lanubile, Federico Maiorano, and Nicole Novielli. Sentiment polarity detection for software development. *Empirical Software Engineering*, 23(3):1352–1382, 2018.

[CLN17] Fabio Calefato, Filippo Lanubile, and Nicole Novielli. Emotxt: A toolkit for emotion recognition from text. In *Proceedings of the 7th International Conference on Affective Computing and Intelligent Interaction Workshops and Demos (ACII 2017)*, pages 79–80. IEEE Computer Society, 2017.

[CMF18] Maëlick Claes, Mika Mäntylä, and Umar Farooq. On the use of emoticons in open source software development. In *Proceedings of the 12th ACM/IEEE International Symposium on Empirical Software Engineering and Measurement (ESEM 2018)*, pages 50:1–50:4. ACM, 2018.

[CMM12] Anna Corazza, Sergio Di Martino, and Valerio Maggio. LINSEN: an efficient approach to split identifiers and expand abbreviations. In *Proceedings of the 28th IEEE International Conference on Software Maintenance (ICSM 2012)*, pages 233–242. IEEE Computer Society, 2012.

[Coh92] Jacob Cohen. A power primer. *Psychological bulletin*, 112(1):155, 1992.

[Coh13] Jacob Cohen. *Statistical power analysis for the behavioral sciences*. Routledge, 2013.

[Con99] William J. Conover. Practical nonparametric statistics. 1999.

[CS07] Jack G. Conrad and Frank Schilder. Opinion mining in legal blogs. In *Proceedings of the 11th International Conference on Artificial Intelligence and Law (ICAIL 2007)*, pages 231–236. ACM, 2007.

[CSM19] Di Chen, Kathryn T. Stolee, and Tim Menzies. Replication can improve prior results: a github study of pull request acceptance. In Yann-Gaël Guéhéneuc, Foutse Khomh, and Federica Sarro, editors, *Proceedings of the 27th International Conference on Program Comprehension (ICPC 2019)*, pages 179–190. IEEE / ACM, 2019.

[CSPG17] Adelina Ciurumelea, Andreas Schaufelbühl, Sebastiano Panichella, and Harald C. Gall. Analyzing reviews and code of mobile apps for better release planning. In *Proceedings of the IEEE 24th International Conference on Software Analysis, Evolution and Reengineering (SANER 2017)*, pages 91–102. IEEE Computer Society, 2017.

[CT00] Bruno Caprile and Paolo Tonella. Restructuring program identifier names. In *Proceedings of the 2000 International Conference on Software Maintenance (ICSM 2000)*, pages 97–107. IEEE Computer Society, 2000.

[CT17] Brock Angus Campbell and Christoph Treude. NLP2Code: Code snippet content assist via natural language tasks. In *Proceedings of the 33rd IEEE International Conference on Software Maintenance and Evolution (ICSME 2017)*, pages 628–632, 2017.

[CW13] Laura V. Galvis Carreño and Kristina Winbladh. Analysis of user comments: an approach for software requirements evolution. In *Proceedings of the 35th International Conference on Software Engineering (ICSE 2013)*, pages 582–591. IEEE Computer Society, 2013.

[DH09]   Lipika Dey and S. K. Mirajul Haque. Opinion mining from noisy text data. *International Journal on Document Analysis and Recognition*, 12(3):205–226, 2009.

[DLP03] Kushal Dave, Steve Lawrence, and David M. Pennock. Mining the peanut gallery: opinion extraction and semantic classification of product reviews. In *Proceedings of the Twelfth International World Wide Web Conference (WWW 2003)*, pages 519–528. ACM, 2003.

[DMBK01] Arie Deursen, Leon M.F. Moonen, A. Bergh, and Gerard Kok. Refactoring test code. Technical report, Amsterdam, The Netherlands, The Netherlands, 2001.

[DOB⁺18] Giuseppe Destefanis, Marco Ortu, David Bowes, Michele Marchesi, and Roberto Tonelli. On measuring affects of github issues' commenters. In *Proceedings of the 3rd International Workshop on Emotion Awareness in Software Engineering (SEmotion 2018)*, pages 14–19. ACM, 2018.

[DP06]   Florian Deissenboeck and Markus Pizka. Concise and consistent naming. *Software Quality Journal*, 14(3):261–282, 2006.

[DRD99] Stéphane Ducasse, Matthias Rieger, and Serge Demeyer. A language independent approach for detecting duplicated code. In *Proceedings of the 1999 International Conference on Software Maintenance (ICSM 1999)*, pages 109–118. IEEE Computer Society, 1999.

[DRF17] Ermira Daka, José Miguel Rojas, and Gordon Fraser. Generating unit tests with descriptive names or: would you name your children thing1 and thing2? In *Proceedings of the 26th ACM SIGSOFT International Symposium on Software Testing and Analysis (ISSTA 2017)*, pages 57–67. ACM, 2017.

[DSJ⁺13] Cristian Danescu-Niculescu-Mizil, Moritz Sudhof, Dan Jurafsky, Jure Leskovec, and Christopher Potts. A computational approach to politeness with application to social factors. In *Proceedings of the 51st Annual Meeting of the Association for Computational Linguistics (ACL 2013)*, pages 250–259. The Association for Computer Linguistics, 2013.

[DY13]   Rahim Dehkharghani and Cemal Yilmaz. Automatically identifying a software product's quality attributes through sentiment analysis of tweets. In *Proceedings of the 1st International Workshop on Natural Language Analysis in Software Engineering (NaturaLiSE 2013)*, pages 25–30, 2013.

[EH04]   M Awad Elias and M Ghaziri Hassan. Knowledge management, 2004.

[EHPV09] Eric Enslen, Emily Hill, Lori L. Pollock, and K. Vijay-Shanker. Mining source code to automatically split identifiers for software analysis. In *Proceedings of the 6th International Working Conference on Mining Software Repositories (MSR 2009)*, pages 71–80. IEEE Computer Society, 2009.

[FA11] Gordon Fraser and Andrea Arcuri. Evosuite: automatic test suite generation for object-oriented software. In Tibor Gyimóthy and Andreas Zeller, editors, *Proceedings of the 19th ACM SIGSOFT Symposium on the Foundations of Software Engineering and 13th European Software Engineering Conference (SIGSOFT/FSE 2011)*, pages 416–419. ACM, 2011.

[FGR+18] Alessio Ferrari, Gloria Gori, Benedetta Rosadini, Iacopo Trotta, Stefano Bacherini, Alessandro Fantechi, and Stefania Gnesi. Detecting requirements defects with NLP patterns: an industrial experience in the railway domain. *Empirical Software Engineering*, 23(6):3684–3733, 2018.

[Fie13] Andy Field. *Discovering statistics using IBM SPSS statistics*. Sage, 2013.

[Fis22] R.A. Fisher. On the interpretation of χ^2 from contingency tables, and the calculation of p. *Journal of the Royal Statistical Society*, 85(1):87–92, 1922.

[FLL+13] Bin Fu, Jialiu Lin, Lei Li, Christos Faloutsos, Jason I. Hong, and Norman M. Sadeh. Why people hate your app: making sense of user feedback in a mobile app store. In *Proceedings of the 19th ACM SIGKDD International Conference on Knowledge Discovery and Data Mining (KDD 2013)*, pages 1276–1284. ACM, 2013.

[FM13] Asger Feldthaus and Anders Møller. Semi-automatic rename refactoring for javascript. In *Proceedings of the 2013 ACM SIGPLAN International Conference on Object Oriented Programming Systems Languages & Applications (OOPSLA 2013)*, pages 323–338. ACM, 2013.

[FMAA18] Sarah Fakhoury, Yuzhan Ma, Venera Arnaoudova, and Olusola O. Adesope. The effect of poor source code lexicon and readability on developers' cognitive load. In Foutse Khomh, Chanchal K. Roy, and Janet Siegmund, editors, *Proceedings of the 26th Conference on Program Comprehension (ICPC 2018)*, pages 286–296. ACM, 2018.

[FMS+17] Bjarke Felbo, Alan Mislove, Anders Søgaard, Iyad Rahwan, and Sune Lehmann. Using millions of emoji occurrences to learn any-domain representations for detecting sentiment, emotion and sarcasm. In *Proceedings of the 2017 Conference on Empirical Methods in Natural Language Processing (EMNLP 2017)*, pages 1615–1625. Association for Computational Linguistics, 2017.

[GAB15] Emitza Guzman, Omar Aly, and Bernd Bruegge. Retrieving diverse opinions from app reviews. In *Proceedings of the 2015 ACM/IEEE International Symposium on Empirical Software Engineering and Measurement (ESEM 2015)*, pages 21–30. IEEE Computer Society, 2015.

[GAL14] Emitza Guzman, David Azócar, and Yang Li. Sentiment analysis of commit comments in github: an empirical study. In *Proceedings of the 11th Working Conference on Mining Software Repositories (MSR 2014)*, pages 352–355. ACM, 2014.

[GAS17] Emitza Guzman, Rana Alkadhi, and Norbert Seyff. An exploratory study of twitter messages about software applications. *Requirements Engineering*, 22(3):387–412, 2017.

[GB13] Emitza Guzman and Bernd Bruegge. Towards emotional awareness in software development teams. In *Proceedings of the Joint Meeting of the European Software Engineering Conference and the ACM SIGSOFT Symposium on the Foundations of Software Engineering (ESEC/FSE 2013)*, pages 671–674. ACM, 2013.

[GK05] Robert J Grissom and John J Kim. *Effect sizes for research: A broad practical approach.* Lawrence Erlbaum Associates Publishers, 2005.

[GK15] Xiaodong Gu and Sunghun Kim. "what parts of your apps are loved by users?". In *Proceedings of the 30th IEEE/ACM International Conference on Automated Software Engineering (ASE 2015)*, pages 760–770. IEEE Computer Society, 2015.

[GM14] Emitza Guzman and Walid Maalej. How do users like this feature? A fine grained sentiment analysis of app reviews. In *Proceedings of the IEEE 22nd International Requirements Engineering Conference (RE 2014)*, pages 153–162. IEEE Computer Society, 2014.

[GMBV12] Michael Goul, Olivera Marjanovic, Susan Baxley, and Karen Vizecky. Managing the enterprise business intelligence app store: Sentiment analysis supported requirements engineering. In *Proceedings of the 45th Hawaii International International Conference on Systems Science (HICSS-45 2012)*, pages 4168–4177. IEEE Computer Society, 2012.

[GMPV13] Samir Gupta, Sana Malik, Lori L. Pollock, and K. Vijay-Shanker. Part-of-speech tagging of program identifiers for improved text-based software engineering tools. In *Proceedings of the IEEE 21st International Conference on Program Comprehension (ICPC 2013)*, pages 3–12. IEEE Computer Society, 2013.

[GPAG13] Latifa Guerrouj, Massimiliano Di Penta, Giuliano Antoniol, and Yann-Gaël Guéhéneuc. TIDIER: an identifier splitting approach using speech recognition techniques. *Journal of Software: Evolution and Process*, 25(6):575–599, 2013.

[GS10]   Mark Gabel and Zhendong Su. A study of the uniqueness of source code. In *Proceedings of the 18th ACM SIGSOFT International Symposium on Foundations of Software Engineering (FSE 2010)*, pages 147–156. ACM, 2010.

[GS17]   Anjali Goyal and Neetu Sardana. Nrfixer: Sentiment based model for predicting the fixability of non-reproducible bugs. *e-Informatica*, 11(1):103–116, 2017.

[GSGO18] Giovanni Grano, Simone Scalabrino, Harald C. Gall, and Rocco Oliveto. An empirical investigation on the readability of manual and generated test cases. In *Proceedings of the 26th Conference on Program Comprehension (ICPC 2018)*, pages 348–351. ACM, 2018.

[GZS13]   David García, Marcelo Serrano Zanetti, and Frank Schweitzer. The role of emotions in contributors activity: A case study on the GENTOO community. In *Proceedings of the 2013 International Conference on Cloud and Green Computing (CGC 2013)*, pages 410–417. IEEE Computer Society, 2013.

[HBL+14] Emily Hill, David W. Binkley, Dawn J. Lawrie, Lori L. Pollock, and K. Vijay-Shanker. An empirical study of identifier splitting techniques. *Empirical Software Engineering*, 19(6):1754–1780, 2014.

[HBS+12] Abram Hindle, Earl T. Barr, Zhendong Su, Mark Gabel, and Premkumar T. Devanbu. On the naturalness of software. In *Proceedings of the 34th International Conference on Software Engineering (ICSE 2012)*, pages 837–847. IEEE Computer Society, 2012.

[HCC17]   Ya-Han Hu, Yen-Liang Chen, and Hui-Ling Chou. Opinion mining from online hotel reviews - A text summarization approach. *Information Processing and Management*, 53(2):436–449, 2017.

[HCX+18] Yi Huang, Chunyang Chen, Zhenchang Xing, Tian Lin, and Yang Liu. Tell them apart: distilling technology differences from crowd-scale comparison discussions. In *Proceedings of the 33rd ACM/IEEE International Conference on Automated Software Engineering (ASE 2018)*, pages 214–224. ACM, 2018.

[HFB+08] Emily Hill, Zachary P. Fry, Haley Boyd, Giriprasad Sridhara, Yana Novikova, Lori L. Pollock, and K. Vijay-Shanker. AMAP: automatically mining abbreviation expansions in programs to enhance software maintenance tools. In *Proceedings of the 2008 International Working*

Conference on Mining Software Repositories (MSR 2008), pages 79–88.
ACM, 2008.

[HG14]   Clayton J. Hutto and Eric Gilbert. VADER: A parsimonious rule-based
         model for sentiment analysis of social media text. In *Proceedings of
         the 8th International Conference on Weblogs and Social Media (ICWSM
         2014)*. The AAAI Press, 2014.

[HL04]   Minqing Hu and Bing Liu. Mining and summarizing customer reviews.
         In *Proceedings of the 10th ACM SIGKDD International Conference on
         Knowledge Discovery and Data Mining (SIGKDD 2004)*, pages 168–177.
         ACM, 2004.

[HM96]   Martin Hitz and Behzad Montazeri. Chidamber and kemerer's met-
         rics suite: A measurement theory perspective. *IEEE Transactions on
         Software Engineering*, 22(4):267–271, 1996.

[HØ09a] Einar W. Høst and Bjarte M. Østvold. Debugging method names. In
         *Proceedings of the 23rd European Conference on Object-Oriented Pro-
         gramming (ECOOP 2009)*, volume 5653 of *Lecture Notes in Computer
         Science*, pages 294–317. Springer, 2009.

[HØ09b] Einar W. Høst and Bjarte M. Østvold. Software language engineer-
         ing. chapter The Java Programmer's Phrase Book, pages 322–341.
         Springer-Verlag, Berlin, Heidelberg, 2009.

[Hol79] Sture Holm. A simple sequentially rejective multiple test procedure.
         Scandinavian journal of statistics, pages 65–70, 1979.

[HSH17] Johannes Hofmeister, Janet Siegmund, and Daniel V. Holt. Shorter
         identifier names take longer to comprehend. In *Proceedings of the
         IEEE 24th International Conference on Software Analysis, Evolution and
         Reengineering (SANER 2017)*, pages 217–227. IEEE Computer Society,
         2017.

[IAZ19] Md Rakibul Islam, Md Kauser Ahmmed, and Minhaz F. Zibran. Mar-
         valous: machine learning based detection of emotions in the valence-
         arousal space in software engineering text. In *Proceedings of the 34th
         ACM/SIGAPP Symposium on Applied Computing (SAC 2019)*, pages
         1786–1793. ACM, 2019.

[IH13]   Claudia Iacob and Rachel Harrison. Retrieving and analyzing mobile
         apps feature requests from online reviews. In *Proceedings of the 10th
         Working Conference on Mining Software Repositories (MSR 2013)*, pages
         41–44. IEEE Computer Society, 2013.

[IMGM18] Nasif Imtiaz, Justin Middleton, Peter Girouard, and Emerson R. Murphy-Hill. Sentiment and politeness analysis tools on developer discussions are unreliable, but so are people. In *Proceedings of the 3rd International Workshop on Emotion Awareness in Software Engineering (SEmotion 2018)*, pages 55–61. ACM, 2018.

[IZ17] Md Rakibul Islam and Minhaz F. Zibran. Leveraging automated sentiment analysis in software engineering. In *Proceedings of the 14th International Conference on Mining Software Repositories (MSR 2017)*, pages 203–214. IEEE Computer Society, 2017.

[IZ18a] Md Rakibul Islam and Minhaz F. Zibran. DEVA: sensing emotions in the valence arousal space in software engineering text. In *Proceedings of the 33rd Annual ACM Symposium on Applied Computing (SAC 2018)*, pages 1536–1543. ACM, 2018.

[IZ18b] Md Rakibul Islam and Minhaz F. Zibran. Sentistrength-se: Exploiting domain specificity for improved sentiment analysis in software engineering text. *Journal of Systems and Software*, 145:125–146, 2018.

[JH07] Patricia Jablonski and Daqing Hou. Cren: a tool for tracking copy-and-paste code clones and renaming identifiers consistently in the IDE. In *Proceedings of the 2007 OOPSLA workshop on Eclipse Technology eXchange (ETX 2007)*, pages 16–20. ACM, 2007.

[JSDS17] Robbert Jongeling, Proshanta Sarkar, Subhajit Datta, and Alexander Serebrenik. On negative results when using sentiment analysis tools for software engineering research. *Empirical Software Engineering*, 22(5):2543–2584, 2017.

[KBLN04] Miryung Kim, Lawrence D. Bergman, Tessa A. Lau, and David Notkin. An ethnographic study of copy and paste programming practices in OOPL. In *Proceedings of the 2004 International Symposium on Empirical Software Engineering (ISESE 2004)*, pages 83–92. IEEE Computer Society, 2004.

[KG04] Cory Kapser and Michael W. Godfrey. Aiding comprehension of cloning through categorization. In *Proceedings of the 7th International Workshop on Principles of Software Evolution (IWPSE 2004)*, pages 85–94. IEEE Computer Society, 2004.

[KG06a] Cory Kapser and Michael W. Godfrey. "cloning considered harmful" considered harmful. In *Proceedings of the 13th Working Conference on Reverse Engineering (WCRE 2006)*, pages 19–28. IEEE Computer Society, 2006.

[KG06b] Cory Kapser and Michael W. Godfrey. Supporting the analysis of clones in software systems. *Journal of Software Maintenance*, 18(2):61–82, 2006.

[KK16] Suntae Kim and Dongsun Kim. Automatic identifier inconsistency detection using code dictionary. *Empirical Software Engineering*, 21(2):565–604, 2016.

[KM17] Zijad Kurtanovic and Walid Maalej. Automatically classifying functional and non-functional requirements using supervised machine learning. In *Proceedings of the 25th IEEE International Requirements Engineering Conference (RE 2017)*, pages 490–495. IEEE Computer Society, 2017.

[KP09] Chris F. Kemerer and Mark C. Paulk. The impact of design and code reviews on software quality: An empirical study based on PSP data. *IEEE Transactions on Software Engineering*, 35(4):534–550, 2009.

[KRB⁺18] Oleksii Kononenko, Tresa Rose, Olga Baysal, Michael W. Godfrey, Dennis Theisen, and Bart de Water. Studying pull request merges: a case study of shopify's active merchant. In *Proceedings of the 40th International Conference on Software Engineering: Software Engineering in Practice (ICSE-SEIP)*, pages 124–133. ACM, 2018.

[KXLW19] Javed Ali Khan, Yuchen Xie, Lin Liu, and Lijie Wen. Analysis of requirements-related arguments in user forums. In *Proceedings of the 27th IEEE International Requirements Engineering Conference (RE 2019)*, pages 63–74. IEEE, 2019.

[LA19] Marc J. Lanovaz and Bram Adams. Comparing the communication tone and responses of users and developers in two R mailing lists: Measuring positive and negative emails. *IEEE Software*, 36(5):46–50, 2019.

[LB11] Dawn J. Lawrie and David W. Binkley. Expanding identifiers to normalize source code vocabulary. In *Proceedings of the IEEE 27th International Conference on Software Maintenance (ICSM 2011)*, pages 113–122. IEEE Computer Society, 2011.

[LFB07a] Dawn J. Lawrie, Henry Feild, and David W. Binkley. An empirical study of rules for well-formed identifiers. *Journal of Software Maintenance*, 19(4):205–229, 2007.

[LFB07b] Dawn J. Lawrie, Henry Feild, and David W. Binkley. Quantifying identifier quality: an analysis of trends. *Empirical Software Engineering*, 12(4):359–388, 2007.

[Liu11]   Bing Liu. *Web Data Mining: Exploring Hyperlinks, Contents, and Usage Data. Second Edition*. Data-Centric Systems and Applications. Springer, 2011.

[Liu15]   Bing Liu. *Sentiment Analysis - Mining Opinions, Sentiments, and Emotions*. Cambridge University Press, 2015.

[LLLL19]   Yuzhou Liu, Lei Liu, Huaxiao Liu, and Suji Li. Information recommendation based on domain knowledge in app descriptions for improving the quality of requirements. *IEEE Access*, 7:9501–9514, 2019.

[LLMZ06]   Zhenmin Li, Shan Lu, Suvda Myagmar, and Yuanyuan Zhou. Cp-miner: Finding copy-paste and related bugs in large-scale software code. *IEEE Transactions on Software Engineering*, 32(3):176–192, 2006.

[LLY+18]   Xueqing Liu, Yue Leng, Wei Yang, Chengxiang Zhai, and Tao Xie. Mining android app descriptions for permission requirements recommendation. In *Proceedings of the 26th IEEE International Requirements Engineering Conference (RE 2018)*, pages 147–158. IEEE Computer Society, 2018.

[LMFB06]   Dawn J. Lawrie, Christopher Morrell, Henry Feild, and David W. Binkley. What's in a name? A study of identifiers. In *Proceedings of the 14th International Conference on Program Comprehension (ICPC 2006)*, pages 3–12. IEEE Computer Society, 2006.

[LNB+]   Bin Lin, Csaba Nagy, Gabriele Bavota, Andrian Marcus, and Michele Lanza. Replication package of the study "on the quality of identifiers in test code". https://identifierquality.bitbucket.io.

[LNB+19]   Bin Lin, Csaba Nagy, Gabriele Bavota, Andrian Marcus, and Michele Lanza. On the quality of identifiers in test code. In *Proceedings of the 19th International Working Conference on Source Code Analysis and Manipulation (SCAM 2019)*, pages 204–215. IEEE, 2019.

[LNBL19]   Bin Lin, Csaba Nagy, Gabriele Bavota, and Michele Lanza. On the impact of refactoring operations on code naturalness. In *Proceedings of the 26th IEEE International Conference on Software Analysis, Evolution and Reengineering (SANER 2019)*, pages 594–598. IEEE, 2019.

[LPM+]   Bin Lin, Luca Ponzanelli, Andrea Mocci, Gabriele Bavota, and Michele Lanza. Replication package of the study "on the uniqueness of code redundancies". https://icpc-redundancy.github.io/icpc-2017.zip.

[LPM+17]   Bin Lin, Luca Ponzanelli, Andrea Mocci, Gabriele Bavota, and Michele Lanza. On the uniqueness of code redundancies. In *Proceedings of the*

25th International Conference on Program Comprehension (ICPC 2017), pages 121–131. IEEE Computer Society, 2017.

[LSM⁺] Bin Lin, Simone Scalabrino, Andrea Mocci, Rocco Oliveto, Gabriele Bavota, and Michele Lanza. Replication package of the study "investigating the use of code analysis and NLP to promote a consistent usage of identifiers". `https://scam-identifier.github.io/replication.zip`.

[LSM⁺17] Bin Lin, Simone Scalabrino, Andrea Mocci, Rocco Oliveto, Gabriele Bavota, and Michele Lanza. Investigating the use of code analysis and NLP to promote a consistent usage of identifiers. In *Proceedings of the 17th IEEE International Working Conference on Source Code Analysis and Manipulation (SCAM 2017)*, pages 81–90. IEEE Computer Society, 2017.

[LYY⁺17] Zhixing Li, Yue Yu, Gang Yin, Tao Wang, and Huaimin Wang. What are they talking about? analyzing code reviews in pull-based development model. *Journal of Computer Science and Technology*, 32(6):1060–1075, 2017.

[LZB⁺a] Bin Lin, Fiorella Zampetti, Gabriele Bavota, Massimiliano Di Penta, and Michele Lanza. Replication package of the study "pattern-based mining of opinions in q&a websites". `https://pome-repo.github.io/`.

[LZB⁺b] Bin Lin, Fiorella Zampetti, Gabriele Bavota, Massimiliano Di Penta, Michele Lanza, and Rocco Oliveto. Replication package of the study "sentiment analysis for software engineering: how far can we go?". `https://sentiment-se.github.io/replication.zip`.

[LZB⁺18] Bin Lin, Fiorella Zampetti, Gabriele Bavota, Massimiliano Di Penta, Michele Lanza, and Rocco Oliveto. Sentiment analysis for software engineering: how far can we go? In *Proceedings of the 40th International Conference on Software Engineering (ICSE 2018)*, pages 94–104. ACM, 2018.

[LZB⁺19] Bin Lin, Fiorella Zampetti, Gabriele Bavota, Massimiliano Di Penta, and Michele Lanza. Pattern-based mining of opinions in q&a websites. In *Proceedings of the 41st International Conference on Software Engineering (ICSE 2019)*, pages 548–559. IEEE / ACM, 2019.

[LZO⁺18] Bin Lin, Fiorella Zampetti, Rocco Oliveto, Massimiliano Di Penta, Michele Lanza, and Gabriele Bavota. Two datasets for sentiment analysis in software engineering. In *Proceedings of the 2018 IEEE International Conference on Software Maintenance and Evolution (ICSME 2018)*, page 712. IEEE Computer Society, 2018.

[mav]   Apache Maven Central Repository. `http://central.maven.org/`
           `maven2/maven/`. last access 24.08.2018.

[MCP⁺09]   Alessandro Murgia, Giulio Concas, Sandro Pinna, Roberto Tonelli, and
           Ivana Turnu. Empirical study of software quality evolution in open
           source projects using agile practices. In *Proceedings of the 1st Interna-
           tional Symposium on Emerging Trends in Software Metrics (ETSM 2009)*,
           pages 11–22, 2009.

[MKAH14]   Shane McIntosh, Yasutaka Kamei, Bram Adams, and Ahmed E. Hassan.
           The impact of code review coverage and code review participation on
           software quality: a case study of the qt, vtk, and ITK projects. In *Pro-
           ceedings of the 11th Working Conference on Mining Software Repositories
           (MSR 2014)*, pages 192–201. ACM, 2014.

[MKNS16]   Walid Maalej, Zijad Kurtanovic, Hadeer Nabil, and Christoph Stanik.
           On the automatic classification of app reviews. *Requirements Engineer-
           ing*, 21(3):311–331, 2016.

[ML09]   Mika Mäntylä and Casper Lassenius. What types of defects are really
           discovered in code reviews? *IEEE Transactions on Software Engineer-
           ing*, 35(3):430–448, 2009.

[MMK15]   Rodrigo Morales, Shane McIntosh, and Foutse Khomh. Do code review
           practices impact design quality? A case study of the qt, vtk, and ITK
           projects. In *Proceedings of the 22nd IEEE International Conference on
           Software Analysis, Evolution, and Reengineering (SANER 2015)*, pages
           171–180. IEEE Computer Society, 2015.

[Moc07]   Audris Mockus. Large-scale code reuse in open source software. In *Pro-
           ceedings of the 1st International Workshop on Emerging Trends in FLOSS
           Research and Development (FLOSS 2007)*, pages 7–7. IEEE, 2007.

[Mot10]   Harvey Motulsky. *Intuitive biostatistics: a non-mathematical guide to
           statistical thinking*. Oxford University Press, 2010.

[MPB12]   Emerson R. Murphy-Hill, Chris Parnin, and Andrew P. Black. How we
           refactor, and how we know it. *IEEE Transactions on Software Engineer-
           ing*, 38(1):5–18, 2012.

[MSB⁺14]   Christopher D. Manning, Mihai Surdeanu, John Bauer, Jenny Rose
           Finkel, Steven Bethard, and David McClosky. The stanford corenlp
           natural language processing toolkit. In *Proceedings of the 52nd Annual
           Meeting of the Association for Computational Linguistics (ACL 2014)*,
           pages 55–60. The Association for Computer Linguistics, 2014.

[MT04]   Rada Mihalcea and Paul Tarau. Textrank: Bringing order into text. In *Proceedings of the 2004 Conference on Empirical Methods in Natural Language Processing (EMNLP 2004)*, pages 404–411. ACL, 2004.

[MTAO14]   Alessandro Murgia, Parastou Tourani, Bram Adams, and Marco Ortu. Do developers feel emotions? an exploratory analysis of emotions in software artifacts. In *Proceedings of the 11th Working Conference on Mining Software Repositories (MSR 2014)*, pages 262–271. ACM, 2014.

[NCL15]   Nicole Novielli, Fabio Calefato, and Filippo Lanubile. The challenges of sentiment detection in the social programmer ecosystem. In *Proceedings of the 7th International Workshop on Social Software Engineering (SSE 2015)*, pages 33–40. ACM, 2015.

[NNN+12]   Anh Tuan Nguyen, Tung Thanh Nguyen, Hoan Anh Nguyen, Ahmed Tamrawi, Hung Viet Nguyen, Jafar M. Al-Kofahi, and Tien N. Nguyen. Graph-based pattern-oriented, context-sensitive source code completion. In *Proceedings of the 34th International Conference on Software Engineering (ICSE 2012)*, pages 69–79. IEEE Computer Society, 2012.

[NNN16]   Anh Tuan Nguyen, Hoan Anh Nguyen, and Tien N. Nguyen. A large-scale study on repetitiveness, containment, and composability of routines in open-source projects. In *Proceedings of the 13th International Conference on Mining Software Repositories (MSR 2016)*, pages 362–373. ACM, 2016.

[NNNN13]   Tung Thanh Nguyen, Anh Tuan Nguyen, Hoan Anh Nguyen, and Tien N. Nguyen. A statistical semantic language model for source code. In *Proceedings of the Joint Meeting of the European Software Engineering Conference and the ACM SIGSOFT Symposium on the Foundations of Software Engineering (ESEC/FSE 2013)*, pages 532–542. ACM, 2013.

[NY03]   Tetsuya Nasukawa and Jeonghee Yi. Sentiment analysis: capturing favorability using natural language processing. In John H. Gennari, Bruce W. Porter, and Yolanda Gil, editors, *Proceedings of the 2nd International Conference on Knowledge Capture (K-CAP 2003)*, pages 70–77. ACM, 2003.

[OAD+15]   Marco Ortu, Bram Adams, Giuseppe Destefanis, Parastou Tourani, Michele Marchesi, and Roberto Tonelli. Are bullies more productive? empirical study of affectiveness vs. issue fixing time. In *Proceedings of the 12th IEEE/ACM Working Conference on Mining Software Repositories (MSR 2015)*, pages 303–313. IEEE Computer Society, 2015.

[OMD+16]   Marco Ortu, Alessandro Murgia, Giuseppe Destefanis, Parastou Tourani, Roberto Tonelli, Michele Marchesi, and Bram Adams. The emotional side of software developers in JIRA. In *Proceedings of the 13th International Conference on Mining Software Repositories (MSR 2016)*, pages 480–483. ACM, 2016.

[OMT19] Marco Ortu, Michele Marchesi, and Roberto Tonelli. Empirical analysis of affect of merged issues on github. In *Proceedings of the 4th International Workshop on Emotion Awareness in Software Engineering (SEmotion 2019)*, pages 46–48. IEEE / ACM, 2019.

[Opp92] A. N. Oppenheim. *Questionnaire Design, Interviewing and Attitude Measurement*. Pinter Publishers, 1992.

[Par13] Terence Parr. *The definitive ANTLR 4 reference*. Pragmatic Bookshelf, 2013.

[PBL13] Luca Ponzanelli, Alberto Bacchelli, and Michele Lanza. Leveraging crowd knowledge for software comprehension and development. In *Proceedings of the 17th European Conference on Software Maintenance and Reengineering (CSMR 2013)*, pages 57–66. IEEE, 2013.

[PBS19] Rajshakhar Paul, Amiangshu Bosu, and Kazi Zakia Sultana. Expressions of sentiments during code reviews: Male vs. female. In *26th IEEE International Conference on Software Analysis, Evolution and Reengineering, SANER 2019, Hangzhou, China, February 24-27, 2019*, pages 26–37. IEEE, 2019.

[PH14] Ferran Pla and Lluís F. Hurtado. Political tendency identification in twitter using sentiment analysis techniques. In *Proceedings of the 25th International Conference on Computational Linguistics (COLING 2014)*, pages 183–192. ACL, 2014.

[PL07] Bo Pang and Lillian Lee. Opinion mining and sentiment analysis. *Foundations and Trends in Information Retrieval*, 2(1-2):1–135, 2007.

[PLV02] Bo Pang, Lillian Lee, and Shivakumar Vaithyanathan. Thumbs up? sentiment classification using machine learning techniques. In *Proceedings of the 2002 Conference on Empirical Methods in Natural Language Processing (EMNLP 2002)*, pages 79–86. Association for Computational Linguistics, July 2002.

[PM18] Panthip Pooput and Pornsiri Muenchaisri. Finding impact factors for rejection of pull requests on github. In *Proceedings of the VII International Conference on Network, Communication and Computing (ICNCC 2018)*, pages 70–76. ACM, 2018.

[PP11]   Marco Pennacchiotti and Ana-Maria Popescu. Democrats, republicans and starbucks afficionados: user classification in twitter. In *Proceedings of the 17th ACM SIGKDD International Conference on Knowledge Discovery and Data Mining (KDD 2011)*, pages 430–438. ACM, 2011.

[PPZ+16] Fabio Palomba, Annibale Panichella, Andy Zaidman, Rocco Oliveto, and Andrea De Lucia. Automatic test case generation: what if test code quality matters? In *Proceedings of the 25th International Symposium on Software Testing and Analysis (ISSTA 2016)*, pages 130–141. ACM, 2016.

[PSG+15] Sebastiano Panichella, Andrea Di Sorbo, Emitza Guzman, Corrado Aaron Visaggio, Gerardo Canfora, and Harald C. Gall. How can I improve my app? Classifying user reviews for software maintenance and evolution. In *Proceedings of the 2015 IEEE International Conference on Software Maintenance and Evolution (ICSME 2015)*, pages 281–290. IEEE Computer Society, 2015.

[PSG+16] Sebastiano Panichella, Andrea Di Sorbo, Emitza Guzman, Corrado Aaron Visaggio, Gerardo Canfora, and Harald C. Gall. Ardoc: app reviews development oriented classifier. In *Proceedings of the 24th ACM SIGSOFT International Symposium on Foundations of Software Engineering (FSE 2016)*, pages 1023–1027. ACM, 2016.

[PVG+11] Fabian Pedregosa, Gaël Varoquaux, Alexandre Gramfort, Vincent Michel, Bertrand Thirion, Olivier Grisel, Mathieu Blondel, Peter Prettenhofer, Ron Weiss, Vincent Dubourg, Jake VanderPlas, Alexandre Passos, David Cournapeau, Matthieu Brucher, Matthieu Perrot, and Edouard Duchesnay. Scikit-learn: Machine learning in python. *Journal of Machine Learning Research*, 12:2825–2830, 2011.

[PVH+11] Lori L. Pollock, K. Vijay-Shanker, Emily Hill, Giriprasad Sridhara, and David C. Shepherd. Natural language-based software analyses and tools for software maintenance. In *Software Engineering - International Summer Schools, ISSSE 2009-2011, Salerno, Italy. Revised Tutorial Lectures*, volume 7171 of *Lecture Notes in Computer Science*, pages 94–125. Springer, 2011.

[PVS14]   Daniel Pletea, Bogdan Vasilescu, and Alexander Serebrenik. Security and emotion: sentiment analysis of security discussions on github. In *Proceedings of the 11th Working Conference on Mining Software Repositories (MSR 2014)*, pages 348–351. ACM, 2014.

[RAC+15] Gabriele Ranco, Darko Aleksovski, Guido Caldarelli, Miha Grčar, and Igor Mozetič. The effects of twitter sentiment on stock price returns. *PloS one*, 10(9), 2015.

[RC08] Chanchal Kumar Roy and James R. Cordy. An empirical study of function clones in open source software. In *Proceedings of the 15th Working Conference on Reverse Engineering (WCRE 2008)*, pages 81–90. IEEE Computer Society, 2008.

[RCK09] Chanchal Kumar Roy, James R. Cordy, and Rainer Koschke. Comparison and evaluation of code clone detection techniques and tools: A qualitative approach. *Science of Computer Programming*, 74(7):470–495, 2009.

[Rei07] Steven P. Reiss. Automatic code stylizing. In *Proceedings of the 22nd IEEE/ACM International Conference on Automated Software Engineering (ASE 2007)*, pages 74–83. ACM, 2007.

[RGS08] Peter C. Rigby, Daniel M. Germán, and Margaret-Anne D. Storey. Open source software peer review practices: a case study of the apache server. In *Proceedings of the 30th International Conference on Software Engineering (ICSE 2008)*, pages 541–550. ACM, 2008.

[RHG+16] Baishakhi Ray, Vincent Hellendoorn, Saheel Godhane, Zhaopeng Tu, Alberto Bacchelli, and Premkumar T. Devanbu. On the "naturalness" of buggy code. In *Proceedings of the 38th International Conference on Software Engineering (ICSE 2016)*, pages 428–439. ACM, 2016.

[RR13] Peter C. Rigby and Martin P. Robillard. Discovering essential code elements in informal documentation. In *Proceedings of the 35th International Conference on Software Engineering (ICSE 2013)*, pages 832–841. IEEE Computer Society, 2013.

[RR14] Mohammad Masudur Rahman and Chanchal K. Roy. An insight into the pull requests of github. In *Proceedings of the 11th Working Conference on Mining Software Repositories (MSR 2014)*, pages 364–367. ACM, 2014.

[RRK15] Mohammad Masudur Rahman, Chanchal K. Roy, and Iman Keivanloo. Recommending insightful comments for source code using crowd-sourced knowledge. In *Proceedings of the 15th IEEE International Working Conference on Source Code Analysis and Manipulation (SCAM 2015)*, pages 81–90. IEEE Computer Society, 2015.

[RS11] Peter C. Rigby and Margaret-Anne D. Storey. Understanding broadcast based peer review on open source software projects. In *Proceedings of the 33rd International Conference on Software Engineering (ICSE 2011)*, pages 541–550. ACM, 2011.

[RUY+19] Waheed Yousuf Ramay, Qasim Umer, Xu-Cheng Yin, Chao Zhu, and Inam Illahi. Deep neural network-based severity prediction of bug reports. *IEEE Access*, 7:46846–46857, 2019.

[RVY14] Veselin Raychev, Martin T. Vechev, and Eran Yahav. Code comple-
tion with statistical language models. In *Proceedings of the ACM SIG-
PLAN Conference on Programming Language Design and Implementation
(PLDI 2014)*, pages 419–428. ACM, 2014.

[SBR⁺19] Simone Scalabrino, Gabriele Bavota, Barbara Russo, Massimiliano Di
Penta, and Rocco Oliveto. Listening to the crowd for the release
planning of mobile apps. *IEEE Transactions on Software Engineering*,
45(1):68–86, 2019.

[SBS19] Jingyi Shen, Olga Baysal, and M. Omair Shafiq. Evaluating the performance of machine learning sentiment analysis algorithms in software
engineering. In *2019 IEEE Intl Conf on Dependable, Autonomic and
Secure Computing, Intl Conf on Pervasive Intelligence and Computing,
Intl Conf on Cloud and Big Data Computing, Intl Conf on Cyber Science
and Technology Congress (DASC/PiCom/CBDCom/CyberSciTech 2019)*,
pages 1023–1030. IEEE, 2019.

[SCC⁺17] Ranjan Satapathy, Iti Chaturvedi, Erik Cambria, Shirley S Ho, and
Jin Cheon Na. Subjectivity detection in nuclear energy tweets. *Com-
putación y Sistemas*, 21(4):657–664, 2017.

[SCON18] Mateus F. Santos, Josemar Alves Caetano, Johnatan Oliveira, and
Humberto T. Marques Neto. Analyzing the impact of feedback in github
on the software developer's mood. In *Proceedings of the 30th International Conference on Software Engineering and Knowledge Engineering
(SEKE 2018)*, pages 445–444. KSI Research Inc. and Knowledge Systems Institute Graduate School, 2018.

[SdLJMP15a] Daricélio Moreira Soares, Manoel Limeira de Lima Júnior, Leonardo
Murta, and Alexandre Plastino. Acceptance factors of pull requests
in open-source projects. In *Proceedings of the 30th Annual ACM Symposium on Applied Computing (SAC 2015)*, pages 1541–1546. ACM,
2015.

[SdLJMP15b] Daricélio Moreira Soares, Manoel Limeira de Lima Júnior, Leonardo
Murta, and Alexandre Plastino. Rejection factors of pull requests filed
by core team developers in software projects with high acceptance
rates. In *Proceedings of the 14th IEEE International Conference on Machine Learning and Applications (ICMLA 2015)*, pages 960–965. IEEE,
2015.

[SIH14] Siddharth Subramanian, Laura Inozemtseva, and Reid Holmes. Live
API documentation. In *Proceedings of the 36th International Conference
on Software Engineering (ICSE 2014)*, pages 643–652. ACM, 2014.

[SK03]   Ramanath Subramanyam and Mayuram S. Krishnan. Empirical analysis of CK metrics for object-oriented design complexity: Implications for software defects. *IEEE Transactions on Software Engineering*, 29(4):297–310, 2003.

[SLS16]   Vinayak Sinha, Alina Lazar, and Bonita Sharif. Analyzing developer sentiment in commit logs. In *Proceedings of the 13th International Conference on Mining Software Repositories (MSR 2016)*, pages 520–523. ACM, 2016.

[spa]   Spacy. `https://spacy.io`.

[SPW⁺13] Richard Socher, Alex Perelygin, Jean Wu, Jason Chuang, Christopher D. Manning, Andrew Y. Ng, and Christopher Potts. Recursive deep models for semantic compositionality over a sentiment treebank. In *Proceedings of the 2013 Conference on Empirical Methods in Natural Language Processing (EMNLP 2013)*, pages 1631–1642. ACL, 2013.

[SPZ⁺18] Davide Spadini, Fabio Palomba, Andy Zaidman, Magiel Bruntink, and Alberto Bacchelli. On the relation of test smells to software code quality. In *Proceedings of the 2018 IEEE International Conference on Software Maintenance and Evolution (ICSME 2018)*, pages 1–12. IEEE Computer Society, 2018.

[SS17a]   Navdeep Singh and Paramvir Singh. How do code refactoring activities impact software developers' sentiments? - an empirical investigation into github commits. In Jian Lv, He Jason Zhang, Mike Hinchey, and Xiao Liu, editors, *Proceedings of the 24th Asia-Pacific Software Engineering Conference (APSEC 2017)*, pages 648–653. IEEE Computer Society, 2017.

[SS17b]   Rodrigo R. G. Souza and Bruno Silva. Sentiment analysis of travis CI builds. In *Proceedings of the 14th International Conference on Mining Software Repositories (MSR 2017)*, pages 459–462. IEEE Computer Society, 2017.

[SSP19]   Faiz Ali Shah, Kairit Sirts, and Dietmar Pfahl. Using app reviews for competitive analysis: tool support. In *Proceedings of the 3rd ACM SIGSOFT International Workshop on App Market Analytics (WAMA 2019)*, pages 40–46. ACM, 2019.

[SSPV15] Ryan Serva, Zachary R. Senzer, Lori L. Pollock, and K. Vijay-Shanker. Automatically mining negative code examples from software developer Q & A forums. In *Proceedings of the 30th IEEE/ACM International Conference on Automated Software Engineering Workshops (ASE Workshops 2015)*, pages 115–122. IEEE Computer Society, 2015.

[SVT16] Marcelino Campos Oliveira Silva, Marco Tulio Valente, and Ricardo Terra. Does technical debt lead to the rejection of pull requests? In *Proceedings of the XII Brazilian Symposium on Information Systems: Information Systems in the Cloud Computing Era-Volume 1 (SBSI 2016)*, pages 248–254, 2016.

[TBP$^+$10] Mike Thelwall, Kevan Buckley, Georgios Paltoglou, Di Cai, and Arvid Kappas. Sentiment strength detection in short informal text. *Journal of the Association for Information Science and Technology*, 61(12):2544–2558, 2010.

[TDH14] Jason Tsay, Laura Dabbish, and James D. Herbsleb. Influence of social and technical factors for evaluating contribution in github. In *Proceedings of the 36th International Conference on Software Engineering (ICSE 2014)*, pages 356–366. ACM, 2014.

[TJA14] Parastou Tourani, Yujuan Jiang, and Bram Adams. Monitoring sentiment in open source mailing lists: exploratory study on the apache ecosystem. In *Proceedings of the 24th Annual International Conference on Computer Science and Software Engineering (CASCON 2014)*, pages 34–44. IBM / ACM, 2014.

[TME$^+$18] Nikolaos Tsantalis, Matin Mansouri, Laleh Mousavi Eshkevari, Davood Mazinanian, and Danny Dig. Accurate and efficient refactoring detection in commit history. In *Proceedings of the 40th International Conference on Software Engineering (ICSE 2018)*, pages 483–494. ACM, 2018.

[TPB$^+$16] Michele Tufano, Fabio Palomba, Gabriele Bavota, Massimiliano Di Penta, Rocco Oliveto, Andrea De Lucia, and Denys Poshyvanyk. An empirical investigation into the nature of test smells. In *Proceedings of the 31st IEEE/ACM International Conference on Automated Software Engineering (ASE 2016)*, pages 4–15. ACM, 2016.

[TR10] Andreas Thies and Christian Roth. Recommending rename refactorings. In *Proceedings of the 2nd International Workshop on Recommendation Systems for Software Engineering (RSSE 2010)*, pages 1–5. ACM, 2010.

[TR16] Christoph Treude and Martin P. Robillard. Augmenting API documentation with insights from stack overflow. In *Proceedings of the 38th International Conference on Software Engineering (ICSE 2016)*, pages 392–403. ACM, 2016.

[TSD14] Zhaopeng Tu, Zhendong Su, and Premkumar T. Devanbu. On the localness of software. In *Proceedings of the 22nd ACM SIGSOFT International*

Symposium on Foundations of Software Engineering (FSE 2014), pages 269–280. ACM, 2014.

[Tuk77] John W. Tukey. *Exploratory data analysis*. Addison-Wesley series in behavioral science: quantitative methods. Addison-Wesley, 1977.

[Tur02] Peter D. Turney. Thumbs up or thumbs down? semantic orientation applied to unsupervised classification of reviews. In *Proceedings of the 40th Annual Meeting of the Association for Computational Linguistics (ACL 2002)*, pages 417–424. ACL, 2002.

[UK] Gias Uddin and Foutse Khomh. The opiner tool. goo.gl/2EnL78.

[UK17a] Gias Uddin and Foutse Khomh. Automatic summarization of API reviews. In *Proceedings of the 32nd IEEE/ACM International Conference on Automated Software Engineering (ASE 2017)*, pages 159–170. IEEE Computer Society, 2017.

[UK17b] Gias Uddin and Foutse Khomh. Mining API aspects in API reviews. Technical report, 2017.

[UK17c] Gias Uddin and Foutse Khomh. Opiner: an opinion search and summarization engine for apis. In *Proceedings of the 32nd IEEE/ACM International Conference on Automated Software Engineering (ASE 2017)*, pages 978–983. IEEE Computer Society, 2017.

[UK19] Gias Uddin and Foutse Khomh. Automatic mining of opinions expressed about apis in stack overflow. *IEEE Transactions on Software Engineering*, Early Access, 2019.

[ULS18] Qasim Umer, Hui Liu, and Yasir Sultan. Emotion based automated priority prediction for bug reports. *IEEE Access*, 6:35743–35752, 2018.

[VBR⁺16] Lorenzo Villarroel, Gabriele Bavota, Barbara Russo, Rocco Oliveto, and Massimiliano Di Penta. Release planning of mobile apps based on user reviews. In *Proceedings of the 38th International Conference on Software Engineering (ICSE 2016)*, pages 14–24. ACM, 2016.

[Wan10] Wei Wang. Sentiment analysis of online product reviews with semi-supervised topic sentiment mixture model. In *Proceedings of the 7th International Conference on Fuzzy Systems and Knowledge Discovery (FSKD 2010)*, pages 2385–2389. IEEE, 2010.

[Wer18] Karl Werder. The evolution of emotional displays in open source software development teams: an individual growth curve analysis. In *Proceedings of the 3rd International Workshop on Emotion Awareness in Software Engineering (SEmotion 2018)*, pages 1–6. ACM, 2018.

[WHGW17] Wentao Wang, Nesrin Hussein, Arushi Gupta, and Yinglin Wang. A regression model based approach for identifying security requirements in open source software development. In *Proceedings of the IEEE 25th International Requirements Engineering Conference Workshops (RE 2017 Workshops)*, pages 443–446. IEEE Computer Society, 2017.

[Wil45] Frank Wilcoxon. Individual comparisons by ranking methods. *Biometrics bulletin*, 1(6):80–83, 1945.

[WND08] Peter Weißgerber, Daniel Neu, and Stephan Diehl. Small patches get in! In *Proceedings of the 2008 International Working Conference on Mining Software Repositories (MSR 2008)*, pages 67–76. ACM, 2008.

[WPWZ19] Shaohua Wang, NhatHai Phan, Yan Wang, and Yong Zhao. Extracting API tips from developer question and answer websites. In *Proceedings of the 16th International Conference on Mining Software Repositories (MSR 2019)*, pages 321–332. IEEE / ACM, 2019.

[WYT13] Edmund Wong, Jinqiu Yang, and Lin Tan. Autocomment: Mining question and answer sites for automatic comment generation. In *Proceedings of the 2013 28th IEEE/ACM International Conference on Automated Software Engineering (ASE 2013)*, pages 562–567. IEEE, 2013.

[YZL18] Geunseok Yang, Tao Zhang, and Byungjeong Lee. An emotion similarity based severity prediction of software bugs: A case study of open source projects. *IEICE Transactions*, 101-D(8):2015–2026, 2018.

[Zel09] Andreas Zeller. *Why Programs Fail - A Guide to Systematic Debugging, 2nd Edition*. Academic Press, 2009.

[ZH13] Yingying Zhang and Daqing Hou. Extracting problematic API features from forum discussions. In *Proceedings of the IEEE 21st International Conference on Program Comprehension (ICPC 2013)*, pages 142–151. IEEE Computer Society, 2013.

[ZRvDD11] Andy Zaidman, Bart Van Rompaey, Arie van Deursen, and Serge Demeyer. Studying the co-evolution of production and test code in open source and industrial developer test processes through repository mining. *Empirical Software Engineering*, 16(3):325–364, 2011.

www.ingramcontent.com/pod-product-compliance
Lightning Source LLC
Chambersburg PA
CBHW081508220526
45467CB00010B/2836